D1565737

WITHDRAWN

*Dostoevsky's Religion*

# Dostoevsky's Religion

*Steven Cassedy*

STANFORD UNIVERSITY PRESS

STANFORD, CALIFORNIA

2005

Stanford University Press
Stanford, California

Printed in the United States of America on acid-free, archival-quality paper

Library of Congress Cataloging-in-Publication Data
Cassedy, Steven.
  Dostoevsky's religion / Steven Cassedy.
    p. cm.
  Includes bibliographical references and index.
  ISBN 0-8047-5137-4 (cloth : alk. paper)
  1. Dostoyevsky, Fyodor, 1821–1881—Religion. I. Title.
PG3328.Z7R42247 2005
891.73'3—dc22                          2004028724

Original Printing 2005

Last figure below indicates year of this printing:
14   13   12   11   10   09   08   07   06   05

Typeset by Classic Typography in 11/14 Adobe Garamond

For Patrice, Mike, and Eva

# Contents

# Preface

To judge from the past, there is a natural and powerful impulse to characterize the "religion" in Dostoevsky's writings as a set of beliefs (which we may list and describe) and then to attribute them all to the author, or to identify a subset that we may attribute to the author, or to state that the author repudiated all the beliefs we've listed. In any case, it always seems to boil down to the question, "What did Dostoevsky himself really believe?"

That's where the trouble begins. People who pose this question don't expect an answer like "Dostoevsky believed that all religion is essentially a product of our tendency to produce myths" or "Dostoevsky believed that religion serves a socializing function in human civilization." They expect an answer like "Dostoevsky was a devout Christian and believed in personal immortality," or the opposite, "Dostoevsky was a tried-and-true atheist and did not believe in much of anything at all." If they decide that he was a religious (specifically Christian) person and not an atheist, they expect further details about what, in his view, good Christians should believe and how they should behave. They expect, in short, a kind of theology and corresponding guide to living that represents "what Dostoevsky believed."

There are two problems with this approach. The first is that even if we do wish to know (and think it's important to know) what Dostoevsky believed when it came to religion, we'll quickly be disappointed to find he "believed" a welter of diverse ideas that, taken as a whole, are shot through with flagrant contradictions and inconsistencies. Readers of Dostoevsky who declare, for example, that their novelist embraced and promoted a kind of nationalist Russian Orthodox Christianity are telling the truth—it's easy to find passages to support this claim—but they're overlooking the passages where he *ridicules* this type of belief. Those who declare that Dostoevsky was a sworn enemy of socialism, seen as the antithesis of "his" Christianity, are telling the truth, too—it's easy to find passages to support *this* claim—but they forget the

occasions when he passionately defended individual proponents of this ideology. Those who declare that, underneath it all, Dostoevsky was a deeply
religious man are ignoring the power with which he was able to endow
counterarguments to religious beliefs of various sorts. In fact, when it comes
right down to it, those who name almost any issue, religious or not, and
firmly declare that Dostoevsky held a certain position on it are failing to
take into account that he almost certainly took an opposite position in some
other place.

The second problem is that the question "What did Dostoevsky himself
really believe?" is not the only one to ask if we're talking about religion in his
works. Here are some others:

· When Dostoevsky talked about religion or dramatized it in his fiction,
  what exactly was his understanding of what he was talking about or
  dramatizing?
· How did he dramatize religious issues in his fiction, and what may we
  infer from his dramatization of those issues?
· To what extent was his understanding of religion determined by con-
  temporary thought, Russian and non-Russian?
· To what extent was his understanding of religion determined by the
  Russian Orthodox tradition in which he was raised?
· If, for the purpose of understanding "Dostoevsky's religion," we seek a
  conception of Russian Orthodox Christianity, are our sources reliable?
· To what extent was his understanding of religion the product of his
  own idiosyncratic mind?
· What, in his view, was the nature of belief itself?

After all, here are the simple facts: Dostoevsky explicitly said and wrote
some things about religious issues, he invented fictional characters that he
caused to express some views on religious issues, and he created fictional situations that bore an association with some religious issues. Since (as I see it)
he's made it impossible for us to state what his personal religious beliefs are
in the sense I have mentioned, then all we can talk about is what he *does*
when the topic of religion comes up in his writing. So it's fine if we make
statements like "He frames religious issues as antinomies" or "He invents situations that test his characters' religious beliefs." But if we really want to
make a statement about what Dostoevsky *believed*, the most we'll be able to

say is probably something like "He believed that when we think about religion we become involved in antinomies" or "He believed that belief itself is the principal issue in any discussion of religion." But these statements are completely different from a statement about whether or not Dostoevsky embraced certain religious beliefs and practices. So in the end, it seems to me, what we're left with is the speculations and reflections on religion to which Dostoevsky has led us.

What to say about them?

Before we even try to say something about them, we need to realize that, to a considerable extent and especially in the West, we're prisoners of the interpretations that some of Dostoevsky's better-known readers have served up since his works were published. The explanations of Dostoevsky's religious thought, both in Russia and in the West, make up a remarkable—and often truly funny—story. Dostoevsky, very much like his admirer Nietzsche, is one of those writers in whom many readers see reflections of themselves and then mistake those reflections for the writers—and this is only one part of the story. I've attempted a short version of it in Chapter One.

If someone in Dostoevsky's milieu, a member of the educated Russian class of the midnineteenth century, had turned his or her attention to the subject of religion, what issues would have been likely to come to mind simply in virtue of the intellectual climate? An educated American of almost any religious persuasion in the late 1960s, for example, on thinking about religion in general, could not avoid thinking about the famous "Is God Dead?" cover of *Time* magazine in April 1966, or the naughty "God is dead" T-shirts a few years later. An educated Protestant living in Geneva in 1600 could hardly avoid thinking about the issue of predestination, owing to the power of the Calvinist tradition in that city. Educated Russians living in Moscow or Saint Petersburg in the 1840s would perhaps think of their own Russian Orthodox upbringing, if in fact they had one (as Dostoevsky did, while many of his contemporaries did not), they might think of the movement of religious nationalism called Slavophilism, and they might think of certain indigenous sectarian movements. But they would also be conditioned to bring to a discussion of religious issues a host of romantic and secularizing concepts that writers in Western Europe were busy introducing (and that Russian university students were busy snapping up). In this environment, "Christ was an eternal ideal toward which man strives and, by a law of nature, must strive" is not an innocent statement. All this is the subject of Chapter Two.

But inevitably we are brought back to the peculiarity of our author and the impossibility of answering a question that proves so much less complicated for so many other writers: What did he believe? It turns out that the nature of belief itself was a central preoccupation for Dostoevsky, and that the content of religious belief for him often takes second place to the odd ways in which belief functions. We can certainly say with confidence that even when Dostoevsky was not consciously speculating about belief, his conduct showed that it was a central issue in his character; he was incapable of sustaining the same position on an issue, religious or not, for any significant length of time, and yet he was capable of expressing views with what seems for all the world to be the utmost conviction and sincerity. This is what Chapter Three is about.

If Dostoevsky always found himself torn between opposing beliefs, it's no doubt because he viewed belief—especially religious belief—as something essentially contradictory, paradoxical, and antinomic. No one will be surprised to hear that Dostoevsky was fascinated with contradictions and conflicting points of view. But I'm not persuaded that he ever truly resolved many of the contradictions that fascinated him, and many of these contradictions end up specifically as antinomies, that is, pairs of mutually contradictory and equally compelling claims. I don't see, for example, how the conflict in *The Brothers Karamazov* between the views of Ivan and those of Father Zosima is definitively resolved in favor of the former (as so many readers claimed in the early decades after Dostoevsky's death) or in favor of the latter (as so many readers have claimed for the last few decades). Instead I see in Dostoevsky the real possibility of sincerely asserting one thing today and sincerely asserting its opposite tomorrow. This binds the expression of a conviction to the situation in which we express it and suggests a curiously modernist view of language and belief. That's Chapter Four.

When it came to metaphysical questions, Dostoevsky betrayed a turn of thought that renders his conception of belief yet more complicated. He seems early on to have become fascinated with the idealist notion of infinite progress toward an unattainable goal. The perfectly selfless Christian love whose practical unrealizability was the subject of more than one remarkable text is a good example. Reaching such a goal brings about the destruction of the self. Another example is perfect belief, or perfect faith. Like perfectly selfless love, perfect faith stands at the end of a path that comes ever closer to this end but never reaches it. The same applies to perfect lack of faith. Faith and faithlessness, good and evil are pairs of opposing ideals, all of them un-attainable by finite beings living in a finite world.

The idealism that characterizes Dostoevsky's conception of religion leads to an odd paradox about the nature of the individual, one particularly evident in the pair of novels *The Idiot* and *The Devils*. In those works, reflections about ideal love and faith—but also about ideal evil—lead to the conclusion that the "perfect" state for the individual (whether the individual seeks absolute good or absolute evil) is a state of complete dissolution. Perfect Christian love, as *The Idiot* illustrates, necessitates the evaporation of the ego, and perfect evil, as *The Devils* illustrates, leads to personal destruction. Dostoevsky's understanding of freedom, however, leads to the conclusion that the individual must remain whole and that a breakdown of the individual arises from moral and personal failures. The ideality of belief and the paradox of the individual are what I discuss in Chapter Five.

So belief is contextual, antinomic, and ideal. The status of the individual is deeply paradoxical. All this suggests more than ever that the topic of Dostoevsky's religion does not mean simply a list of the author's personal beliefs. But surely Dostoevsky must at least have conceived of some religious worldview with a content that's independent of the question of whether he or anyone else can fully believe any or all of its constituent parts. The closest thing to such a worldview in a work of fiction is the one we find in Father Zosima (and Zosima's disciple Alesha) in *The Brothers Karamazov*. But there's not much about this worldview that's Christian, or even for that matter consistent. It represents a strange blend of almost pagan earth worship and religious nationalism, as Zosima makes the slippery transition from asking us to adore the earth generally to asking us to adore the *Russian* earth specifically. This leads to asserting a special status for Russians in the divine scheme and consequently to endorsing a view that contradicts some of the historically fundamental aspects of Christianity. This is the focus of attention in Chapter Six.

Dostoevsky is a little like Nietzsche in this respect (among so many others); he's left us a large body of thought on religion, one that probes the foundations of religion in general and Christianity in particular but without offering a plausible worldview of its own. Like Nietzsche's, this is a highly critical body of thought that can point us toward the reevaluation of our most basic conceptions about religion. A key difference between the two is that Nietzsche didn't think he was proposing the content of a positive religion, while Dostoevsky apparently did.

This book is not meant to be a systematic study of Dostoevsky's fiction, focusing on the religious content of each work. Nor, for the reasons I've just given, is it a systematic study of his nonfiction, focusing on the things he said in his "own" voice (and therefore truly *thought*). It's meant to expose the body of thought on religion that emerges both from the actual content of his writing and from how he presented religious issues in works of various sorts.

I've written this book not just for specialists but also for general readers who are interested in Dostoevsky. I've assumed familiarity with four of Dostoevsky's works: *Crime and Punishment*, *The Idiot*, *The Devils*, and *The Brothers Karamazov*. When I mention a character or a scene from those books, I generally don't take the time to explain who the character is or to set the scene.

I've used the Library of Congress system for transliterating Cyrillic, though I've generally used the commonly recognized spellings of names (*Dostoevsky*, not *Dostoevskii*) in the text. All translations in the book, unless I've indicated otherwise, are my own.

## ACKNOWLEDGMENTS

Many friends and colleagues have helped me with this book. Donald Fanger, Gary Rosenshield, Judith Deutsch Kornblatt, Gary Saul Morson, Paul Valliere, James Scanlan, Robert Louis Jackson, John Burt Foster, Harriet Murav, David Goodblatt, Richard Elliott Friedman, and others graciously answered countless queries. Irina Paperno, Harsha Ram, Vladimir Alexandrov, Catherine Evtuhov, Olga Meerson, Ronald Vroon, Gail Lenhoff, Michael Heim, Anne Lounsbery, Catherine Nepomnyashchy, Richard Gustafson, Gary Rosenshield, and Judith Deutsch Kornblatt helped arrange guest lectures at their institutions over the last few years. The questions that they, their colleagues, and their students asked were enormously valuable to me as I formulated my ideas and organized the book.

I'd like to thank Gabriella Safran for giving Stanford University Press and me an extremely helpful, critical reading of the manuscript.

Special thanks to Caryl Emerson for finding the time and energy, in the midst of her customarily and unbelievably exhausting schedule, to give advice on the manuscript and its publication. Early on, with her amazing ability to get right to the heart of any matter, she helped me formulate the central points of the book and avoid some embarrassing missteps.

Special thanks to Jim Scanlan for advice and dialogue over the years. Though he may disagree with much of what I've said here, I trust he'll know how highly I esteem him and his work.

My most heartfelt thanks go to the man who introduced me to the works of Dostoevsky almost thirty years ago. Joseph Frank has been for me the model of the American intellectual in its consummate form: multilingual so as to be the envy of any European scholar, steeped broadly in the intellectual history of the West, firmly rooted in the concrete and empirical, skeptical of fashionable trends that divert attention from what's truly important, synoptic (a word that Frank himself admiringly applied long ago to Erich Kahler) in approach, and always sensitive to the political dimension of culture. Like so many others of his generation, he never doubted that his calling was a noble one, that to have attained the status of "an Intellectual" was to have earned a privilege to be taken very seriously. It's no wonder he was drawn to Dostoevsky. It would be hard to find an author—a human being, for that matter—for whom the world of *ideas* was filled with such tumultuous passion and dramatic excitement. Joseph Frank taught all his students what it is to live in such a world.

*Dostoevsky's Religion*

## CHAPTER ONE

# Historical Problems
# of Understanding

History has played an odd little trick with the topic of "Dostoevsky's religion," as it has with almost everything that happened in Russia before the October Revolution. Dostoevsky died in 1881, at the pinnacle of fame in his own country but much less well known outside. After his death, almost two generations of Russians came to love or hate as much of his work as was available, while the West was slowly discovering him. Many of his best-known Russian readers in those days were religious thinkers who made a name for themselves partly by writing about the religious ideas they saw in Dostoevsky's works.

Then came the October Revolution, and Dostoevsky became a problem. During the Soviet years, it was dicey to discuss him at all, let alone to attribute religious ideas to him. If the availability of his various works is any indication, the official—but not officially expressed—view seems to have been that he was a dangerously conservative thinker. Editions of *The Devils*, his most clearly political novel, were printed in the Soviet Union and promptly shipped abroad. Officially sanctioned commentary on Dostoevsky in this era tended either to treat him as an outmoded historical phenomenon or to make of him something more palatable to the Leninist outlook than a reading of, say, *The Devils* might lead one to suppose. The English-speaking world has had a taste of the first approach since 1964, when Norton published its Critical Edition of *Crime and Punishment*. The appendix to that edition included excerpts from the USSR Ministry of Culture's official guide for the teaching of Dostoevsky in Soviet universities. In 1953, the ministry characterizes his works in wholly negative terms as the "expression of reactionary bourgeois-individualistic ideology," while in 1955 it sees them somewhat more favorably as "a critical reflection of the deep inner contradictions which were corroding the Russian aristocratic-bourgeois society in the second stage of the liberating movement."[1] The more enlightened editorial staff of the *Polnoe sobranie sochinenii* (*Complete Works*), published between 1972 and 1990, took the second approach. In the first volume of the projected set, the staff introduced their author with the remarkable claim that "despite numerous historically conditioned errors and delusions" he had advanced essentially the same attitudes as those that the Great October Revolution had brought to life: mistrust of bourgeois civilization and belief in the Russian people.[2]

As to Dostoevsky's religious ideas, before the collapse of the Soviet Union one tactic was to chalk them up to the author's allegedly reactionary outlook. Another was to pretend they weren't there at all. Nowhere is this more evident than in two classic Soviet-era cinematizations of Dostoevsky's novels. Ivan Pyr'ev's screen version (1968) of *The Brothers Karamazov*, though including scenes in Father Zosima's monastery, an abbreviated version of Ivan's conversation from the "Rebellion" chapter, and other scenes in which Ivan discusses his views on God and immortality, omits "The Grand Inquisitor," the entire section devoted to Father Zosima's life, and even Alesha's funeral speech, concluding instead with an exuberant farewell scene in which Dmitry, after his murder trial, joyfully goes off to Siberia and Grushenka follows him. Lev Kulidzhanov's rendering (1969) of *Crime and Punishment*, though almost four agonizingly tedious hours long and mindlessly faithful to many parts of the novel, omits the Epilogue and, of course, the scene in which Sonia reads the Gospel story of the raising of Lazarus.

So the tale of the open discussion of Dostoevsky's religion in his own country includes a lengthy hiatus, during which not only was the discussion largely suspended but in addition the works of his early religious commentators were banned. Once the discussion resumed in the 1990s, it could not simply pick up where it had left off.

In the West, however, there were few constraints of the sort that the Soviet regime imposed on its people. Starting at the end of the nineteenth century, Dostoevsky's popularity grew in Europe and the United States, and an increasing number of his works became available in translation. During seventy years of virtual silence in Russia on the topic of Dostoevsky's religion, Westerners had plenty to say. Until relatively recently, most Western commentators did not trouble to learn much of anything about Dostoevsky's native religious tradition. When they did, they generally relied, directly or indirectly, on the tradition that Dostoevsky's early Russian commentators initiated after his death. But these commentators had their own peculiar biases.

## DOSTOEVSKY'S RELIGION THROUGH
## RUSSIAN ORTHODOX EYES

If we wanted to know the "truth" about Dostoevsky's religion, we would probably turn first to writers who shared Dostoevsky's nationality and religion— that is, to writers who approached Dostoevsky from the perspective of Russian Orthodox Christianity. Unfortunately there are numerous perils here, for the Russian Orthodox Christianity that so many Russian writers use as a foundation for an understanding of Dostoevsky's religion turns out to be to some extent Dostoevsky's own idiosyncratic creation. There's another fact that complicates matters further. By the turn of the twentieth century, much of Russian intellectual life had been thoroughly infected with the Nietzsche bacillus. After the philosopher died in 1900, his spirit was suddenly everywhere. Of course, no two people could agree on what Nietzsche's views were, but everyone seemed to have a strong opinion (favorable or unfavorable) about him. His early infatuation with Wagner and his promotion of the "Dionysian" spirit in *The Birth of Tragedy* impressed some. His vitriolic comments on religion in general and Christianity in particular impressed or enraged others. His remarks on the will to power intoxicated many. His style—his fondness for aphorism and for the bold, sweeping, and completely unsupported claim—inspired many to follow his example. Much of the commentary on Dostoevsky from this era, in Russia and in Western Europe, bears the heavy imprint of the naughty boy who proclaimed (as many others had already done to much less fanfare) the death of God.

The man who was responsible for reinvigorating (some might say for actually creating) Russian Orthodox theology at the end of the nineteenth century was also the man who gave the earliest and strongest impetus to the tradition of reading Dostoevsky's works through Orthodox eyes: Vladimir Solov'ev (1853–1900), the dazzlingly precocious philosopher who was a friend and companion to Dostoevsky from 1873 till the end of the novelist's life. Solov'ev was the talk of the town in 1878, when he began delivering his *Lectures on Godmanhood* and transfixing his audience with his vision of a humanity divinized and a deity humanized through the incarnation. His name came to be associated with the concept of the Universal Church, a human brotherhood brought about, once again, by the incarnation. He is also usually credited with inaugurating the Russian "religious renaissance," the movement that produced a flood of important writings on Russian Orthodox Christianity from the end of the nineteenth century till the Revolution. The intellectual relationship between Solov'ev and Dostoevsky was said to be reciprocal, and some have said that Solov'ev was the real-life prototype for both Alesha and Ivan Karamazov.[3]

After Dostoevsky died, the religious philosopher paid tribute to him in his *Three Discourses in Memory of Dostoevsky*, published between 1881 and 1885. Solov'ev attempts to define what kind of Christianity his late friend represented. There are three possible types of Christianity, Solov'ev explains: what he calls temple (*khramovoe*) Christianity, domestic (*domashnee*) Christianity, and universal (*vselenskoe*) Christianity. For now, we needn't concern ourselves with the meaning of the first two (I'll return to the subject in Chapter Six). Dostoevsky's is of the third type, which is to say "a free, all-humankind [*vsechelovecheskoe*] unity, an all-world [*vsemirnoe*] brotherhood in Christ's name."[4] Many would recognize this as a classic Lutheran idea, but Solov'ev calls it simply a "Christian idea" and attributes it to Dostoevsky. It makes sense that Dostoevsky should have embraced this version of Christianity, Solov'ev thinks, since at the heart of the novelist's personal and social outlook lay the religious conviction that "separate individuals, even the best people, do not have the right to coerce society in the name of their individual superiority," that "social truth is not made up by separate minds but rooted in collective feeling."[5] This in turn makes sense because Dostoevsky was able to see the Godly in both man and nature and was thus able to appreciate the truth of the claim that the Universal Church represents the "living body of the God-man."[6]

Naturally these assertions might surprise some readers, since Dostoevsky at least created fictional characters who expressed views very different from the ones that Solov'ev is sure he espoused. In Solov'ev's eyes, Dostoevsky's ironic distance from these characters must have been great indeed—and must have been beyond all doubt. Many of the ideas Solov'ev mentions may be found in book six of *The Brothers Karamazov*, "The Russian Monk." At one point in that book, in a description of his years of wandering, Father Zosima tells of an encounter with a former servant. Years earlier he beat the servant and then asked the servant's forgiveness, before abandoning his own worldly affairs and beginning his monastic calling. The servant, seeing that his former master is now poor, gives him alms. Here is Zosima's comment: "I had been his master and he my servant, but now, as he and I kissed each other with love and spiritual tenderness, a great human unity arose between us. I've thought about this a great deal, but now here are my thoughts: can it really be inaccessible to the mind that this great, simple-hearted unity might arise, in its own time and universally, among our Russian people?" Father Zosima doesn't use phrases like "free, all-humankind unity," but the collective spirit, the flattening out of social distinctions, the universality are all there in his comment. So the question is whether "temple Christianity" is a preexisting, generically Christian notion that shows up in Dostoevsky or whether Solov'ev derived the notion from Dostoevsky's fiction. If it's true, as some say, that the exchange of ideas between Dostoevsky and his younger friend reached its height of activity when Dostoevsky was working on *The Brothers Karamazov*, then it would not be surprising that Solov'ev and one of Dostoevsky's characters should have similar views about what constitutes a certain type of religion.

Curiously enough, Solov'ev would later turn his attention to Nietzsche, though not directly in connection with his understanding of Dostoevsky's religion. But given Solov'ev's formulation of Dostoevsky's fundamental religious conviction ("separate individuals, even the best people, do not have the right to coerce society in the name of their individual superiority"), his interest in the German philosopher is hardly surprising. What catches Solov'ev's attention in Nietzsche is precisely questions of power and will, and his response to Nietzsche's positions on these questions (at least as Solov'ev represents those positions) is invariably constructed from the religious outlook that he regarded himself as sharing with Dostoevsky. Consequently he permitted himself to make such amazing claims as these: Nietzsche erred by celebrating strength and beauty in and for themselves, failing to realize that "there exists a Divinity both strong and beautiful, whose strength does not weaken and whose beauty does not die, because with Him both strength and beauty are inseparable from the good";[7] and we can reinterpret Nietzsche and conclude that the Superman is simply one who has done what is natural to all humans—namely, attempt to be higher and better than reality, to conquer death through resurrection in Christ.[8]

The first important book-length study devoted to the subject of Dostoevsky and religion was *Dostoevsky and the Legend of the Grand Inquisitor* (1891), by Vasily Rozanov (1856–1919). Rozanov devoted the bulk of his book to a kind of retelling, with commentary, of two consecutive chapters in *The Brothers Karamazov*: "Rebellion" and "The Grand Inquisitor." As one who considered debate about Dostoevsky to be debate about where the author stood on issues of great import—in this case, did he side with Ivan, or did he side with Alesha?—Rozanov clearly counted himself among those who believed Dostoevsky sided with the former. The "Legend" is infused with the spirit of death and hopelessness; it is "the lone synthesis in history of the most ardent thirst for the religious together with a complete incapacity for it."[9] Rozanov then goes on, however, to propose an historical account of the Russian Orthodox Church, explaining that the "Romance races" showed a predilection for externally imposed universalism, as expressed in the Roman Catholic Church; the Germanic races showed a predilection for subjective individualism, as expressed in Lutheranism; and the Russian race is filled with "clarity, harmony, an attraction to the inward agreement both of ourselves with everything around us and of everything around us with and through itself," as expressed in Russian Orthodoxy.[10] Of the three spirits, the Orthodox is the one that corresponds most closely to the Gospel and the spirit that shines in it, Rozanov declares, because Orthodox believers are animated simply by *faith*.[11]

What's curious about this bit of dialectical analysis, as Rozanov himself points out in an extended note to his discussion, is that it comes from Dostoevsky himself, who devoted a few pages of the January 1877 issue of *Diary of a Writer* to just this subject. To believe the editorial staff of the *Polnoe sobranie sochinenii*, Dostoevsky himself borrowed the ideas from the religious philosopher Aleksei Stepanovich Khomiakov (1804–60), who had helped create a highly nationalistic vision of Russian Christianity in the first half of the nineteenth century.[12] To Rozanov's mind, however, the ideas belonged to Dostoevsky, and he makes no effort to ground them in any evidence or authority earlier than the author of *The Brothers Karamazov*.

Rozanov mentions Nietzsche only once in *Dostoevsky and the Legend of the Grand Inquisitor*, in a footnote.[13] There is no evidence that his approach in this work is dominated by Nietzsche. For other Russian commentators of the Russian religious renaissance, however, the figure of Nietzsche and the question of Dostoevsky's religion became somehow inseparable, and after Rozanov virtually every major figure of this movement who turned his attention to Dostoevsky viewed the late novelist through a Nietzschean lens. The question generally became not whether a Nietzschean worldview would help us to understand Dostoevsky (the answer was yes) but whether Dostoevsky personally embraced the views that various fictional characters expressed in his works (a question that commentators tended to settle simply by declaring *ex cathedra* which fictional characters represented the author's personal views).

Take the great poet and religious philosopher Dmitry Merezhkovsky (1865–1941), for example. Having spent his early career as an aesthete and a popularizer of French symbolism, Merezhkovsky turned to religion in 1899 and founded the Religious Philosophical Society of Saint Petersburg in 1901. He also explored the idea of founding a new church and even went so far as to compose a liturgy for it. From 1900 to 1902, he published his first important work of literary criticism, *L. Tolstoy and Dostoevsky*. Nietzsche, long a constant presence in Merezhkovsky's personal world, infuses his reading of Dostoevsky to a degree that, a century later, can only make one's head spin. Nietzsche's notebook scribblings on *The Devils* were not published till 1970, so in 1900 no one knew for certain whether the philosopher of the anti-Christ had read this novel. But even in the absence of evidence, Merezhkovsky was sure there was a resemblance between Nietzsche and the atheist-humanist character Kirillov. That someone might be struck by the resemblance is not necessarily astonishing. What is astonishing is that Merezhkovsky thinks the teachings of both essentially coincide with those of Jesus. Here's what he says: Kirillov preaches the man-God and the physical transformation of man and the world; Nietzsche preaches the superman but simply has not taken his idea to the same extreme as Kirillov; Christianity preaches the kingdom of resurrected flesh; all three doctrines contain the idea of the transformation of man, and this idea is "something supra-experiential, supra-physical, 'metaphysical' and even mystical."[14]

It would be a great challenge to explain fully and precisely just how and why these statements are so bizarre. The implicit suggestion that Dostoevsky uses Kirillov as a spokesman for his own views (Merezhkovsky explicitly says that Kirillov's ideas are evidence of "the coincidence of Dostoevsky with Nietzsche"[15]); the attribution to Kirillov of a Christian outlook that is so often attributed to Dostoevsky himself; the idea, proposed without irony, that the physical transformation of man is unequivocally a Christian one—one could go on and on. As to the Nietzschean elements, Merezhkovsky was writing in the spirit of an age during which many of his fellow Russian intellectuals

(Western European intellectuals too, for that matter) felt that Nietzsche had to be an integral part of a discussion about pretty much anything.

Elsewhere in the book on Tolstoy and Dostoevsky, Merezhkovsky gives us a fascinating glimpse into his peculiar vision of Christianity. He is discussing the notion of equality as it appears in the teachings of Tolstoy, Nietzsche, and Jesus. Tolstoy and Nietzsche, he says, understand the notion simplistically and too literally. He then says this:

> But equality, the equivalence of human individuals in God, is only *one of two poles* of the teaching of Christ: all are equal in God, because all may and must be equal. At one time they were, and at some time they will be equal, but for now they are not. All are going from God back to God, but they have not yet gotten there . . . one has gone off ahead, while another has stayed behind, and if we fail to recognize this "ahead" and "behind," then all movement comes to a stop. Moreover the teaching of Christ is not a flat path on a flat plane, either earthly or heavenly, but an eternal ascent and descent, a ladder from earth to heaven and from heaven to earth. A ladder is a series of steps. Everyone may rise to the highest step, and there we find equality. But not everyone has yet gotten there, and anyone who does get there will be higher up than those who have stayed behind.[16]

These statements by themselves might be surprising only in their claim to represent "the teaching of Christ," as if all Christians would immediately accept Merezhkovsky's way of formulating that teaching. It's what follows, however, that is truly unbelievable. Merezhkovsky gives the source of his remarks about equality. It is, once again, Christ's own teaching, and for support he quotes Luke 19:26: "To all those who have, more will be given; but from those who have nothing, even what they have will be taken away." Then, in an echo of Father Zosima's wonder at the mysteries of Scripture, Merezhkovsky exclaims, "What an incomprehensible and intolerable aristocratism, what a mystical injustice!" So he "corrects" the words of Jesus to read, "To all those who have not will be given; and from those who have, even what they think they have will be taken away, so that all should have in equal measure." The point, he goes on to say, is that Christ's teaching must be understood not as a reaffirmation of all the old aristocratic values but rather as a "revaluation of these values."[17]

Never mind whether any of this makes the least bit of sense (how could it?). What matters is that Merezhkovsky is glibly proposing it as "the teaching of Christ." That teaching requires us to see ourselves as both mired in the imperfection of earthly life, where nothing is equal, and on our way to an ideal realm where everything is. We go from earth to heaven and back. We marvel at the mystery of inequality on earth and bow before the grandeur of Christ's inexplicable "revaluation of values." How is this simply the teaching of Christ, as if it were universally accepted as such? No, this sounds like the teaching of Christ filtered through Father Zosima (marveling at the mysteries of the earth), which means filtered through Dostoevsky (whether Dostoevsky believed in it or not). It is also, of course, the teaching of Nietzsche, in its affirmation of the earth and earthly life (to which Nietzsche, in so many of his writings, including *The Anti-Christ*, accused historical Christianity of being hostile) and in its affirmation of the revaluation of values.

The year after Merezhkovsky published his study of Tolstoy and Dostoevsky, Sergei Bulgakov (1871–1944), another central figure in the Russian religious renaissance (and one whose résumé included a period of solid commitment to Marxism), published a study called "Ivan Karamazov as a Philosophical Type." Like Merezhkovsky, Bulgakov noticed the resemblance between Nietzsche and some of Dostoevsky's characters. Like Merezhkovsky, he believed Dostoevsky, through such characters, and Nietzsche elaborated a worldview that at least on first inspection conflicts radically with Christianity. Ivan's literary creation, the Grand Inquisitor, finds a reason to denounce the equality of traditional Christianity and, like Nietzsche, to propose a sharp social division in humankind between the masses and a small, elite group of powerful men. The Grand Inquisitor is, in short, Nietzsche's anti-Christ. But instead of torturing logic and good sense in order to fit these impious conceptions into a Christian worldview, as Merezhkovsky did, Bulgakov announces that Ivan and Nietzsche—both children of socialism, the ultimate secular equalizing ideology—are complete skeptics. It's just that Ivan's creator, Dostoevsky, transcended his character's skepticism, while Nietzsche never transcended his own. Bulgakov can say this because he's quite certain that Dostoevsky is essentially the same person as Alesha Karamazov, and Ivan represents nothing more than an abstract intellectual problem.[18]

If anyone solidified and canonized the tendency to examine Dostoevsky's religion, generalize from it to Russian Orthodoxy, and talk about Nietzsche all at the same time, it was Nikolai Berdiaev (1874–1948), who, like so many others of his generation, went through his Nietzschean period before seeing the light and "returning" to the Orthodox Church (while never entirely abandoning Nietzsche). In *Dostoevsky's Worldview* (1921), published the year before the new Soviet state sent Berdiaev into exile for his subversive views, the Nietzscheanism is hard to miss. Tolstoy is an Apollonian, theological thinker, while Dostoevsky is a Dionysian, anthropological thinker.[19] For Dostoevsky, love is Dionysian. Prince Myshkin is Dionysian, but his is a Christian Dionysianism (whatever that might mean).[20] Dionysianism is all over the place in Dostoevsky's world, as Berdiaev sees it, yet Dostoevsky is clearly a metaphysician and a Christian. How to square this with his Nietzscheanism *avant la lettre*? Let's not forget that Christianity for Dostoevsky has to do with earth and man. The question of God for Dostoevsky is a human one, and the question of man is a divine one.[21] His metaphysics is concrete, and his ideas have a "vital character."[22]

If Dostoevsky was a Christian, he was of course a Russian Orthodox one. That's why he favors freedom. As Berdiaev explains, the Roman Catholic world has always inclined to the use of force in matters relating to truth and the good, while the Russian Orthodox world has resisted.[23] The path of freedom is the path of the new man of the Christian world, Berdiaev proclaims.[24]

The problem with this account is, first, that these ideas are ideas that *Dostoevsky* explored in his writings, not ideas that are somehow peculiar to Russian Orthodoxy among the world's various versions of Christianity; and, second, that Dostoevsky was not even the first person to express them. But if they were not original to him, he had not learned them simply from "Russian Orthodoxy." The language about freedom, faith, and universal brotherhood that so often finds its way into descriptions of Russian Orthodoxy, as if these features had somehow been ingrained in the Russian folk from the time it was baptized in the tenth century, is essentially the language that Hegel employed to describe Lutheranism (in his case, as if these features were somehow innate to the *German* spirit and as if, through the ineluctable, rational development of Spirit, they had come to fruition in the beliefs of a rebellious Saxon priest in the early sixteenth century). It is also the language that a group of conservative Russian nationalists known as Slavophiles had been using since Dostoevsky was a young man.

Berdiaev's book on Dostoevsky was eventually translated into English, German, and French. It's unlikely that readers of those languages turned to *Dostoevsky's Worldview* if what they wanted primarily was an understanding of Russian Orthodoxy. Many readers of English, however, did learn about this topic from Berdiaev's younger friend, disciple, and fellow Russian émigré George Fedotov (1886–1951), whose *Russian Religious Mind* (1946) was published in English and came to be widely accepted in the West as the authoritative source on Russian Christianity—not just theology, but actually *how the Russian mind works* when it is in a religious mood. Fedotov followed an intellectual path typical for his generation of Russian religious scholars: it included, after a series of German idealist philosophers, Solov'ev and Dostoevsky.[25]

Fedotov is the one who popularized the notion of *kenosis* (the act of "emptying," described in Philippians 2:7, by which Jesus humbled himself and became a man) as a key to that Russian religious mind.[26] The word *kenosis* was never used in Russian till the last decade of the nineteenth century (after Dostoevsky's death), but there's no doubt that the concept had already been around in Fedotov's home country for a generation or two. German Protestant theology developed kenosis as part of a new earth- and human-oriented Christianity, in fact as part of the broad spirit that led so many writers in the nineteenth century to produce books titled *The Life of Jesus*—biographies, that is, of the actual man who (to describe him from a secular point of view) had purportedly walked the earth eighteen hundred years earlier and created a devoted following. But here again we return to Nietzsche and Dostoevsky, both of whom were way stations on the spiritual-intellectual path that Fedotov took.

Why Nietzsche? In the final paragraph of his chapter on "Russian Kenoticism," Fedotov writes this: "Weak and foolish—such is Christ in His kenosis to the eyes of a Nietzsche just as He was to the eyes of the ancient pagan world."[27] It is the only mention of Nietzsche in the book, which means Fedotov expects his readers to find it unsurprising and self-explanatory.

Why Dostoevsky? The man who introduced the word *kenosis* into Russian religious discourse in 1892 was an Orthodox theologian by the name of Mikhail Mikhailovich Tareev. The book in which he first used the term bore the ungainly title *The Temptations of the Godman as the Unique Redemptive Act of the Whole Earthly Life of Christ, in Connection with the History of Pre-Christian Religions and of the Christian Church.* As the title suggests, this is not a work devoted exclusively to Russian Orthodoxy. Yet, as Paul Valliere, one of the few scholars to have written about Tareev, pointed out some years ago, there is every likelihood that Tareev's views of Christ's *kenosis*, and particularly his emphasis on humility as one of Christ's cardinal virtues, were inspired at least in part by Dostoevsky. Tareev takes as the point of departure for his discussion of humility the temptation narrative in the Gospels, but his approach to this narrative is untraditional: as Valliere shows, it leaves out such issues as incarnation, passion, and resurrection, focusing instead, like Dostoevsky in "The Grand Inquisitor," on the earthly ministry of Jesus.[28] That earthly ministry includes not only Christ's humility but his suffering too. In the second edition to *The Temptations of the Godman*, Tareev, in order to emphasize Christ's earthly status, points out that in the Greek original of the temptation narrative the Savior is addressed not as *the* son of God but simply as "son of God" (Matthew 4:6), meaning *any* one of many sons of God. Like all sons of God, Christ must suffer, and in fact his suffering is a precondition to his believing in God's love for him: "In order for a man whom the sufferings of life have tormented and made into an enemy of God and slave of the devil to come to believe in God's love for him," Tareev writes, "for this the Son of God must appear in the conditions of human life, filled as they are with suffering from evil."[29]

Tareev wrote a fairly lengthy article on Dostoevsky in which, while also defining Russian religious thought in general, he touched on themes that would become standard in scholarship on Dostoevsky's religious views: "Christian humility," love for life, life as an immediate path to God, "real life" as combined with the "highest good," the highest good as part of Godmanhood (as Solov'ev used the word).[30] Tareev's other Russian source for the notion of the kenosis (but without the use of this word) as connected with the temptation narrative is Solov'ev's *Lectures on Godmanhood.* Kenosis (under this name) subsequently shows up in the works of the brilliant philosopher and theologian Pavel Florensky (1882–1937), Sergei Bulgakov, and Fedotov, though Fedotov specifically stresses voluntary, innocent suffering as a kenotic virtue.[31] Tareev's tendency to emphasize humility and suffering as Christian virtues and Fedotov's tendency to see an admiration for humility and voluntary suffering as a cardinal, indigenous attribute of the popular Russian religious temperament, stretching all the way back to the Christianization of Kievan Rus in the tenth century, thus apparently have something to do with the creator of Sonia Marmeladova, Prince Myshkin, and Alesha Karamazov. I'll return to this topic in Chapter Six.

It would be wrong and unfair to say that writers such as Solov'ev, Tareev, and Fedotov were completely ignorant of the character of Christianity—the Russian sort or any other sort—as it existed before Dostoevsky and that their conceptions of the Russian tradition were wholly formed from the odd imaginings of an author of fiction. It would be equally wrong and unfair to suggest that no reader in Russia or the West had access to any source of insight into Dostoevsky's religion, or for that matter into Russian Christianity, other than works by the writers I have just mentioned. Still, Dostoevsky appears to have contributed heavily to a set of themes and emphases that appear, in this peculiar combination, after his death, and the writers I have mentioned exerted a powerful force in shaping critical commentary on this dimension of Dostoevsky's works. To the extent that any writers have mistaken Dostoevsky's own fictional themes for historical fact, the views of those writers are not entirely reliable. This is why it's appropriate to say that, whatever one's final view of this dimension might be (even if one is unable to establish a final view), this part of the history of reading Dostoevsky has helped *obscure* matters. The history of reading him in the West obscured them even more.

## DOSTOEVSKY'S RELIGION
## THROUGH WESTERN EYES

The West has always loved feeling perplexed about Russia, and no figure has inspired more perplexity than Dostoevsky. His contemporary Tolstoy, always stealing the spotlight (not to mention commanding much higher fees for his writing), could boast an international following for the last fifteen years of his life, when it was possible throughout the Western world and beyond to describe oneself as a "Tolstoyan." This is because, even in the West, people felt (rightly or wrongly) that they knew what Tolstoy believed. With Dostoevsky, they were often not so sure. Some sensed that religion was in some way an important element in his books, not to mention in his own strange personality. Others overlooked it almost entirely. Nietzsche, no less popular in Western Europe than in Russia for the first few decades of the twentieth century, puts in frequent appearances.

The man who, more than anyone else, was responsible for introducing Dostoevsky to France as well as to Western Europe was Eugène Melchior, vicomte de Vogüé. He was well placed to speak with authority about things Russian, especially literature. He served for six years (1876–82) as an attaché in the embassy in Saint Petersburg, married the sister of an illustrious Russian general, devoted years to the study of the Russian language and Russian literature, and was personally acquainted with Dostoevsky. In 1886, he published the fruit of his years of study, a book called *The Russian Novel*, in which he included a chapter on Dostoevsky. The title he gave this chapter would probably surprise no one today, but since at that stage so little had been written about Tolstoy's lesser-known countryman, it set the tone for years to come: "The Religion of Suffering—Dostoevsky."

The more we read de Vogüé's chapter, however, the more it appears he made an odd choice of title. De Vogüé himself is said to have been a deeply religious man, yet he seems not to have considered the religious dimension in Dostoevsky to be especially important. He notes that Dostoevsky read the Gospel every night during his term in prison camp.[32] When he speaks of the prisoners that Dostoevsky describes in *Notes from the House of the Dead*, "these men who go to servitude with a Gospel," he characterizes them as "extreme souls penetrated by the spirit of a Gospel that passed through Byzantium, shaped by this spirit for asceticism and martyrdom."[33] But he does not say what he means by "passed through Byzantium." For de Vogüé, when it comes right down to it Dostoevsky's thought defies categorization. As the Frenchman tells it, in the 1860s Dostoevsky positioned himself somewhere between the Russian liberals and the Slavophiles, but closer to the Slavophiles. Thus Dostoevsky's is a patriotic religion, "but this religion, full of mysteries, without precise dogmas, in its essence escapes explanation and polemic: one believes in it or does not, and that's all."[34] Presumably a religion of suffering means that Dostoevsky's religion belonged to no recognized tradition within Christianity, that he elevated suffering to a position of great importance, and that as a result suffering became for him an object of religious devotion.

De Vogüé sets the tone for many future Western discussions of Dostoevsky by simply abandoning all hope of truly understanding this novelist or his creations. Having assessed Dostoevsky's contribution to Russian literature almost exclusively on the strength of *Crime and Punishment*, to which he devotes the largest part of his chapter, he dismisses *The Idiot*, *The Devils*, and *The Brothers Karamazov* as tedious, overly long compositions whose only purpose was to serve as vehicles for Dostoevsky's theories.[35] *The Idiot* carries one obsessive idea: "the supremacy of those who are simple of mind and of those who suffer."[36] *The Devils*, "confused, poorly constructed, often ridiculous and encumbered with apocalyptic theories," is little more than a commentary on the revolutionary movement; *The Brothers Karamazov* merits only the two remarks that very few Russians have had the patience to get through it and that it's not worth further discussion. In the end, de Vogüé endorses this statement about Dostoevsky by "one of the masters of contemporary psychology" (whom he does not identify): "This man opens unknown horizons on souls that are different from ours; he reveals to us a new world, natures that are more powerful both for bad and for good, stronger in willing and in suffering."[37]

The German-speaking world produced similarly complicated responses, and in one particularly important case almost as early as France. In addition to giving so many readers, Russian and Western, a set of philosophical concepts (that is, those he did *not* formulate with Dostoevsky in mind) with which to interpret Dostoevsky's works, Nietzsche actually commented on his Russian kindred spirit. He thus directly forms a part of the history of Dostoevsky interpretation. To be sure, his role in this history outside Russia, like his role in the history in Russia, stems mostly from the use to which his future commentators put writings that had nothing to do with Dostoevsky. But Nietzsche's own comments on Dostoevsky are worth mentioning in their own right, and it's certainly safe to say that no other non-Russian did so much to shape (for better, but mostly for worse) the West's understanding of the religious element in Dostoevsky's works.

Anyone who has spent time studying Dostoevsky knows the often-quoted passage from *Twilight of the Idols* (1888) in which the *enfant terrible* of nineteenth-century thought, late in a career soon to be ended by madness, refers to the Russian author as "the only psychologist . . . from whom I had anything to learn."[38] One important Western European writer, Danish critic Georg Brandes, actually had a chance to learn of Nietzsche's views from Nietzsche himself, though he appears to have applied other ideas of Nietzsche to the works of Dostoevsky. Nietzsche corresponded with Brandes, and the same year as *Twilight of the Idols* appeared Brandes wrote Nietzsche a letter in which he described Dostoevsky as a "detestable fellow, completely Christian in his emotional life and at the same time completely sadistic." In sum, Brandes said, "his entire morality is what you have christened 'slave morality.'"[39] Brandes had read *Beyond Good and Evil* (1886) and *The Genealogy of Morality* (1887) with great enthusiasm and was particularly struck by Nietzsche's distinction, introduced in the first of these books, between the powerful morality of masters and the weak morality of slaves. He was equally drawn to Nietzsche's association, in the second of these books, of slave morality with Christianity and with *ressentiment*, the repugnant feeling of injured victimhood that masters inspire in slaves and that has been a guiding spirit in the historical development of Christianity. The previous year Brandes spent three months in Russia and wrote *Impressions of Russia* (published in 1888), which included a chapter on Dostoevsky. He generally followed the lead of de Vogüé, devoting the bulk of his space to a discussion of *Crime and Punishment* and relatively little to the other works of Dostoevsky's mature years. His global comment about the work of the "weird genius" is that it is devoted to the morality of the slave, a concept, Brandes tells us, for whose emergence we are indebted to Nietzsche.[40]

So Brandes's choice of the word "Christian" as a term of contempt in a letter to Nietzsche is hardly arbitrary. In his reply, Nietzsche concurred "absolutely." "Nonetheless," he wrote, "I treasure [Dostoevsky] as the most valuable psychological material I know—I am in a strange way grateful to him no matter how much he runs counter to my most basic instincts."[41]

But to return to Germany: if Nietzsche left a mark on Dostoevsky interpretation out of all proportion to the scant comments he made, the same could probably be said for Freud, whose impact on the future of literary interpretation in general I don't need to document here. Freud's writing on Dostoevsky, his famous essay "Dostoevsky and Patricide" (1928), probably does a better job of offering us something "Freudian" than Nietzsche does of offering something characteristically "Nietzschean" in his own scattered remarks.[42] Predictably, Freud's interest is in the author's personality, which he finds a "bewildering complexity" (*verwirrende Komplikation*).[43] But if the aggregate of "façades" in this personality is bewildering, there is one façade that is not: the neurotic. Freud's analysis of Dostoevsky's epileptic disorder as an expression of an Oedipal wish has been widely known and hotly debated for years. Writing at a time when he had reason to fear that many readers might recoil at the suggestion that patricide is "the chief and primal crime of mankind as of the individual,"[44] Freud assures us (as he assures readers of works more clearly devoted to psychoanalysis itself) that "psychoanalytic experience has placed precisely these matters beyond all doubt."[45] Psychoanalysis, after all, is a science. As to Dostoevsky's religion, Freud offers the analysis that became customary for him: it is founded on filial guilt. This explains both Dostoevsky's attraction to the Christ ideal (as a path toward liberation from guilt) and his celebrated sympathy for the criminal (who takes on the guilt of others and thus represents a Redeemer).[46]

If ever there was a case of reading an author in order to promote one's own ideological program, this is it. Not that there's anything wrong with the program as Freud conceived it. He never pretended he was uncovering the artistic treasures in Dostoevsky's works (though incidentally he considers *The Brothers Karamazov* to be the finest novel ever written). His plan was to uncover something about Dostoevsky himself. Nor was his primary aim to reveal the details of Dostoevsky's religious worldview. But in his effort to carry out his plan to analyze the neurosis that gave rise to the literary works and the religious worldview, he treats the worldview as a pure abstraction: everyone knows what religion is in general, and, what's more, everyone knows what Christianity is specifically. Freud never attempts to identify the peculiarities of Dostoevsky's Christianity, even those that might be of psychoanalytic interest.

Roman Guardini, an Italian Catholic priest and theologian who grew up in Germany and wrote in German, tried his hand at Dostoevsky interpretation in 1932, with the publication of *Man and Faith: Essays on Religious Existence in Dostoevsky's Great Novels*. Guardini makes an admirable effort to approach his subject without the bias of either Western Christianity or Russian Orthodoxy. In fact, as he explains in his preface, he has avoided almost all secondary interpretive literature, relying only on sources that provide factual information. The result is some truly valuable comments simply on the content of the religious ideas that various characters express in Dostoevsky's novels. But despite his method, Guardini was not without bias. He repeatedly observes that the key to a proper understanding of Dostoevsky's religious ideas is Nietzsche. In one footnote, for example, he urges the reader to regard Ivan Karamazov's "rebellion" not as evidence of a paradoxical relation with God, like what we would find in Kierkegaard, but as evidence of the "self-elevation of man against God." It is Nietzsche, he says, who offered the formula for this spirit.[47]

Thomas Mann was drawn to Dostoevsky, especially during World War I, and shared Freud's admiration for his works. Late in his life, after he fled Nazi Germany and settled in the United States, Mann was invited to write the introduction to a collection of Dostoevsky's short fiction in English translation. The introduction is beautifully written and contains gems of expression and insight that will delight anyone familiar with Mann's mind and work.[48] But Mann in part was at the mercy of what by then had become a tradition in the West. He displayed *the* common reaction to the task of writing about Dostoevsky: a combination of fear in the face of perplexity, admiration for disordered genius, and an urge to see his own interests reflected in the Russian novelist's works. He is grateful for the limited nature of his assignment (writing an introduction), since a commentator might have recoiled from "the task of making the entire, tremendous cosmos of Dostoevsky's works the object of his consideration and discussion." Having already written about Tolstoy, Mann shudders at the thought of turning his attention to Tolstoy's contemporary.[49] Just as for others in the West, Dostoevsky's religion is a fleeting object of attention, and as for others there is little attempt in Mann's essay to identify much of anything peculiar to Dostoevsky's version of it.

Nietzsche rears his head here, as Mann overtly displays the common tendency to assimilate the Russian to his accidental German alter ego. In part, Mann's thinking about Dostoevsky has been shaped by his reading of Merezhkovsky, who pointed to the presence of the criminal element, the Superman (both of which Mann explicitly mentions in connection with Merezhkovsky), and disease in Dostoevsky's works (which Mann does not mention in connection with Merezhkovsky).[50] In addition, Mann saw a connection between the two writers because he was under the mistaken impression that Nietzsche had read at least *Crime and Punishment* early enough to offer a shadow image of Raskolnikov in *Thus Spake Zarathustra*.[51] But even without this understandable error and even without the Merezhkovsky connection, it should come as no surprise that the writer who devoted his literary efforts to the marriage of illness and artistic inspiration should not only find the clue to Dostoevsky's genius in the author's physical and mental afflictions but also see the creator of Raskolnikov and Svidrigailov as inseparable from the creator of Zarathustra and the Superman: "Disease . . . First of all, it is a question of who is sick, who is insane, who is epileptic or paralytic: an average dolt, whose disease, of course, lacks all intellectual and cultural aspects—or a Nietzsche, a Dostoevsky. In their cases the disease bears fruits that are more important and more beneficial to life and its development than any medically approved normality."[52]

What about religion? Since Dostoevsky and Nietzsche are "brothers in spirit," there is little to divide them in this connection besides Dostoevsky's being a "Byzantine Christian."[53] The two writers share a moralism that Mann describes as "religious, i.e., satanistic."[54] There is an "aura of devoutness" that surrounds the two and influences their self-consciousness.[55] But religion here is little more than a vaguely construed metaphor for states of mind to which the illnesses of the two men give rise. Even in the case of Dostoevsky's epilepsy (Mann could hardly have chosen the word "aura" without purpose), Mann declares the phase of the illness that follows a seizure, the phase characterized by depression and spiritual darkness, to be far more important than the phase that precedes, which Dostoevsky described in language so overtly religious as to leave no doubt that for *him*, if not for Thomas Mann, his illness carried a significant connection with at least his own understanding of religion.

Back in France, only a few years after the appearance of de Vogüé's book, Marcel Proust discovered Dostoevsky.[56] From the period when he was beginning work on *À la recherche du temps perdu* till the end of his life, he made

numerous references to "le grand Russe," as he called him. By far the most famous is the one that occurs late in *La Prisonnière*, the fifth volume of his novel.
In one of his more contrived scenes, we see the hero and Albertine, his young
mistress, engaged in a four-page conversation transparently constructed to give
the author a pulpit for sharing with us his thoughts on Dostoevsky. Albertine
asks the hero if Dostoevsky had ever murdered anyone. "I don't think so," he
answers. "There is no doubt that, like everyone else, he knew sin in one form or
another, and probably in a form that the law prohibits." He struggles to find
someone with whom he can compare the Russian novelist, but he gives up.

> All this seems as distant from me as possible, unless there are parts of me that
> I don't know. . . . But isn't this a motif, sculptural and simple, that is worthy
> of the most antique art, a frieze that is interrupted and then resumed on
> which Vengeance and Expiation unfold, this crime of the elder Karamazov,
> who gets the poor young madwoman pregnant, the mysterious, animal, un-
> explained movement by which the mother . . . goes to give birth in the home
> of the elder Karamazov?[57]

Proust added the Dostoevsky conversation to the novel almost as an af-
terthought in 1922, the year of his death. Earlier that same year his contemporary André Gide, with a number of prominent literary works to his name
and with the formidable power of his position as a founder of the *Nouvelle
Revue Française*, had presented a series of lectures on Dostoevsky to the
drama school of the Theatre of the Vieux-Colombier in Paris. With no other
credential than his status as a prominent man of letters, Gide adopts an
oddly patronizing tone as he addresses his audience. "I feel overwhelmed by
the number and by the importance of things I have left to tell you," he begins the final lecture of the series. "It's also that, as you've known from the
start, Dostoevsky is often no more than a pretext here for me to express my
own ideas. I would make further excuses for myself if I thought that in so
doing I were distorting Dostoevsky's ideas, but no. . . . "[58]

These are strange words from a man who has shown himself throughout
his course of addresses to be even more flummoxed by his subject than de
Vogüé and Proust were. Fourteen years earlier, in a study of Dostoevsky's
correspondence, Gide had written in celebration of the complexity of the
thought as expressed in the author's letters: "Conservative but not tradition-
alist; Tsarist but a democrat; Christian but not Roman Catholic; liberal but
not a 'progressive,' Dostoevsky remains someone *that one does not know how
to use*."[59] Religion is precisely where the mysterious Russian novelist is at his

most baffling. De Vogüé was right to coin the phrase "religion of suffering," but it was not adequate to contain the many contradictions of Dostoevsky's thought. Gide, himself that rarest of birds, a French Protestant, knew what it was to be "Christian, but not a Roman Catholic." Still, the comments he offers on Dostoevsky's religion in the lecture series, like this comment on the correspondence, betray not only bewilderment in the face of the incomprehensible but inability to escape Western European categories in a futile attempt to fathom that religion.

What else would lead a respected intellectual to offer such ridiculous comments on Dostoevsky's religion as those that fill Gide's lecture series? For example, having observed that "Dostoevsky's heroes inherit the Kingdom of God only by the denial of mind and will and the surrender of personality" (a partly defensible statement), Gide goes on to conclude that Dostoevsky's version of the human comedy springs "from the contact between the Gospels and Buddhism, the Asiatic spirit."[60] Or, having claimed that Russians, by contrast with Westerners, are willing to humble themselves and seek forgiveness, Gide says, "The Greek Orthodox religion is no doubt merely encouraging a national tendency in tolerating, often even in approving of, public confession."[61] Evidence? Definition of "national tendency"? Or again: "I know of no author who is at the same time more Christian and less Catholic." If he's not Catholic and he's not Protestant, then what is he? Someone who takes "the teaching of Christ directly and exclusively from the Gospels," thus someone who leads us to "a sort of Buddhism, or at least a sort of quietism."[62] If Greek Orthodoxy holds the secret to Dostoevsky's religion, then let's find out something about it. If Dostoevsky's religion is a kind of pure Christianity stripped of what a French intellectual would most likely think of—namely, its Roman Catholic trappings—then let's not call it Buddhism.

Again we find Nietzsche. Like so many others, Gide knew full well that a conversation about Dostoevsky had to be at the same time a conversation about the novelist's German soul brother. Gide's remarks are filled with references to Nietzsche—more to Nietzsche, in fact, than to anyone besides Dostoevsky himself (in fact, Nietzsche's famous comment about Dostoevsky the psychologist serves as the epigraph to his book). Where Nietzsche's name comes up is precisely in connection with religion. In Gide's eyes, both men were obsessed with the relation between man and something greater—God or Jesus. His example: in The Devils, Dostoevsky has Stavrogin and his disciple Kirillov ponder the issue of "the man-God's succeeding the God-man." The way Gide sees it, this issue troubled Nietzsche just as much as it did Dostoevsky. To be sure, the reactions of the Russian novelist and the German philosopher differed: Nietzsche devoted his energy to the "affirmation of the self," while Dostoevsky proposed resignation, "bowed deeply before Christ."[63] But to Gide, the religious issues were essentially the same for both writers.

In the English-speaking world, things were much the same as they were in Germany and France. Virginia Woolf devoted an entire beautifully written essay in 1925 to the subject of English bewilderment in the face of Russian literature in general.[64] She does not get into a detailed discussion of religion in Russian literature, but its power to perplex stems from something that at least falls under that topic: the soul. The best example is Dostoevsky. The reason his novels demand such an effort is that they "are composed purely and wholly of the stuff of the soul" and that the soul is entirely alien to the English reader.[65] The exclusive dominance of the soul for Dostoevsky leads to a fictional world filled with contradictions: "Men are at the same time villains and saints; their acts are at once beautiful and despicable. We love and we hate at the same time. There is none of that precise division between good and bad to which we are used."[66] The same dominance also leads Woolf to claim, against the clearest evidence in his novels, that Dostoevsky recognized no social distinctions. "It is all the same to him whether you are noble or simple, a tramp or a great lady."[67]

A few years later, toward the end of his life, D. H. Lawrence wrote an introduction to a separate edition of "The Grand Inquisitor." His own personal journey with Dostoevsky was beset with bumps and false starts. He initially found the story of the Grand Inquisitor to be "rubbish" and was unable to understand all the fuss about it. He then changed his mind, hence his willingness twenty-odd years later to write this preface. In the meantime, Dostoevsky hardly yielded all his secrets and resolved all his contradictions: "His wild love for Jesus is mixed with perverse and poisonous hate of Jesus: his moral hostility to the devil is mixed with secret worship of the devil. Dostoevsky is always perverse, always impure, always an evil thinker and a marvellous seer."[68] On one count, though, Lawrence is confident, and that is the question of the relation between the author and the demon he created (or the demon his character created). It is beyond doubt, he says, that "the Inquisitor speaks Dostoevsky's own final opinion about Jesus." What might that final opinion be? Easy: Jesus is inadequate; men must correct him; when Jesus, without ever having uttered a single word, responds to the Inquisitor's indictment by kissing the old man on the lips, he (Jesus) is showing his acquiescence to the Inquisitor.[69]

If other Western European commentators have brought to their reading of Dostoevsky an understanding of Christianity founded in Western preconceptions, Lawrence brings an understanding of the world founded in his own storied worship of nature and "life." I'm admittedly leaving out a few pages that follow the remarks I have just paraphrased, but the leap in thought from those remarks to the reflections that come at the end of Lawrence's preface is just as extravagant with as without those pages. It's vintage Lawrence, but in a discussion of Dostoevsky it comes across as downright weird: "The earthly bread is leavened with the heavenly bread. The heavenly bread is life, is contact, and is consciousness." Lawrence now feels the moment has arrived to take his readers on a journey through the cycle of the sowing of seed, the springing of the corn, Holy Week and Easter Sunday, and the reaping and the harvest, concluding, "All this is life, life, it is the heavenly bread which we eat in the course of getting the earthly bread. Work is, or should be, our heavenly bread of activity. Contact and consciousness. All work that is not this, is anathema. True, the work is hard, there is the sweat of the brow. But what of it? In decent proportion, this is life. The sweat of the brow is the heavenly butter."[70]

Across the Atlantic, a number of prominent literary scholars decided to tackle the unruly Russian genius. Murray Krieger was among them. In 1960, he published *The Tragic Vision*, a book that used Kierkegaard's *Fear and Trembling* (1843), with its famous notion of choice among resignation, rebellion, and "leap of faith," to establish a theory of "tragic vision" and the cultural type of the "tragic visionary." The tragic vision is "an expression of man only in an extreme situation . . . a vision of extreme cases, a distillate of the rebellion, the godlessness which, once induced by crisis, purifies itself by rejecting all palliatives." The tragic visionary is "the extremist who . . . finds himself transformed from character to parable."[71] Krieger includes, among the heroes of such authors as Malraux, Thomas Mann, Kafka, and Camus, Dostoevsky's Prince Myshkin.[72]

Like all the Western critics I've mentioned, Krieger is handicapped by his inability to read Dostoevsky in the original language and his consequent reliance on a translation. Thus he identifies as a point of departure for any critic of *The Idiot* Dostoevsky's intention "to portray a truly beautiful soul" and speaks of Myshkin's combination of "pity and love" for Nastasia Filippovna. In a discussion that attempts to marry classical tragedy with the Lutheran Christianity of Kierkegaard, accepting "soul" as a translation for the Russian *chelovek* ("person") and "pity" to render the expression *mne zhal' ee* ("I feel sorry for her") can be highly misleading (in fact, even "I feel sorry for her" is not quite right).[73]

So how can we be surprised when Krieger dismisses Myshkin's anti-Catholic tirade as an "errant insertion" in a flawed novel that Dostoevsky filled with similar inconsistencies and infelicities? The tirade may very well be inconsistent with the prince's character, but to describe it as errant is to suggest that it's impossible to explain how it ever got into the novel in the first place. If we can safely perform textual analysis on a translation, why not also assume that Christianity is Christianity and that there's nothing special we need to know about the context in which Dostoevsky wrote what is possibly the most memorable scene in *The Idiot*? Why not react the way so many readers have done and simply describe the book as "confusing?"[74] Dostoevsky was "too much of a Christian not to insist that the fallen world would somehow have to be reflected in its saintly but human intruder." Prince Myshkin is Dostoevsky's attempt at showing "man as Jesus," and the attempt failed so much that Dostoevsky had to try all over again in *The Brothers Karamazov*.[75] But *what kind of* Christian? *What* Jesus? If we were writing about Saint Augustine, would we casually use the term "Christian" without bothering to describe what this term might mean for a churchman living in the Roman Empire in the fourth and fifth centuries C.E.? If we were writing about Nietzsche, would we casually mention Jesus without bothering to describe what this figure means to a German (and *this* German!) living at the end of the nineteenth century? Then how can "Christian" and "Jesus" have a merely generic meaning to a man who was raised in Russian Orthodoxy and at the same time exposed to a host of conflicting religious doctrines (Russian and Western European) in mid-to-late-nineteenth-century Russia?

Before the 1970s, most of the full-length critical-biographical treatments of Dostoevsky by academic authors either gave scant treatment to religious issues or followed the author's early nonspecialist Western readers in speaking generically of Christian themes and concepts. Ernest J. Simmons, for example, in *Dostoevsky: The Making of a Novelist* (1950), refers to the Russian Orthodox Church many times but never gives any indication of learning much more about it than that Dostoevsky frequently shows it to be in conflict with Roman Catholicism and believes it represents a purer form of Christian faith than its Western counterpart. In other words, Simmons essentially restricts his own knowledge of Russian Orthodoxy to what he can read in Dostoevsky's text. This is certainly blameless as far as it goes, but it does not tell us whether Dostoevsky's own references to Russian Orthodoxy rest on any solid foundation or whether they merely stem from an outlook that is peculiar to him. To judge only from the few references, in the text and in the bibliography, to scholars who wrote about Christian themes in Dostoevsky, Simmons must have confined his reading to the Russians I mentioned earlier: Merezhkovsky, Rozanov, and Berdiaev.

Since 1970, scholars in the West have paid more attention to the religious element in Dostoevsky's work, and some of them have largely avoided the pitfalls of assuming a generic Christianity and relying on a tradition shaped in part by Dostoevsky and Nietzsche. There is a book-length study in French, by Jean Drouilly, which I will have occasion to mention later on.[76] The English-speaking world in the same period has produced a number of works that prominently feature the religious dimension in Dostoevsky's work or that are exclusively devoted to it. Ellis Sandoz's *Political Apocalypse: A Study of Dostoevsky's Grand Inquisitor* (1971), as its title indicates, is a study of Dostoevsky's political thought, but the nature of Ivan Karamazov's famous "poem" requires the author to speak at length about religion. In a chapter titled "Philosophical Anthropology," Sandoz turns to Russian Orthodox Christianity. He relies heavily on the Fedotov tradition, as his references (none of them in Russian) and his discussion of kenoticism clearly indicate. We find, for example, these statements:

> Revealed in the Christ of the Legend [of the Grand Inquisitor] is the Russian Christ as meditated by contemplatives from the time of [early Russian saints] Boris and Gleb. It is the kenotic Christ of self-humiliation, suffering, love, humility, and voluntary sacrificial death. . . . The picture of Christ, thus, weaves together the principal elements of Russian devotion. . . . The highest expression of the Russian religious soul is the "following" of Christ . . . by sharing his passion. This kenotic ideal is the expression of *agape*, the simple caritative (not mystical) love immediately evident in the biblical Christ.[77]

The sources for these remarks? Not surprisingly, they are Fedotov's *Russian Religious Mind* and a book by the twentieth-century Russian scholar Nicolas Zernov. Zernov's book is titled, revealingly, *Three Russian Prophets: Khomiakov, Dostoevsky, Soloviev* and forms part of the powerful tradition of treating Dostoevsky's fiction as an integral part of the history of Russian Orthodoxy.

A. Boyce Gibson's *The Religion of Dostoevsky* (1973) too contains very few references to Russian sources. The author, a professor of philosophy, indicates through his sources that he has learned about Russian Christianity largely through some of the Russian thinkers I have already mentioned; the standard three-volume English-language anthology of Russian philosophy;

and another work by Nicolas Zernov, titled *Eastern Christendom*. It's easy to see the limitations of his approach (to choose only one example) when he claims that the central religious concept for Dostoevsky in his later years was *sobornost'*, which "was a vital part of the Orthodox tradition."[78] *Sobornost'* (often left in its original form, as here) is sometimes translated as "conciliarity." Since the word is constructed from *sobor*, which means "council" or "assembly" (in secular and ecclesiastical senses), it refers to a spirit of universal brotherhood, a kind of noninstitutional, universal church, much like the one that Vladimir Solov'ev spoke of. It is the invention of Dostoevsky's older compatriot Aleksei Khomiakov, whom I mentioned earlier. Like *kenosis*, *sobornost'* may well refer to a trend that existed in Russian Christianity for some time without being thus named, but as a term with its own set of emphases it was in Dostoevsky's day a very recent creation. The great historian of Russia Nicholas Riasonovsky, in fact, wrote some time ago that *sobornost'* was essentially half Russian Orthodoxy and half early-nineteenth-century European romanticism.[79]

Joseph Frank's recently completed five-volume critical biography contains no doubt a more sober and thorough treatment of Dostoevsky's religious thought than any of its predecessors in the West. Frank, taking a masterfully broad view of the author and his works, integrates Dostoevsky's religion into a worldview that includes the social-historical world contemporary to Dostoevsky as well as the specifically political world. James Scanlan's *Dostoevsky the Thinker: A Philosophical Study* (2002) contains some extremely valuable chapters on religious thought, though Scanlan is more convinced than I am of the possibility of attributing to Dostoevsky a coherent set of beliefs.

Once again, I don't pretend to be giving a complete survey of the commentary, scholarly and nonscholarly, on Dostoevsky's religious thinking. I don't wish to claim that the works I've mentioned are without merit, and I certainly don't mean to suggest that almost no one in the West has had anything of value to say about the religious dimension in Dostoevsky's works. I merely wish to say that the task of understanding this dimension in the West has been complicated by the peculiar history of the commentary on it—doubly complicated, in fact, because so often the "reliable" Russian sources to which Western writers turn for information about Dostoevsky's religion are tainted in the way I described earlier. What complicates the picture even more is that Dostoevsky's ideas about religion *were* partly shaped by Western Christian conceptions—but not in the way that most Western commentators suspected.

## CHAPTER TWO

# Dostoevsky and Religion: The Context

For now, let's set aside the question of whether or not Dostoevsky embraced religious beliefs that his characters expressed in his stories and novels or that he himself expressed in his nonfiction writings. When he thought about religion in general and Christianity in particular, what questions and issues, given his circumstances, were likely to arise in his mind, and why?

Of course it's impossible to give a completely solid answer to this question. To begin with, Dostoevsky's thoughts about religion (and everything else, for that matter) contain a healthy proportion of his own idiosyncratic personality, and surely there's no reliable way to measure that proportion. In addition, when we examine intellectual trends that might have helped shape his thoughts, we're forced to draw some fairly speculative inferences about what he knew or was "exposed to." Naturally this is true for anyone who's dead and consequently unable to answer questions, but it's especially true in Dostoevsky's case, because he appears to have read very little serious philosophy of any significant level of difficulty. Shortly after he was released from prison camp in 1854, for example, he wrote his brother to request, among other things, a copy of Hegel's *History of Philosophy*, saying that his "entire future is bound up with this."[1] There's some question about whether he actually even received the books he requested, but as far as anyone has been able to tell if he ever received the Hegel he never cracked it. Yet there can be little doubt, as I'll show in a moment, that Dostoevsky had in his head at least a popularized notion of certain Hegelian phrases and concepts, because he is so good at presenting them in an amusingly distorted and satirical form.

Still, it's quite possible to see what the questions and issues were, just as it is to see why an educated Russian who came of age in the 1840s might have thought about these questions and issues in connection with religion. Many of them were framed by Western European, primarily German thinkers. Others were framed by Russian thinkers who were either directly borrowing from Western European thinkers or adapting the ideas of these thinkers to their own national context. I quote from these thinkers as extensively as I do because I wish to offer a sense of the language in which educated people in Russia and Western Europe expressed ideas about religion just before and during Dostoevsky's life. No matter what Dostoevsky himself may or may not have read, we find this language over and over again in his works. It should be easy to see why this context helped create as tortured and ambivalent an attitude toward religion as was Dostoevsky's, and why that attitude is consequently so difficult to isolate and describe.

## WESTERN EUROPE AND HOW GOD CAME TO BE A MERELY HUMAN ATTRIBUTE

I'm definitely not the first one to tell some version of this story. A few provisos: first, I'm telling a version of it that I've tailored to "Dostoevsky's religion." For this reason, I'm leaving out many figures we would find in a version by, say, an historian of religion telling the story for its own sake. Second, I'm not claiming Dostoevsky actually read texts by all the figures I'm including. Third, I don't mean to suggest that the philosophers I'm about to speak of belonged to the same "school" or generally thought the same way about religion. What I'm looking at are two closely related tendencies: to regard God and Jesus as purely human attributes and to regard religion either as a natural, predictable human phenomenon or as something having a primarily practical function for human life. Some of these philosophers profess contempt for religion, others admiration and respect. But what all have in common, to varying degrees, is a vantage point (or, at the least, language that leads many readers to discern such a vantage point) detached from personal religious faith, a vantage point from which, if one is not directly attacking religion, one looks at it objectively and dispassionately, attempting to account for its puzzling nature rather than attempting, say, to convert the reader or to reveal religion's secrets from the inside.

Let me start with a point of reference in Dostoevsky's own works. *The Devils* (published in 1871) contains a chapter called "Night," in which Nikolai Stavrogin, the hero, pays a visit to his two former disciples, Kirillov and Shatov. Kirillov is an atheist and a humanist, which to him means that he doesn't believe in God (except in a rather peculiar way) and that he reduces experience to the uniquely human. Yet in an earlier conversation, Kirillov revealed his notion that if he were to kill himself specifically "to kill fear," he would *become* God.

He has an extraordinary view of God, history, and the future: "There is no God, but he exists. . . . History will divide itself into two parts: from the gorilla to the annihilation of God and from the annihilation of God . . . to the transformation of the earth and the physical transformation of man."[2] During Stavrogin's nocturnal visit, Kirillov now professes his love for things of the earth (specifically leaves) and speaks of the "man-God." Stavrogin asks Kirillov if he means the "God-man," and Kirillov insists that he means just what he said. He evades the question whether he has started to believe, saying instead that he prays to everything, for example, a spider crawling on the wall.[3]

Shatov is a Slavophile, which to him means someone who combines a fervent love of Russia with the belief that there is a distinctly Russian God and that the Russian people are the lone God-bearing people on earth, "coming to renew and save the world with the name of the new God." "God," he says, "is the synthetic personality of the entire people, taken from their beginning to their end." "The people are the body of God." Shatov rails against the Catholic Church, equating it with atheism and socialism: "I believe in Russia and her [Russian] Orthodoxy . . . I believe in the body of Christ . . . I believe that the second coming will take place in Russia." This last set of remarks comes in response to Stavrogin's question whether he (Shatov) believes in God. Since it's clear from what Shatov has been saying that one can't embrace his system of beliefs without believing in God, Stavrogin tauntingly presses him and asks once again if he believes. Shatov's comical answer: "I . . . I will believe in God."[4]

The worldviews that Kirillov and Shatov each claim to embrace appear at first to be mutually contradictory, at least in the fundamental respect that Kirillov's rests on a rejection of God (as traditionally understood) and has no room for a national god, while Shatov's rests on belief in God and includes a national god. We learn from Kirillov and Shatov that Stavrogin has been a mentor to both. Shatov puts it bluntly and unequivocally, saying that the Slavophile phrases he utters are Stavrogin's own, that Stavrogin was the teacher and Shatov the pupil, and that Kirillov is Stavrogin's creation. Nevertheless, not one of the three men truly believes. Stavrogin says so explicitly when, defending himself against (but not refuting) the claim that he created Kirillov, he explicitly admits to being an atheist now and to having been one at the time he taught Shatov and Kirillov.[5] Given the lack of faith in all three men, it's possible to surmise that in some respects the theories of Shatov and Kirillov are not so different from each other as they might initially appear and that Stavrogin was not being entirely inconsistent in teaching the two theories.

Stavrogin himself had a mentor. We learn early in the novel that Stepan Verkhovensky, that archetypal representative of the 1840s generation of Russian romantic idealists, was the young Nikolai's tutor and that the two grew very attached to one another.[6] What did the older man believe? Let's speak only about religion. A couple of pages before telling us about the teacher-disciple relationship, the narrator says that the "teacher believed in God," but the details he gives immediately show that this statement is not true in any traditional sense. Either the narrator is speaking ironically, or he has a poor understanding of Verkhovensky's beliefs. Here's exactly what the old man himself says: "I don't understand why everyone here regards me as a godless man. . . . I believe in God, *mais distinguons*, I believe in him as in a being conscious of himself in me only. . . . As regards Christianity, notwithstanding my sincere respect for it, I am not a Christian. I'm rather an ancient pagan, like the great Goethe or an ancient Greek."[7]

I'll explain shortly what Dostoevsky was likely thinking of when he put these words into the mouth of his character. For now, however, all that matters is the patent absurdity of Verkhovensky's statements. To describe God as "a being conscious of himself in me only" is to describe him in a manner that, at least before the nineteenth century, would have been incomprehensible to almost any Christian. Verkhovensky represents God as a being endowed with an attribute that is distinctly human, namely consciousness. To claim to believe in God and then claim to be a pagan like Goethe or an ancient Greek is implicitly to say that you are simultaneously a monotheist and a pantheist. What Verkhovensky says makes no sense on the face of it.

To be sure, the narrator nowhere explicitly tells us that Verkhovensky taught these exact ideas to Stavrogin, but the old man was the dominant influence in the boy's life, while Stavrogin, in turn, appears to have been the dominant influence in the lives of Kirillov and Shatov. Different though the worldviews of the four men might appear to be on the surface, they share two features: all explicitly or implicitly deny the existence of, or fail to believe in, God (or at least *one* God), and all ultimately are rooted in the human and secular. Verkhovensky's "God" exists only as a function of his (God's) relationship with Verkhovensky personally. Stavrogin, a confessed atheist, spends the entire novel in pursuit of earthly and human experiences. Kirillov believes in God only if God results from the physical transformation of man. Shatov believes in a God who, as his teacher Stavrogin points out, is a "simple attribute of the folk [*narodnost'*]."[8]

So where does all this come from?

A good place to begin is the work of Immanuel Kant (1724–1804). The letter in which Dostoevsky requested a copy of Hegel's *History of Philosophy* contains also a request for Kant's *Critique of Pure Reason* (1781, 1787). It's highly unlikely he ever read this work. The *Critique of Pure Reason* is devoted to the subject of epistemology. Kant's most sustained discussion of religion appears in a work that he wrote well after the *Critique of Pure Reason*. In *Religion Within the Boundaries of Reason Alone* (1793), Kant's aim is to build a case for a religion of morality based on reason (where the word has been redefined to refer to the faculty of mind that allows us to think about such suprasensible ideas as "the good"). His approach is therefore detached and pragmatic, since he regards religion as something essentially senseless in and for itself but helpful in establishing Kant's type of morality in humankind. He has little admiration either for rituals and observances connected with institutional religions or for most religions themselves. Consider this statement about miracles:

> If a moral religion (one that is to be based not in statutes and observances but in the heart's attitude toward compliance with all of man's duties, seen as divine commands) needs to be founded, then all *miracles* that history connects with the establishment of that religion must themselves in the end make belief in miracles in general unnecessary. . . . Still, it is appropriate to man's style of thinking that, if a religion of mere cult and observances comes to its end, so that one founded in spirit and truth . . . needs to be established,

the introduction of the latter, even though it does not require it, should be accompanied and at the same time adorned in history by miracles, in order that it might proclaim the ending of the former, which without miracles would have lacked all authority.[9]

One could spend pages listing and discussing all the elements in this passage (and this is not one of the most often quoted passages in Kant's study) that would be inconsistent with the principles of almost any religion. But to be brief, I'll mention only three. Kant's framing of the topic betrays a perspective detached from any given religion, since he poses the problem of establishing a purely hypothetical religion that would satisfy certain purely hypothetical criteria. He states outright that a religion like the one he has in mind would have no need of miracles. He allows, however, that miracles, unnecessary though they might be, can have a certain pragmatic value. The suggestion is that some human intelligence might very well design a religion and make conscious choices about which elements to include and which elements to exclude.

Here's how Kant speaks of the God-man (the Son of God):

> But in the appearance of the God-man, there is nothing of him that falls to the senses or that can be recognized through experience; there is instead the prototype that lies in our reason and that we attribute to the God-man (since, as far as can be perceived from his example, he is found to be in conformity with the prototype), truly the object of beatific faith. And such a faith is the same thing as the principle of life conduct that is pleasing to God.[10]

I would expect many Christian believers to take great offense at the suggestion that the Savior is nothing more than an idea formed in human reason, that life conduct pleasing to God is nothing more than a principle, and that faith in the Son of God is nothing more than this principle.

Finally, there is Kant on the New Testament. Let's suppose we've decided to talk about the general idea of a revealed religion. We're likely to want an example or two from history, since in order to make ourselves understood we would need to think of some actual cases to serve as examples. "We could not do better than to accept, as a medium for the elucidation of our idea of a revealed religion in general, some book, any book [*irgend ein Buch*], that contained such cases, especially a book that is most fervently interwoven with teachings that are moral and consequently related to reason."[11] It would be hard to imagine a more shocking manner of relativizing the authority of the Holy Scriptures than this.

Six years after Kant published *Religion Within the Boundaries of Reason Alone*, Friedrich Schleiermacher (1768–1834), sometimes described as the nineteenth century's chief theologian of Protestantism, made a name for himself by publishing *On Religion: Speeches to Its Cultivated Despisers* (1799). Schleiermacher's intent was to reject Kant's insistence that moral reason was the highest human faculty and, as his title suggests, to defend religion against its cultivated despisers.

His defense rests on the claim that we humans are religious by nature. Here is how he supports this claim. Religion, he says, must be distinguished from both metaphysics and (this is his refutation of Kant) morality: "The essence of religion is neither thinking [that is, metaphysics] nor acting [that is, morality], but intuition and feeling."[12] Religion is a "sense and taste for the infinite."[13] These statements might appear innocent enough at first glance, but Schleiermacher soon makes clear, first, that what counts for him is *religion* (in the singular) as a universal phenomenon, not specific (or what he calls "positive") *religions* (in the plural); second, that the "sense and taste for the infinite" is the central factor in religion and thus the common factor among individual, positive religions; and third, that the infinite is not the same thing as God.

God and for that matter immortality are in fact completely unnecessary to religion: "God is manifestly nothing other than the genius of mankind. Man is the prototype of this God."[14] There can be no God without the world, Schleiermacher says, implicitly rejecting the notion of a divine creation of the world.[15] As to the individual religions, they are nothing more than "distinct [*bestimmt*] forms in which infinite religion is represented."[16] The basic intuition of religion, after all, is "any intuition of the infinite in the finite."[17] Schleiermacher's comment on holy scripture (that is, the sacred writing of *any* religion) is even more denigrating than Kant's comment on the New Testament. "Every holy scripture," says Schleiermacher, "is only a mausoleum of religion, a monument to the circumstance that a great spirit was there that is no longer there. . . . He who believes in a holy scripture is not he who has religion; rather it is he who has no need of such scripture and who could, perhaps, write one himself."[18]

But Schleiermacher was trying to *defend* religion. How can he do so when his defense appears to rise from a view that is so utterly skeptical about any particular religion? What good does it do to tell your readers that religion, *any* religion, is a fine thing and that, given human nature, it is a perfectly predictable thing, if what underlies these claims is so obviously the patronizing attitude of a man completely free from an endorsement of any religion those readers themselves might embrace? "I have everywhere presupposed the multiplicity of religions and their certain diversity as something necessary and inevitable," he says.[19] It is difficult if not impossible to reconcile this statement with a commitment, on the part of the author, to any particular religion. "Go ahead," he might as well have said, "and show an unquestioning faith in a religion, *any* religion, and do so with my blessing. But I won't join you." It's no surprise that Schleiermacher is credited with founding the comparative study of religions as a scholarly field. The true comparative student of religions must approach the subject dispassionately, and admiration either for religion in general or for any particular religious tradition can stem from nothing more than a faithless, supercilious act of judgment.

But the greatest assault on Christianity as a particular religion, and by implication on religion in general, at least to those inclined to read him in this way, came from Hegel (1770–1831). Whether he intended it or not, he more than anyone was responsible for reducing religious experience to a phenomenon of *human consciousness.*

This is not the place to give a summary of Hegel's philosophy—his philosophy of religion or his philosophy of anything else. Hegel devoted an entire, long work, his *Lectures on the Philosophy of Religion,* specifically to this subject. But he mentioned religion—and gave it an exalted place—in virtually everything he wrote.

Having read Hegel's best known works, a true skeptic might be tempted to claim that the great philosopher had written the same thing five or six times over. It's true that his *Phenomenology of Spirit* (or *Phenomenology of Mind,* 1807), *Science of Logic* (1812–16), *Encyclopedia of the Philosophical Sciences* (1817, including a revised version of the *Science of Logic*), *Philosophy of History* (1822, published posthumously in 1837), *Lectures on Aesthetics* (1818–29), and *History of Philosophy* (published posthumously, 1833–36) all tell a story more or less modeled on the process of development that he described in the *Phenomenology of Spirit.* In that work, Hegel traced the human mind/Spirit (*Geist* in German means both, but I'll use "Spirit," capitalized, to translate this word) through its various phases of development, beginning with simple consciousness (based on "sense certainty," that is, the most rudimentary sensual awareness of one's surroundings); passing through self-consciousness, reason, and Spirit (the last two being understood in specialized senses); then reaching religion; and the final, highest phase, what

Hegel calls "absolute knowing." Since Hegel's aim is to establish a philosophy in which the individual self is integrated into the world through Spirit (not separated from it, not incapable of knowing it directly, as Kant had claimed we all are), the various processes of development that Hegel describes in subsequent works—whether he's talking about progress to what he calls the "Absolute Idea" in the *Logic* and the *Encyclopedia*, or history itself, or the development of art, or the development of philosophy—all have to do with the development of Spirit.

In the *Phenomenology*, Hegel makes it clear that religion has to do not just with consciousness but ultimately with consciousness in its next-higher phase, self-consciousness. In lower phases of spiritual development, religion appears as "consciousness of the absolute being," but religion *as its own phase in the development of Spirit* appears as the "self-consciousness of Spirit," while absolute being appears in and for itself.[20] "Spirit that knows itself becomes in religion immediately its own pure *self-consciousness*," he says.[21] He even describes Jesus in terms that can easily be construed as reducing the Son of God to a mere phenomenon of self-consciousness: "The divine man or human God who has died is *in himself* universal self-consciousness."[22]

There has been considerable disagreement among Hegel's readers over whether the master may be considered a believer, that is, whether he accepts God as a preexistent being. Many passages in his works appear to point to this interpretation; others can be easily read as pointing toward the view that God and religion simply form a phase in the development of Spirit (though some see Spirit and God as part of the same world), and still others appear to point in both directions. At the very end of the *Philosophy of History*, Hegel says that world history consists in the "course of development of the Idea that realizes itself," leading us to think that the highest point of development is merely "the Idea" and not something called God. But he then goes on to say that this fact represents "the true *theodicy*, the justification of God in history," suggesting that God preexists and that history justifies him.[23] Elsewhere in the same series of lectures, Hegel says that "God rules the world," but only after having said that God is "reason in its most concrete representation."[24]

There is a classic statement on God in the *Encyclopedia*, one that turns up, mischievously distorted, in Verkhovensky's remark about God as "a being conscious of himself in me only." Hegel's version reads like this: "God is God only in so far as he knows himself; his self-knowing, furthermore, is [both] his self-consciousness in man and man's knowing *of* God, which leads to the self-knowing of man *in* God."[25] This maddening language is typical for Hegel; but in addition to all the self-reflexivity (knowing *oneself, self-*consciousness, *self-*knowing), there is an utter lack of clarity on the issue of the preexistent God. Hegel refers to God at the outset but then assigns attributes to him (self-knowing, self-consciousness) that we would normally associate only with humankind. At the very end of the entire *Encyclopedia,* Hegel does not mention God at all, referring instead to "the eternal Idea, existing in and for itself." He describes this Idea as "absolute Spirit."[26]

So it goes throughout Hegel's mature works. Here he is in the *Lectures on Aesthetics*: "God in his truth is therefore no mere ideal that is begotten of fantasy; instead, he inserts himself into the midst of the finitude and outward contingency [*Zufälligkeit*] of existence yet still knows himself in [that finitude and contingency] as a divine subject that remains in itself infinite and makes this infinity for itself."[27] Here he is in the *Philosophy of History,* on the legacy of the Reformation: "Luther's simple teaching is that the *this,* infinite subjectivity, that is, true spirituality, Christ, in no way is externally present and real but instead is to be attained, as the spiritual, only in reconciliation with God, *in faith and in enjoyment.*"[28] In other words, "infinite subjectivity" and "Christ" are synonymous expressions, and religion has now become a phenomenon of subjective consciousness. One could cite many such passages.

It should therefore be no surprise that some of Hegel's successors took his comments to mean (or *corrected* them to mean, or expressly defied him in asserting) that religion can be reduced to consciousness or self-consciousness and that it has to do with such notions as the absolute and the infinite. One of them was a man whose work Dostoevsky probably read (at least we know he borrowed a French translation of it in 1847) and whose work he loved to hate (or so he said).[29] David Friedrich Strauss (1808–74) was the author of one of the many books published beginning in the late eighteenth century under the title *The Life of Jesus.* By the early nineteenth century, the quest for the historical Jesus was an established field of study. For Christian purists, it intrinsically represented an assault on faith. The aim of such study was, after all, to write a *biography* of Jesus, and writing a biography of Jesus presupposes his existence as a mere man whose life story can be recorded. The initiator of the trend is said to be the German theologian Hermann Samuel Reimarus (1694–1768), who wrote a critique of Christianity that was published posthumously, under the title *Fragments of an Unknown* (1774–77). Reimarus's thesis, extraordinarily radical at the time, was that Jesus was a mere human susceptible to strange and irrational visions. Hegel at the age of twenty-four had written an essentially Kantian *Life of Jesus* (1795). In 1828, the prominent German theologian Heinrich Paulus wrote a *Life of Jesus as the Foundation of a Pure History of Primal Christianity*. In 1832, just three years before Strauss published his own book, Schleiermacher gave a series of lectures on the life of Jesus.

Strauss's two-volume work, whose full title was *The Life of Jesus Treated Critically (Das Leben Jesu kritisch bearbeitet)*, was published in 1835–36. The author started out as an orthodox Hegelian, and even though some might regard his conclusions as being opposite to Hegel's teachings, his underlying belief is that Christianity can ultimately be reduced to the functioning of normal human consciousness. Despite the great length of Strauss's book, his point and his method are quite easy to grasp. His point is that the Gospel stories are mere myths. His method lies in subverting the factual authenticity of those stories by exposing flaws and inconsistencies (both logical and historical), refuting natural interpretations (for example, those that attempt to explain miracles by claiming they were natural events misinterpreted or purposely reinterpreted), refuting historical interpretations (those attempting to explain Gospel events by showing that they have a true, though possibly distorted, basis in historical fact), and then applying his mythic interpretation. Mythic interpretation frequently leads to the conclusion that the true origin of a Gospel story is the need of Jesus' followers to believe certain things about him. In some cases, this involves appropriating concepts and phrases either from the Hebrew Bible or generally from Jewish tradition, and in others it involves reinterpreting such concepts and phrases. Strauss analyzes, for example, the temptation narratives in the Gospels and shows that all the important elements in them (not just Jesus' responses to the devil) are derived from the Hebrew Bible. Take, for example, the expression "Son of God," as applied to Jesus in the Gospel stories (as, once again, in the temptation narratives). In Strauss's view (a view that scholars today do not take seriously), Jews before the era of Jesus used this expression in a purely theocratic or purely figurative sense, that is, in order to identify certain people or pagan gods as greatly favored or to express admiration for physical beauty. But Jesus' followers were intent on establishing a Messianic tradition, so they came to use the phrase in a literal sense.[30] From this practice comes the fundamental Christian concept of Jesus as literally the son of God and as thus possessing a dual nature. In fact, a bit later in the book Strauss explicitly comments on the dual nature of Christ, saying that it represents the result of an entirely natural process arising from the *needs* of Jesus' followers. The early Christian community found it necessary to hold a conception of Jesus as mediator between the divine and the human.[31] "Certain advantages" arise from the union of the divine and human in Christ, Strauss says, suggesting that early Christians had the freedom to choose which qualities they would assign to their savior.[32]

They *did* have this freedom, if Strauss is correct in the way he describes the conditions necessary for the emergence of Christianity. It all has to do with human consciousness and the human needs of a particular community. The community that was prepared to accept Jesus' teachings, Strauss says in his ultimate defense of his mythical method, lacked a truly historical consciousness (something that never exists in its pure form anyway) but manifested a consciousness that remained open to belief in miracles. "Should such a consciousness, in which the gate to the miraculous is not yet shut, be wholly drawn into a state of religious enthusiasm, it will find anything believable . . . . The miracles of evangelical history were in no way necessary, in the form of a preceding cause, for the purpose of exciting such enthusiasm. Rather all that was needed was, on the one side, the well-known religious impoverishment of that time . . . and, on the other, the powerful sense of religious satisfaction that the belief in the resurrected Messiah together with the essential content of Jesus's teaching offered."[33] It could hardly get clearer than this: people and their needs come before the beings in which religion requires us to believe, not the other way around.

Like Kant and Schleiermacher before him, Strauss claims to be no enemy of Christianity. In the preface to the first edition of his book, he says, "The author knows that the inner core of the Christian faith is entirely independent of his critical investigations. Christ's supernatural birth, his miracles, his resurrection and ascension remain eternal truths, no matter how much doubt may have been cast on their reality as historical facts. . . . A discussion at the end of this work will show that the dogmatic content of Jesus' life has suffered no injury."[34] But once again, to a true believer, these are words of condescension. "No one with a smidgen of good sense would ever believe any of this," he appears to be saying, "but still I admire those who do."

Dostoevsky had no trouble picking up on the dual message in Strauss. In the *Diary of a Writer*, he refers to a common opinion about the author of the *Life of Jesus*. Though Strauss was clearly someone who "hates Christ and has set as a goal for his whole life ridiculing Christianity and spitting upon it," nonetheless, this opinion holds, the great proponent of the mythic interpretive method "worships mankind in its entirety, and his teaching is as exalted and noble as can be." Dostoevsky goes on to speak scornfully of the mitigating claim about Strauss's worshiping mankind, saying that once we allow people like the biographer of Jesus to destroy the old society and construct a new one, complete chaos will descend upon us.[35]

The best known and most unguarded champion of the idea that religion (specifically Christianity) is reducible to human consciousness dispensed with the pleasantries about the beneficial qualities of religious faith (though he took care to point out that his attitude was "critical" rather than "negative").[36] This was the great Apostle of Materialism, Ludwig Feuerbach (1804–72), author of the much admired, much reviled, but unquestionably famous book *The Essence of Christianity* (1841). You don't need to read very far in this fairly short and conceptually simple book to get the point. In the first two pages, the author tells us that consciousness is the feature that distinguishes man from beast and then states unabashedly that religion is merely "consciousness of the infinite," that is, "man's consciousness of his own . . . infinite being [*Wesen*]."[37] God? He is man's own being, so consciousness of God is man's self-consciousness.[38] God as a morally perfect being is "nothing more than the realized idea, the personified law of morality, the moral being of man established as absolute being."[39] The true turning point in history will occur when man recognizes "that consciousness of God is nothing other than consciousness of the species."[40]

For this reason, predictably, prayer is just a conversation between man and himself, between man and his heart, and the basic dogmas of Christianity are simply "fulfilled wishes of the heart."[41] Hegel was thus wrong when he claimed that man's consciousness of God was the same as the self-consciousness of God and that human consciousness is thus the same as divine consciousness. Turn this around and you have the truth—namely, that knowledge of God is man's knowledge of himself.[42] In short, "Man is the beginning of religion, man is the middle-point of religion, and man is the end of religion."[43] It's hard to be more explicit than that.

Still, Feuerbach did believe in *something*, and the something was love. But let's not forget that his religion was ultimately the religion of materialism (which is essentially to say no religion at all), so love must not be understood in any sense higher than the purely material. "What the old mystics said of God, namely, that he was the *highest* and yet the *most common* being, in truth holds for love. But not for some visionary, imaginary love, no, for real love, for love that has flesh and blood."[44] It is love, not faith, that is the constructure force for man. "Love," says Feuerbach, "identifies man with God, God with man, thus man with man; faith separates God from man, thus man from man. For God is nothing other than the mystical species concept of mankind, and the separation of God from man is therefore the separation of man from man."[45] The high priest of the finite and earthly concludes his book this way: "Let the bread thus be holy to us, let the wine be holy, but let also the water be holy! Amen."[46]

Believe it or not, within four years of the publication of *The Essence of Christianity* there was a far more intemperate and ill-spirited assault on religion than anything that even Feuerbach had concocted. This came from the nineteenth century's proto-Nietzschean bad boy, Max Stirner, in a book called *The Individual and His Own* (1844, usually translated into English as *The Ego and His Own*). Stirner's book is commonly discussed in connection with the philosophy of egoism, but the author had some memorable comments about God and religion. His ideas can be stated very quickly. Since his principal aim is to establish a right of ownership (or "ownness") that belongs to him who dares to seize what he wants, the world is for Stirner a constant Hobbesian state-of-nature war of egoist against egoist. One very prominent egoist is God: "Now it is clear that God worries only about what is his, is concerned only with himself, thinks only of himself, and keeps only himself in mind; woe to those who are not agreeable to him. He serves nothing [or no one] higher and satisfies only himself. His business is—a purely egoistic business."[47] Stirner's answer: "For my part, I take a lesson from [these egoists] and, rather than selflessly serve these great egoists any more, I want to be the egoist myself."[48] Stirner has earned a little corner in intellectual history for proclaiming, long before Nietzsche did so in *The Gay Science*, the death of God (though Hegel had referred to the death of God in at least two senses beginning in 1802, as did Lutheran hymns, in the sense of Christ's death on the cross, a couple of centuries before Hegel).[49] Stirner's claim is oblique but unmistakable. "At the entrance to modern times stands the God-man" says Stirner. "At their exit, will only the God in the God-man vanish, and can the God-man actually die if only the God in him dies?. . . . How can you believe that the God-man has died before the man in him, in addition to God, has died?"[50]

Ownness as a category transcends freedom, which Stirner regards as the doctrine of Christianity and therefore something that resides in the realm of dreams.[51] As if to show that Feuerbach was not adequately radical in his approach to religion, Stirner tells us that egoism transcends love.[52]

It's quite possible that Stirner was not entirely serious when he wrote his highly provocative book. Whether he was or not, his views on religion exceed the reach of my description of a process that reduced God and religion to human attributes. Stirner did not waste his time accounting for religion as a phenomenon; his only interest was to render it and God impotent.

Finally, there is Ernest Renan (1823–92), the author of the other truly famous *Life of Jesus* (1863) in the nineteenth century. Dostoevsky is said to have read the book almost immediately after its publication, and he mentions both the book and its author many times in his fiction and nonfiction writings.[53] Of the secular defenders of Christianity, Renan was perhaps the most enthusiastic, but for this very reason his defense came across to his enemies as all the more patronizing, disingenuous, and even downright dishonest.

Here's the basis for Renan's approach: "Man, as soon as he distinguished himself from animals, was religious, that is to say, he saw in nature something beyond reality and, for himself, something beyond death." His religious impulse expressed itself in numerous ways in human history, but one event needs to be set aside in a category of its own. "The chief event in the history of the world," Renan says, "is the revolution by which the noblest portions of humanity made the passage from those ancient religions comprised in the vague name 'paganism' to a religion founded on divine unity, the trinity, the incarnation of the Son of God."[54] In Renan's book, the second sentence I've quoted precedes the first, but without the statement about man's innately religious nature, we're likely to misconstrue the statement about the unique character of Christianity. Renan, like Schleiermacher, is taking the comparative approach, which is to say standing back and dispassionately evaluating a collection of religions before arriving at an assessment of Christianity in particular (highly favorable though that assessment may ultimately be). Any such assessment of Christianity can thus be based on nothing more exalted than a kind of anthropological analysis.

What about the Gospels? Of what historical value are they? The form of the question already determines the type of answer Renan gives: "They are neither biographies in the manner of Suetonius nor fictional legends in the manner of Philostratus; rather they are legendary biographies."[55] It would be difficult to come up with a passage expressing a more skeptical, more secularizing, more pragmatic attitude than the one in which Renan likens the Gospel stories to "naïve [which is to say purely legendary] narratives" about more recent historical figures (for example, narratives of the sort that old soldiers twenty years earlier might have constructed from their distant memories of Napoleon): "One could say the same of the Gospels [that they are naïve narratives]. Intent solely on putting in relief the master's excellence, his miracles, his teaching, the Evangelists display complete indifference toward anything that does not form part of Jesus's own mind [*esprit*]. Contradictions with respect to times, places, and people were regarded as insignificant, for the higher the degree of inspiration that one accorded to Jesus's sayings, the farther one was from attributing this inspiration to the authors."[56]

Let there be no question about the likelihood of our actually *believing* in Jesus as the Son of God: "He is the Son of God, but then all men are, or can become, Sons of God to varying degrees." In his closing paean to the Savior, Renan says this: "This sublime person, who every day continues to preside over the destiny of the world—it is permissible to call him divine, not in the sense that Jesus absorbed all of the divine or was identical to it, but in the sense that Jesus is the individual who caused his species to take the biggest step toward the divine."[57] Renan *loves* Jesus and apostrophizes him as we might address a dearly departed child who had made us especially proud. "Rest now in thy glory, thou noble initiator," he writes. "Thy work is done; thy divinity is established. . . . At the cost of several hours of suffering, which never even threatened thy great soul, thou hast purchased the most complete immortality."[58]

In the very first installment of his *Diary of a Writer*, Dostoevsky characterizes Renan as "proclaiming in his *Vie de Jésus*, a book filled with faithlessness, that Christ was nonetheless an ideal of human beauty, an unattainable type that can never again be repeated, even in the future." It's hard to say just what to make of this remark. Dostoevsky slips in the phrase "a book filled with faithlessness" as though it contained an established fact, yet he goes on to describe Renan's Jesus in words ("ideal," "unattainable") very close to those that he (Dostoevsky) was fond of using in connection with the same topic. One thing, however, appears certain. Whatever Dostoevsky's ultimate personal views on faith might have been, he regards Renan's faithlessness as beyond all dispute.

It would be silly to take all the ideas I've just discussed and say that all educated people in Russia or Western Europe in the midnineteenth century had exactly these ideas in their minds, that they thought about religion only in connection with these ideas, or that there were no other ideas being expressed. It's simply that the trend I've described was something quite new, something likely to attract the attention of educated readers, something that formed the topic of much conversation, and something that provoked numerous written

comments, both casual and scholarly. An informal measure of Renan's notoriety in the popular mind, a full half-century after the publication of his
*Life of Jesus*, is that D. H. Lawrence mentions the book in *Sons and Lovers*
(1913). Paul Morel, one of the "sons," and his lady friend Miriam have been
questioning their religious faith. "They were at the Renan 'Vie de Jésus'
stage," Lawrence says. He does not feel the need to offer so much as a word
of explanation.

It's very easy to document Dostoevsky's "contact" with these ideas. Any
biographical account of his early adult years will include the story of his relationship with Russia's reigning progressive literary (and by extension social) critic of the 1840s, Vissarion Belinsky (1811–48).[59] Despite his faulty
command of German, Belinsky read much of the philosophy that was in
vogue among Russian intellectuals during the 1830s and 1840s and, in the
late 1840s, discussed it with Dostoevsky, then a fledgling writer. In the chapter of *Diary of a Writer* where Dostoevsky mentions Renan, it is in a discussion of Belinsky. Dostoevsky reports all the blasphemous things Belinsky
said about Christ and religion, listing the writers that most attracted the
great critic in connection with this topic. Among the names are Feuerbach
and Strauss.[60]

There's some scholarship on Dostoevsky's knowledge of Hegel.[61] Of course,
it's largely inconclusive, if what we're looking for is hard evidence that the
novelist actually sat down and studied the *Encyclopedia*'s fifteen hundred
pages of dry and impenetrable prose. But, as with many of the figures I have
just talked about, there's plenty of evidence that Dostoevsky at least engaged
in conversations with people who knew their Hegel. The hastiest survey of
the period's "thick journals" (a peculiarly Russian phenomenon: magazines
devoted to fiction and brainy discussions of mostly contemporary social, political, artistic, and philosophical issues) will show how much energy Russian
intellectuals spent on Hegel and other Western European thinkers. Nikolai
Chernyshevsky (1828–89), the reigning left-wing literary critic/novelist/essayist/
social activist of the generation immediately succeeding Belinsky's, dedicated
dozens and dozens of pages to highly learned and informed analyses of Hegel's
thought.

All this is easy to document. But we should allow Dostoevsky's work to
speak for itself, so let's return to *The Devils*. We'll start with the source,
Stepan Verkhovensky. When Dostoevsky has him describe God as "a being
conscious of himself in me only," he appears somehow to have the elderly
gentleman paraphrase Hegel's passage from the *Encyclopedia* (the one I cited

earlier) about God's "self-consciousness in man" (though Dostoevsky probably would have known Hegel's idea only by hearsay), but with an important
distortion. "In man" becomes "in me only." Thus in Verkhovensky Hegel's
universal claim about humankind becomes a claim about only Verkhovensky
himself, hence an expression of pure egoism.

Even in the last moments of his life, in what is always called the "conversion" scene, Verkhovensky does not alter his beliefs. I've never been able to
understand why so many readers take this scene seriously and accept the notion that the old man has undergone a genuine, dramatic change from spiritual indifference to true faith. To my way of seeing, nothing even close to
this happens. The narrator has just told us that in fact Verkhovensky was beginning to believe, but he adds that this was possibly because the ceremony
of the sacraments aroused the dying man's artistic sensibilities. Listen to
what Verkhovensky now says "with great feeling":

> My immortality is already necessary, because God will not wish to act falsely
> and extinguish completely in my heart the fire of a love for him that has just
> been kindled. And what is dearer than love? Love is higher than being, love
> is the crown of being, and is it possible that being would not be subservient
> to love? If I have come to love him and rejoice in my love, is it possible that
> he would extinguish me and my joy and turn us both into nothingness? If
> God exists, then I am immortal! *Voilà ma profession de foi.*[62]

If this is a profession of faith, then it sounds like the faith of a man who
has taken Feuerbach and a philosophy of egoism, put them into a tall glass,
stirred them, and drunk them down in one draught. What starts out as love
for God quickly becomes just love in the abstract, which Verkhovensky says
is higher than being itself. God's function is nothing more than to keep love
alive in one's heart, together with the pleasurable sensation that love arouses.
If God's existence has to do only with my own needs and my desire for immortality, then what kind of God is he, and how can someone like Stepan
Verkhovensky really believe in him? His old friend, Stavrogin's mother, one
of the author's classic vixen-matrons, gets it just right: "God exists, Stepan
Trofimovich," she says in response to his profession of faith; "I assure you he
exists." The narrator (remember that the narrator in this novel is an actual
character and is not to be confused with the author) gets it slightly wrong:
"It appears she did not entirely understand his *profession de foi.*" Maybe she
hasn't followed everything her friend has said—that's not the sort of mind she
has. But with her earthy, childlike worldview, she has certainly understood,

as the narrator has *not*, the basic point: that her old friend doesn't truly believe in God.

It gets more ridiculous. Verkhovensky continues his profession:

> For a man, far more necessary than his own happiness is to know and at every moment believe that somewhere there is a perfect and peaceful happiness, for all and everything. . . . The entire law of man's being rests in man's constant ability to bow before something immeasurably great. If you deprive people of the immeasurably great, then they won't go on living and will die in despair. The immeasurable and infinite is just as necessary to man as the minor planet on which he lives. . . . My friends, all my friends, long live the Great Thought. The eternal, immeasurable Thought. Every man, no matter who he is, must bow before that which is the Great Thought.[63]

The phrase "Great Thought" is often translated into English as "Great Idea." Whether "Thought" is a reference to Hegel's Idea, as this word occurs in the *Encyclopedia* in the phrase "absolute Idea" (of course Dostoevsky would probably have known it only at second hand), or whether it means nothing more than just "thought," it is hardly something that would stand at the pinnacle of a Christian religious system. It is ultimately human-based.

Who would be surprised? Only a short while earlier, in the peasant cottage where Verkhovensky is soon to die, an itinerant book-seller offered him a copy of the Gospels. He reflected at that moment that he had not read the Gospels in at least thirty years and that what little he remembered of it stemmed from his reading Renan's *Life of Jesus* seven years earlier.[64] If his notions of religion have been shaped by Hegel, *together with* Feuerbach and Renan, it's hard to see how he could suddenly embrace something that recognizably forms a part of any traditional Christian system of belief. To be sure, conversion is precisely the embracing now of something one did not embrace a little while ago. But in this case, so much of Hegel, Feuerbach, and Renan is carried over into the "new" beliefs as to make them practically identical to the old ones.

Then there is Verkhovensky's spiritual/intellectual son, Stavrogin, and grandchildren, Kirillov and Shatov (this is not to mention his actual son, the godless, unprincipled, cynical anarchist Peter). The legacy is clear. Stavrogin explicitly identifies himself as an atheist in the passage I quoted earlier. The moment at which we see him closest to an expression of religious faith occurs in the chapter "At Tikhon's," which Dostoevsky was forced by his editor to omit from his novel and which was published for the first time in 1922. Stavrogin goes to the local monastery and shows the bishop who resides there a written confession of some of his (Stavrogin's) very dark deeds. It quickly becomes clear that for Stavrogin everything is ultimately reducible to the fundamental Feuerbachian category, consciousness. His confession includes this statement, for example:

> Every extraordinarily shameful, immeasurably degrading, base, and (most important) ridiculous situation in which I have chanced to find myself in my life has always aroused in me, together with immeasurable rage, unbelievable delight. . . . If I were to steal something, I would feel, on the commission of the theft, rapture at the consciousness of the depth of my baseness. It was not the baseness that I loved . . . my rapture pleased me because of the agonizing *consciousness* of my meanness. . . . This feeling never overcame me completely, for there always remained consciousness of the fullest sort (and after all everything was based on consciousness!).[65]

In a passage omitted from some editions, Stavrogin "strictly" formulates to himself what has been the guiding principle in his life: "that I do not know or feel evil or good and that not only had I lost all sense of them, but there is no such thing as evil or good (and this was pleasant for me), only prejudice; that I could be free from all prejudice, but that, if I should ever attain that freedom, I would perish. It was the first time I had been conscious of this in a formula."[66]

Toward the end of the scene, Stavrogin announces that he seeks forgiveness, and Tikhon tells him that if he truly believes in the possibility of forgiveness, then he already believes in *everything*. But when Stavrogin asks, "By the way, won't Christ forgive?" he does so with a "light shade of irony" and soon storms out of the bishop's cell.

Kirillov requires almost no comment. Like so many other characters in Dostoevsky's works, he names God while showing an underlying inability truly to believe in him. Kirillov undermines any possibility of belief, because what he says on the subject (his use of the phrase "man-God," his claim to be able to become God by shooting himself) emphasizes God's ultimately physical and human origin.

Kirillov has perhaps borrowed a page from *The Essence of Christianity*. Feuerbach translated the Christian notion of Judgment Day into the moment in history when man realizes the central truth of Feuerbach's book: that consciousness of God is nothing more than consciousness of the human species. For Kirillov, the turning point occurs between the two phases of history, the first of which ("from the gorilla to the annihilation of God") represents a weird marriage between Darwin and Feuerbach (or Stirner, for that matter) and the second of which ("from the annihilation of God . . . to the physical transformation of man") represents an absurdly materialized version of the Apocalypse. Oddly, Nietzsche would say something quite similar in *Ecce homo* (1888), where he divides history into two periods separated by his own "discovery of Christian morality" (the discovery that it is a "decadence morality" and that it stands against life itself).[67]

With Shatov, we find ourselves in a quandary regarding Dostoevsky's own beliefs. I'll speak of quandaries like this one in the next chapter. But it's not difficult to find in Dostoevsky's writings ideas quite similar to those Shatov expresses to Stavrogin. Prince Myshkin's tirade in the famous vase-smashing scene has language almost identical to what we find in Shatov's speech. If all we had were Myshkin's and Shatov's remarks, we could easily dismiss Slavophile ideology (in the way it's presented in Dostoevsky's works) as an expression of illness (Myshkin) or faithless stupidity (Shatov). But it appears again and again in the *Diary of a Writer*, where Dostoevsky implicitly claims to be speaking in his own voice. "The Russian man," he writes in the September 1876 issue, "knows nothing higher than Christianity, nor can he even conceive of anything higher. His whole land, his whole community, all Russia he calls Christianity [*khristianstvo*], 'peasantry' [*krest'ianstvo*—the two words sound almost identical in Russian]."[68] The following year the novelist describes the fundamental belief of the type of Slavophilism to which he himself purportedly subscribes: "that our great Russia, at the head of the united Slavs, will proclaim to the whole world, to all European mankind, and to its civilization the new, robust word still unheard by the world."[69] After one of many hysterical passages in which Dostoevsky attacks the Catholic Church, he adds this about the Russian people (*narod*, "folk," "peasantry"): "For now, our people are only bearers of Christ, and they place their hopes only in him. They call themselves peasants [*krest'ianin*], which is to say Christians [*khristianin*—again two words that sound almost identical]."[70] The entire meaning of Russia is "all-world-ness" (*vsemirnost*), "common-to-all-humankind-ness" (*obshchechelovechnost*), he says in a notebook entry from 1876–77.[71] Or, as he puts it in *Diary of a Writer*, "common-to-all-humankind-ness" is (paradoxically) the "Russian national idea."[72]

When Shatov calls God "the synthetic personality of the entire people" and Stavrogin mocks him for reducing the divinity to a "simple attribute of the folk [*narodnost*]," Stavrogin's right. This is exactly what Shatov has done. But look who's doing the mocking! It's Stavrogin, who has just readily admitted to being an atheist. And talk about reducing God to a mere attribute of the folk! It's precisely what Dostoevsky does in the shrill diatribes he published, ostensibly representing his own heartfelt views, in the *Diary of a Writer*.

Never mind, for the moment, what really is Dostoevsky's "own," "true" belief in this welter of conflicting arguments and hopelessly mixed signals (his attitude is complicated, as I'll explain in the next chapter). For now, what matters is that if reducing God to a mere attribute of the folk is something that a would-be believer (Shatov), an avowed nonbeliever (Stavrogin), and someone representing himself *as* a believer (the author of *Diary of a Writer*) can all do, then the most we can say about this feature of Slavophilism, as Dostoevsky presents it, is that it has the potential to be relativized to such a degree that no single system of belief would ever entertain any hope of claiming the feature as exclusively its own. A corollary to this last statement, of course, is that, understood in Stavrogin's way, Shatov's remark about God and the people does nothing loftier than reduce God and religion to something completely temporal and secular (no matter what we decide Dostoevsky was thinking when he wrote roughly the same thing in *Diary of a Writer*). How else can we ever make sense of the seemingly absurd claims that there is a distinctly *Russian* God or Christ and that this God or Christ is also somehow universal *because* he's Russian?

To someone living and flourishing entirely in the intellectual climate of Western Europe at the end of the 1860s, many of the ideas that Dostoevsky's characters express in *The Devils* would not appear entirely outlandish (though the characters themselves and how they express themselves might appear quite outlandish). The notion that any religious figure, any set of religious beliefs, and any conversation about religion could ultimately be submitted to a sort of scholarly scrutiny leading ultimately to the observation that all such matters are a natural result of human, all-too-human causes might have *offended* lots of Western Europeans in this era (I'm speaking only of those whose standing in social life brought them into contact with notions like this), but it would hardly have surprised them.

By the 1860s, it would hardly have surprised an educated Russian, either. The new radical movement that Dostoevsky encountered shortly after his return from exile in 1850, dubbed "Nihilism" by Turgenev, took Western Europe's spiritual relativism to the next level. The intellectual darlings of this era, especially Nikolai Chernyshevsky, devoted a good part of their energies to expressly denying the existence of anything whose existence cannot be

demonstrated empirically. Thus not only God but any sort of spiritual belief, any quality that cannot be examined under a microscope, was relegated
to the category of "prejudice" (*predrassudok*, a favorite, recurring word in
this generation). I'll return to "prejudice" in a few chapters.

In *Fathers and Sons* (1862), Turgenev satirized the tendency of the young
generation of the early 1860s to reduce everything to science, leaving no room
(at least in theory) for the soul, for beauty, for romance. The hero, Bazarov,
dissects frogs in order to understand humans and describes a woman with
whom he is clearly smitten as a "specimen" whose body he would love to see
on the dissecting table.

In 1863, Chernyshevsky published *What Is to Be Done?*, quite possibly the
most influential book ever written in Russia. This wooden, impossibly dull,
didactic political treatise dressed up as a novel served the author as a forum
for proposing an ethical system of rational self-interest (or rational egoism,
as someone other than Chernyshevsky named it later on). Since rational self-
interest is a utilitarian ethical theory, it necessarily rejects any spiritual or religious premise, offering instead as a criterion for the advisability of a projected action only the action's carefully considered benefit to its perpetrator.
Three years earlier, Chernyshevsky had vigorously denied the existence of
free will, in a book titled *The Anthropological Principle in Philosophy* (1860).

Dostoevsky's response was *Notes from Underground* (1864), in whose first
part the sardonic narrator savagely ridicules Nihilism. The underground
man's beef with Chernyshevsky and his friends is that, in his eyes, by denying
free will and reducing every moral decision to a utilitarian calculus they are,
first and more important, depriving humankind of its most treasured qualities and, second, simply contravening the obvious truth. The underground
man seeks again and again to prove that, like it or not, we *do* have free will
and we *don't* always act in our own enlightened self-interest; witness our willingness to commit rash and self-destructive acts for the sole purpose of enjoying the exhilarating sensation of freedom. As Dostoevsky makes clear in a
letter to his brother, he himself regarded the Nihilist ideas that his character
ridicules as clearly having to do with religion. He originally included some
passages (now lost) in defense of Christ but noted that the censors, though
allowing the underground man to express (if ironically) all sorts of blasphemous ideas, forbade the author to print the passages in which he "deduced
the necessity of faith and Christ."[73] No doubt the association of Chernyshevsky and other Nihilists (or simply radicals) with socialism was responsi-

ble for Dostoevsky's many shrill and hysterical claims, over the years, that socialism and Christianity are opposites—that Catholicism gave rise to atheism, which in turn gave rise to socialism.

What would likely have surprised those in the late 1860s whose only contact was with strictly Western European intellectual trends were not these clearly Western ideas but the Slavophile ideas that we hear from Shatov and, especially in the following decade, Dostoevsky himself. Dostoevsky, after all, did not live as one of the hypothetical types I've just described, encountering only Western European ideas. There was an indigenous tradition as well, though one that owed much to the Western European discussions I've been describing.

## RUSSIA, AND HOW GOD CAME TO BE A NATIONAL ATTRIBUTE

There are three closely related ideas here, all having to do with the concept of *nation*. The first is the intimate, organic bond between a nation and its people; the second is the ability of the intimately and organically bonded nation and people to develop a religion—or, in this case, a version of an existing religion—that uniquely expresses the spirit of the nation and its people; the third (which appears to contradict the second) is, in the specific case of Russia, the universality of that religion. Though it's impossible ever to trace the true origin of any idea, it's safe to say that the origins of the first two lay outside Russia, probably in Germany, and that Russian writers gave the second idea their own peculiar cast and created the third to serve their own nationalistic interests.

Any number of German philosophers, critics, and poets from the late eighteenth century to the early nineteenth embraced the anti-Enlightenment thought that there is or ought to be an organic connection between a people and the "nation." *Nation* was generally not defined with any precision in this era, especially since the words and phrases that would be used in definitions of it later in the nineteenth century—such as "race" and "ethnic group"—were not in common use at this time. But it is easy in this period to find references to the *Volk* (folk, people), the nation, and the bonds that connect them. One can probably credit Johann Gottlieb Fichte (1762–1814), a luminary of the post-Kantian generation in Germany, with promoting the concept of nation and establishing the connection between nation and folk more forcefully and influentially than anyone else of his generation. His *Speeches to the German Nation*, delivered in 1807 and 1808, during the Napoleonic occupation of Berlin, bluntly repudiated the social contract theory of civil society as an abstractly defined commonwealth of abstractly defined "citizens." The key ideas for Fichte were the *Volk*, the unique character of that *Volk* (in this case, of course, German), and the nation, seen as both the loftiest expression of and the highest authority for the *Volk*. The *Volk*, he says, fulfills a divine mission.[74]

But it was no doubt Hegel and his philosophy of history that had the greatest impact on solidifying the connection between the nation and the spirit of the people. For Hegel, history moves forward in a way that is lawful (in the sense that it obeys laws discernible to people like Hegel), rational (in the sense that our reason can understand those laws), and objective (in the sense that, once reason understands the laws, they become so clear as to be almost like *objects*). Above all, it moves forward in a sequence of discrete stages, each being defined by its spiritual content. The spiritual content is peculiar to the people and civilization whose history we are writing. For example, Hegel's claim that, with Luther, religion becomes a phenomenon of subjective consciousness is a claim about the spiritual development of *Germany* at the time of Luther. In this theory of history, spirit, nation (or civilization), and stage are inextricably, organically intertwined.

This type of thinking is essential to the rise of Slavophilism in Russia, even though many Slavophiles were, by their own account, anti-Hegelian. Slavophilism properly speaking is said to have arisen in the 1830s, but the notion of an organic connection in history between people and nation had already taken hold and would continue to show up in non-Slavophile thinkers.

One of the most influential Russian documents of the entire nineteenth century, I think, is a peculiar thing that came to be named a "Philosophical Letter." It was written in 1829, in French, by Petr Chaadaev (1794?-1856) to a lady friend and then circulated privately for a few years. Its publication in a Russian journal in 1836 led authorities to declare the author insane and to place him under house arrest for over a year. But this merely enhanced the notoriety of both letter and writer, and Chaadaev's "First Philosophical Letter" became for generations a focal point for discussion of Russia and her destiny. Dostoevsky himself, in his *Winter Notes on Summer Impressions* (1863), refers to Chaadaev as second only to the great Belinsky in the ranks of passionate Russians who expressed great contempt for their motherland.[75] I mention this not to comment on the validity of the claim that Chaadaev and Belinsky expressed such contempt but simply to show the stature Chaadaev enjoyed in the eyes of the Russian reading and writing public.

Chaadaev considered himself an enemy of Hegelianism, but you'd hardly know it from the terms in which he describes the current and historical condition of Russia. His letter is a lament that springs from two empirical observations: Russia lives a primitive life in which the past hardly exists, and Russia is hopelessly backward in relation to Western Europe. Put differently, these two observations add up to something of a contradiction. Russia, through her lack of awareness, fails to conform to the laws of history that govern Western Europe, but examined in accordance with those laws of history, she is far behind Western Europe.

What's important here, however, is the sense that the ideal for Chaadaev is a principle of unity that *at any given moment* binds together humankind and its spirit of religion into a "Church" (understood not as an institution but as an assembly of believers) and that *over time* binds together the development of the human spirit.[76] The trouble is that, although Western Europe has come relatively close to this idea, Russia does not even begin to approach it. Russians, living always in the present, have no history. "Our memories date back no farther than yesterday; we are, so to speak, strangers to ourselves."[77] So even though Chaadaev might be describing an ideal that is antinational (he speaks of bringing together all humankind), the current state of affairs as he sees it shows a Russia separated out as a nation from the nations of Europe. If Chaadaev laments the absence of a past among Russians, it's because his underlying assumption is that there needs to be an organic connection between nation and people.

One of the most significant respects in which Russia is set apart is religion. What provoked subsequent Russian nationalists more than anything else in the "First Philosophical Letter" was the invidious comparison the author drew between Catholicism and Russian Orthodoxy (to the detriment of Orthodoxy). I'm the only person I know who believes that Chaadaev was presenting his reader with a paradox about the relations between the Western Church and the Eastern, rather than launching an attack on Orthodoxy and embracing Catholicism. But even if I'm wrong, what unquestionably emerges from Chaadaev's analysis is the strong sense that, at least in the cases he discusses, religion and people are organically bound together. The Catholic Church has succeeded in promoting unity among its followers, while the Russian Orthodox Church has completely failed. In an effort to prove his claim, Chaadaev says something quite absurd:

> The peoples of Europe have a common physiognomy, the appearance of being a family. Despite the general division of these peoples into a Latin and a Teutonic branch, into Southerners and Northerners, there is a common link that unites them all into a single bundle, clearly visible to anyone who has examined their history in depth. You are aware that not long ago all Europe was still called "Christendom" and that this word had its place in public law. Besides this general character, every one of these peoples has its own peculiar character. But all this is nothing more than history and tradition.[78]

I've always thought that the various peoples of Europe had been *disunited* by wars, by perceived ethnic differences, and a by host of other factors—but again my opinion is not what matters. What matters is that Russia has her own peculiar national religious tradition, one that has everything to do with defining her character and that, moreover, has helped to keep her out of the historical process we see in Western Europe.

"Pushed by a fatal destiny," Chaadaev says, referring to the historic split between the Eastern and Western Churches, "we went looking in wretched Byzantium . . . for the moral code that would serve as the foundation of our education. . . . The vivifying principle of unity at that time animated everything in Europe. . . . Since we were confined to our schism, nothing occurring in Europe reached us."[79] Unity is the supreme achievement of Christianity in Europe. "Remember," he says,

> that for fifteen centuries [Europeans] have had only one language for addressing God, one moral authority, one faith. . . . Because the sphere in which the men of Europe live, the sphere that is the only one in which the human species can reach its final destiny, is the result of the influence that religion has exercised on [Europeans], it is clear that if until now the weakness of our beliefs or the inadequacy of our dogma has kept us outside this universal movement in which the social idea of Christianity has developed and been formulated . . . we must seek to reanimate our beliefs by all means possible.[80]

The ideal religious spirit is thus one that expresses the character of a people and that at the same time, by unifying them, becomes universal.

Some twenty years after Chaadaev wrote his letter, a true Slavophile by the name of Ivan Vasil'evich Kireevsky (1806–56) wrote what sounds like a direct rebuttal to the man declared mad by the tsar. "On the Character of Europe's Enlightenment and Its Relation to Russia's Enlightenment" (1852) is mostly a series of unfavorable comparisons between Orthodox Russia and the Catholic West (unfavorable, that is, to the Catholic West), containing much of the language we hear from Dostoevsky's Slavophile characters (Prince Myshkin's rant about the Roman Catholic Church and Shatov's half-witted exaltation of the Russian God and the Russian people). One essential difference between Europe and Russia is the dominance of reason, the "syllogism" in the European way of thinking, by contrast with the Russian tendency to look inward. Chaadaev mentioned the syllogism as something Russia lacked, very much to her detriment. For Kireevsky, this lack is a positive virtue. Kireevsky lists many respects in which Russia and Europe differ, but the global way to characterize the distinction is to say that Europe is ultimately governed by the principle of division, while Russia is governed by the principle of wholeness. "In a word," he says,

> there [in Europe] we have division of the spirit, division of thoughts, division of sciences, division of the state, division of the [social] estates, division of society, division of family rights and duties, division of the moral condition and the condition of the heart, division of the entire aggregate and all the separate types of humankind's being, social and private; in Russia, by contrast, we have a dominant striving toward the wholeness of being, both inward and outward, social and private, intellectual and worldly, productive and moral.[81]

The basis for this claim (which is as extravagant as Chaadaev's converse theory that the West is unified while Russia is not) is Kireevsky's perception that Western European rational thinking has led to a split in the human mind and that this split corresponds to all the other splits we find in Europe: between church and state, intellectual life and moral life, the private individual with his private property on the one hand and the state on the other. Russia, however, has developed somehow more naturally and organically and reveals none of the splits that we find in the West.

Whether or not we see any validity in this claim (it's difficult to countenance the notion, especially as expressed by a member of the Russian upper class, that there is no true, original division between the social estates in Russia), Kireevsky embraces the same underlying notions as the ones we find variously in other Slavophiles and in Chaadaev himself. He has established that at least the Russians enjoy an integral bond with their own spirit, with each other, and with their nation. He now adopts, perhaps from Chaadaev, the word *physiognomy* to claim that each people develops its own peculiar form

of Christianity: "Every people, having chiefly developed in itself one particular side of its intellectual activity, as the consequence of local, tribal, or historical chances, has always, both in its spiritual life and in the writings of its
theologians, had to retain that peculiar character of its own, its natural physiognomy, so to speak, clarified by higher consciousness."[82]

This kind of thinking leads to the same oddly contradictory pair of conclusions that we find in Shatov: there is a peculiarly Russian form of Christianity, and, though it is peculiarly Russian, it is at the same time whole and
universal. The ancient Roman, because of his tendency to treat himself as a
separate, private being, utterly lacked any "immediate feeling of what is
common to all mankind."[83] The Russians, by contrast, adopted a philosophy that was "directly and purely Christian."[84] Thus their religion, owing to
its purity (and, by extension, its lack of peculiar local attributes) showed a
universality that Roman Catholicism did not. Yet Kireevsky spends much of
his essay arguing precisely that Russian Christianity naturally and necessarily shows local attributes peculiar to the Russians as a group.

As well known in Slavophile circles as Kireevsky (in fact, related to Kireevsky
by birth) and mentioned by Dostoevsky even more often than Kireevsky
was Aleksei Khomiakov. I mentioned Khomiakov a couple of times in the
last chapter. Three ideas, essentially his version of the three I've mentioned,
seem to have attracted Dostoevsky and many others to Khomiakov: that
there is an indissoluble connection between a people (*narod*) and the people's nation, that Orthodox Christianity may be represented (though not
strictly in a chronological sense) as the culmination of a process of development from other versions of Christianity, and that the true Christianity, the
sort we find among the Slavs, is universal. Like his contemporary Kireevsky,
Khomiakov seems to have had Chaadaev in mind as he contrasted Russia
and Slavdom with Western Europe. The madman's syllogism apparently became an obsession among Slavophiles. Khomiakov uses the word in a passage designed to show that the true evil of both Catholicism and Protestantism is their underlying rationalism. In a pamphlet titled *A Few Words by
an Orthodox Christian on the Western Faiths*, published in French in 1853,
Khomiakov says that the struggle between the two versions of Christianity
"has continued for centuries and still continues with the help of syllogism,
but the terrain on which this struggle occurs remains the same: it is always
that of rationalism."[85]

What is *narod*? We must first distinguish it from *porod* ("breed" or
"species"). One people is distinguished from another not by physical attrib-

utes or, for that matter, by a peculiar way of thinking. A people's distinctive character is inextricably connected with its history: "To belong to a people [*narod*] means to create and love, with one's complete, rational will, the moral and spiritual law that has revealed itself . . . in that people's historical development."[86]

> The people [*narod*] is the single, constant actor in history. . . . Every people displays a living countenance [remember Chaadaev's and Kireevsky's "physiognomy"] just as does every person, and . . . the inner life of a people is nothing other than the development of some moral or intellectual principle, actualized by society, a principle that determines the fate of states, either exalting and strengthening those states by its inherent truth, or killing them by its inherent lie.[87]

The people is bound to the nation. A fatherland, says Khomiakov, is "the country and the people that created that country, with both of which my entire life, my entire spiritual existence, and the entire wholeness of my human activity have grown together. [The fatherland] is that people with which I am bound by all the veins of my heart and from which I cannot tear myself away."[88]

The Christianity of the Slavs (or specifically of the Russians) as the culmination of a dialectical process of development (not the phrase that Khomiakov uses) shows up a number of times in Khomiakov's writings. The explanation, extremely Hegelian in its conception (and similar to one that Hegel himself presented), is not always entirely systematic, but the essential idea is this: Catholicism presents a combination of unity without freedom, Protestantism presents a combination of individual freedom without unity, and Orthodoxy, in a Hegelian *Aufhebung* (the act of canceling out, negating, and transcending something, while also incorporating elements of it) presents a combination of Catholicism's unity, without its tyranny, and Protestantism's freedom, without its disunity.[89]

Khomiakov's clearest formulation of the difference both between Catholicism and Protestantism and between these two religions and Orthodoxy appears in *A Few Words by an Orthodox Christian on the Western Faiths*. Having rejected the primitive, natural, and living unity of the church, Khomiakov says there, Catholicism sacrificed ecclesiastical liberty for a unity that was "arbitrary and factitious." Protestantism, on the other hand, asserted "liberty and was obliged to sacrifice to it unity."[90] Khomiakov spends much of the essay discussing the natural freedom and unity in the universal Orthodox Church.

We know for certain that this theory of development appealed to Dostoevsky, since, as I mentioned in the last chapter, he spends a few pages on it
in his *Diary of a Writer* for 1877 (for once, offering a more systematically organized argument than we find in the sources from which he borrowed).
Dostoevsky, in fact, fixed Khomiakov's chronological problem by describing
Protestantism as a general movement of protest beginning in the early days
of the Catholic Church.[91] In addition, as we know from a notebook entry
he wrote toward the end of his life, Dostoevsky viewed Khomiakov as a
source of the conception of the church that he, Dostoevsky, so often presented. "The Russian people [*narod*]," he writes, "exists entirely in Orthodoxy and in the idea of Orthodoxy. . . . Orthodoxy is the church, and the
church is the crown of the edifice, and for all eternity. What the church is
comes from Khomiakov."[92] What is not certain is whether Dostoevsky viewed
Khomiakov as a source of the idea that Orthodoxy and the Russian people
are peculiarly and inextricably bound together. Khomiakov explicitly repudiates the idea in the very early essay "The Church is One" (written sometime during the 1840s).

What is certain is that Dostoevsky could easily have found in Khomiakov
the assertion that the Orthodox Church is universal. In fact, one of the best
examples occurs precisely in the passage where Khomiakov repudiates the
national conception of religion: "The Church is called *one, holy, catholic*
(universal), *apostolic*," he says, echoing the Russian version of the Creed ("I
believe . . . in one Holy, Catholic, and Apostolic Church"), "because it is one
and holy, because it belongs to the entire world and not just to one particular locality, because through it all humankind and the entire earth, not just
one particular people or country, are sanctified."[93] Dostoevsky appears not
to have known this essay, but it would have been easy for him to find in
Khomiakov's other writings passages that emphasized the universality of Orthodoxy. In *A Few Words by an Orthodox Christian on the Western Faiths*, for
example, he certainly read a passage containing the ideas that Russia cannot
have her own separate church and that the true church is universal: "The
Russian church does not form a church apart; it is nothing more than a dio-
cese of the universal Church."[94] Thus Dostoevsky found in Khomiakov support for the universality of Russian Christianity, but he was on his own when
it came to the idea that Russian Christianity is a national religion apart.

It's probably safe to say that no Slavophile—or, to put it more accurately,
no one who argued for the organic connection between people and nation,
people and religion, the Russian people and Russian Orthodoxy—aroused

Dostoevsky's passions, both *pro* and *contra*, as much as Nikolai Iakovlevich Danilevsky (1822–85). Danilevsky was the author of *Russia and Europe*, which Dostoevsky read in serial form starting in 1869 (it came out in book form in 1871), during the time he was composing *The Devils*. The editors of Dostoevsky's *Complete Works* have shown how the figure of Danilevsky contributed to the creation of Shatov. They even juxtapose a passage from *The Devils* (the chapter in which Stavrogin visits Kirillov and Shatov) with one from *Russia and Europe* to prove that some of the words Dostoevsky put in Shatov's mouth were heavily borrowed from Danilevsky.[95]

Danilevsky was well aware of the tradition in which he was writing. The terms of his argument and his topics are generally the same as what we've found in Chaadaev, Kireevsky, and Khomiakov. Phrases from these earlier thinkers crop up frequently in *Russia and Europe*. But Danilevsky has introduced a few modifications that he clearly considers to be significant. One in particular was sufficiently significant to arouse Dostoevsky's indignation, despite the novelist's enthusiastic response to most of what his contemporary had to say.

Like the three predecessors I've mentioned, Danilevsky devotes considerable attention to the contrast between Russia and Western Europe, though initially—for the purpose of showing that Russia does not belong to Europe—he claims (disingenuously, perhaps) simply to be showing the contrast without drawing an unfavorable comparison: Russia lacks both Europe's good and Europe's evil.[96] His discussion of Russia and Western Europe is filled with the same sort of organic imagery we found in Chaadaev, Kireevsky, and Khomiakov.

Like the Slavophiles, Danilevsky believes that every people (*narod*) has its own distinct character. But here, as on many other points, he attempts to give his observation a more concrete foundation than what we find in Kireevsky and Khomiakov. Anticipating twentieth-century thinkers who made a name for themselves by repudiating the category of ethnicity or race, Danilevsky says that if we want to divide humankind into groups we must speak not of the customary groups but of "cultural-historical types." This means speaking of various "independent, distinctive levels of development relating to religion, society, everyday life, industry, politics, science, art, in a word, history."[97]

At the same time, Danilevsky avoids applying to Russians (or generally to the Slavs) the jingoistic rhetoric that we find in many Slavophiles and in Dostoevsky himself. In fact, in an open challenge to classic Slavophilism,

Danilevsky ridicules the idea that any one people (or, for that matter, anything human at all) can be called perfect and final, that it can be looked at
as the perpetually flowing river to which every other stream is merely a trib-
utary. The reason this kind of thinking is flawed is precisely that each people, or each cultural-historical type, shows peculiar features that cannot be
applied to others. To say that one group represents the end of all human
striving is implicitly to suggest that this group's features may be used as the
basis of an invidious comparison with other groups.[98]

Nonetheless, there is no doubt that Danilevsky, as secular as his thinking
might be (at least, by comparison with that of many other Slavophiles), emphasizes the peculiar character of any given people. But when it comes to religion, he shows absolutely no hesitation in drawing comparisons that are essentially the same as what we find in Kireevsky and Khomiakov. It couldn't
be simpler: there are four conceptions of Christianity, all having to do with
a concept of the church and with the notion of infallibility. Under the Orthodox conception, the church is "the assembly of all believers of all times
and all peoples, finding itself under the supremacy of Jesus Christ and the
leadership of the Holy Spirit, and ascribing infallibility to the church (the
church, that is, understood in this way)." Catholicism focuses its concept of
the church "in the person of the pope and thereby ascribes to him infallibility." The Protestant concept is one that "transfers onto each member of the
church the right to interpret [divine] revelation, that thereby transfers onto
each individual this infallibility (relative only to this member, of course), or,
what is the same thing, that completely denies any sort of infallibility at all."
(The fourth, comprising Quakerism and a few other sects, is important neither for us nor for Danilevsky's discussion, so we can safely put it aside.)[99]

Like Kireevsky and his characterization of the Russian religion as "directly and purely Christian," Danilevsky has stacked the deck heavily in his
own favor. His description of Orthodoxy, pretending to be merely factual,
naturally serves the purpose of establishing that version of Christianity
(which, of course, happens to be the one the majority of Russians practice)
as the one and only true version. The terms are essentially the same as they
were in Khomiakov's (and as they would be a few years later in Dostoevsky's)
Hegelian-style, dialectical analysis of the historical development of the three
primary branches of Christianity. Catholicism errs by establishing unity
through autocratic tyranny. Protestantism errs by establishing freedom only
to sacrifice unity for individual freedom and subjectivity. Orthodoxy establishes unity *and* individual freedom.

Seen this way, Orthodoxy clearly has a claim to universality. Danilevsky develops his own concept of universality in *Russia and Europe*. Despite his emphasis on cultural-historical types, he aims always for something higher than cultural-historical types or nations. The process of civilization, he insists, must lead to an "all-humankind-ness" (*vsechelovecheskoe*) or the "common-to-all-humankind-ness" (*obshchechelovecheskoe*—Danilevsky uses a slightly different, adjectival form) that Dostoevsky proclaims as the entire meaning of Russia in the *Diary of a Writer* entry I mentioned before.[100]

The element whose absence in Danilevsky led Dostoevsky to protest in letters to his friends was a strong link between the Russian people and its religion, as expressed in the idea of a distinctly Russian Christ. "I'm still not persuaded," he writes to Nikolai Strakhov in 1869, after reading what would appear in *Russia and Europe* as the third and fourth chapters, "that Danilevsky will demonstrate in its *full force* the definitive essence of the calling we have as Russians, an essence that consists in revealing to the world the Russian Christ, who is still unknown to the world and whose principle is contained in our own native Orthodoxy."[101] Having read all of *Russia and Europe* the following year, Dostoevsky writes to his friend Apollon Maikov about Danilevsky, in a letter that also announces the plan for a novel called *The Devils*: "Russia's whole purpose consists in Orthodoxy, in the *light from the East*, which will stream out to humanity in the West, a humanity that has become blind and that has lost Christ. . . . So just imagine, my dear friend, that even among such lofty Russian people as, for example, the author of *Russia and Europe*, I have yet to encounter this thought about Russia, that is, about the exclusively Orthodox purpose she has for humanity."[102] This thought will turn up again and again, often incongruously, in fictional scenes in which religion is at issue.

## MONKS, 'RASKOL'NIKI,' AND (IN GENERAL) SUFFERERS

It would be a great mistake to suggest Dostoevsky's religious thinking stemmed exclusively from ideas that were ultimately Western European in origin (though, as I'd like to show later on, the "contour" of his religious thought is Western through and through). Even though many of the intellectuals he got to know as a young adult, especially in the radical movement in which he participated before his arrest, had secular upbringings, Dostoevsky was raised in the Russian Orthodox tradition. He maintained a kind

of intimacy with certain religious texts for essentially his entire life, returning to this or that favorite for solace at various trying moments. He is said to
have learned to read from a little book titled *A Hundred Four Holy Stories from
the Old and New Testament* (in Russian translation), by a German theologian
named Johannes Hübner. The book, offering simplified retellings of selected
Biblical narratives, is essentially an early-eighteenth-century version of the
modern "Bible stories" books written for children. In the stories, it mingled
actual quotations from the Luther Bible with simple phrases by the author and
even included, at the end of each chapter, a list of "useful lessons"—pedagog-
ical questions designed to elicit from the young reader the moral truths in the
chapter. This book is the source of Dostoevsky's early knowledge of Scripture,
and he was so fond of it that he had Father Zosima, in *The Brothers Karamazov*, recall it as the book from which *he* learned to read.[103]

He was drawn to the writings of Russian monks and saints. Saint Tikhon
of Zadonsk (1724–1883) attracted him especially. Dostoevsky read extensively in a five-volume edition of Tikhon's works that was published in the
early 1860s. The saint is said to be a prototype for Father Zosima and for
Bishop Tikhon in *The Devils*. Humility, a spirit of forgiveness, and a great
love of children are the traits that seem to have caught Dostoevsky's attention. It's no surprise that the author of *The Idiot* was particularly fascinated
by an episode in the life of the saint in which a wealthy aristocrat slapped
him and Tikhon responded by bowing low and begging forgiveness.[104]
George Fedotov includes Saint Tikhon in what he calls the kenotic tradition
(which I mentioned in the preceding chapter). For Fedotov, Christ's kenosis,
an act of "emptying" (of his divinity) or debasement, is merely the archetype
for a host of human traits having to do with humility.[105] No Russian author
in the nineteenth century popularized these traits more than Dostoevsky,
and Tikhon truly is a perfect embodiment of them.

There are many other figures like this—too many to mention them all. In
1856, a monk by the name of Parfeny (in worldly life Petr Aggeev, 1807–78)
published a book about his wanderings in Russia, Moldavia, Turkey, and the
Holy Land. Dostoevsky borrowed heavily from the style of this book when
he created the language Father Zosima uses to tell about his own life.[106]
Theodosius, the eleventh-century Kievan whom Fedotov considers "the first
representative of kenoticism," figures in Dostoevsky's writings, above all in
his plans for *The Devils*.[107]

A source of endless interest for Dostoevsky was the various types of Russian sectarians, above all fanatical groups that had broken with the official

Russian Orthodox Church. He returns again and again to the most prominent of these groups, the *raskol'niki* (schismatics), or "Old Believers," as they
are usually called in English (from the translation of another Russian term
for them). The group arose in the seventeenth century in protest against
changes the church made to religious practices and against corrections it introduced to Russian translations of religious texts. The *raskol'niki* thus became known as religious purists. But it was their willingness to suffer for
their faith that seems to have captured Dostoevsky's imagination as well as
the popular imagination. *Raskol'niki* in the late seventeenth century, for example, were known to practice mass self-immolation.

You will no doubt remember the darkly comical scene in *Crime and Punishment* in which a painter working in the old pawnbroker's building as
Raskolnikov commits his murders suddenly comes forward and confesses to
the crimes. As Raskolnikov and the police inspector Porfiry play their game of
cat and mouse, Raskolnikov hopes to end the investigation by referring to the
painter's confession. Unhappily, Porfiry already knows the score. "But do you
know," he slyly asks, "that he [the painter] is a *raskol'nik* [*on iz raskol'nikov*—
the genitive plural of *raskol'nik* allows Porfiry to pronounce Raskolnikov's
name], or perhaps not exactly a *raskol'nik* but simply one of those sectarians?"
The message in this bit of information? "Do you know, Rodion Romanych
[Raskolnikov], what 'to suffer' means among these people? It's not to do it for
someone but simply 'you must suffer'; that is to say, accept one's suffering,
and if it's brought on by the powers that be, so much the better."[108] In other
words, the painter confessed not because he's truly guilty ("You're the one
who committed the murder, Rodion Romanych"), but because sectarians like
him arbitrarily seek out situations that cause them to suffer. Porfiry then tells
a story essentially identical to one that Dostoevsky himself told in *Notes from
the House of the Dead*, though in that earlier work, the author took care to in-
form his readers that the man in question was not a *raskol'nik* but a "holy
fool" (referring to a class of men who roamed Russia like beggars, behaving
madly, ostensibly for the purpose of humiliating themselves in the image of
Christ). The holy fool is a convict in prison camp who reads the Bible all
night long. One day, he throws a brick at a prison official, intentionally missing his target, for the sole purpose of "accepting his suffering."[109] Let's not
forget, of course, what Sonia, after Raskolnikov ("Mr. Raskol'nik") has confessed his crime to her, admonishes him to do: "Accept your suffering."

It was no doubt this fascination with needless suffering that attracted
Dostoevsky to one of his favorite Biblical characters: Job. Job is the Scriptural

example that serves Father Zosima as a perfect illustration of the *apparent* injustice in God's world (something like the case of Abraham and Isaac for Kierkegaard a generation earlier). The case of Job, a righteous man whom God punished, without explanation, and then restored to health and good fortune, equally without explanation, would be a perfect case to prove Ivan Karamazov's contention that God's world is unjust. For Zosima, it is instead a great mystery and therefore something to be celebrated. Several years before writing *The Brothers Karamazov*, Dostoevsky wrote to his wife about rereading the story in the Hebrew Bible: "I'm reading the Book of Job, and it throws me into a morbid state of rapture: I'll put the book aside and pace the room for an hour, almost crying, and if it weren't for the contemptible notes of the translator, I would perhaps be content. This book, Anna—it's strange—is one of the first that ever affected me in my life, and at the time I was still practically an infant!"[110] The volume in which he first learned about Job was, of course, Hübner's *Hundred Four Holy Stories*.

It's not easy to say what "religion" there is in the texts and figures I've just mentioned. If we're looking for a true theology, then of course we'll be disappointed, because, to judge from what Dostoevsky himself wrote, either theology is missing or he says nothing about it. If we're looking for a set of doctrines (that is, something a little less formal and abstract than a theology), we'll be partially disappointed here too, though Dostoevsky did have a small set of religious ideas (whether or not he accepted them as true)—the connection between morality and belief in immortality, the prospect of personal resurrection, a devotion to the earth—that he found in some of the religious figures he admired. The writings he was so fond of appear to have provided him less with a theology or system of belief than with a set of *practices* and *happenings*. The religious men he read of were interesting more for what they did than for what and how they believed. Humility and a capacity to suffer irrationally are the qualities that drew him to Tikhon, Parfeny, the *raskol'niki*, Job, and many others that I haven't mentioned here. Clearly these qualities were of great religious significance to Dostoevsky. They tell us that there was a close association in his mind between a certain type of narrative and certain personal attributes on the one hand and a type of devoutness and righteousness on the other. But they tell us little about his *beliefs*, unless we count as a "belief" his acceptance of this association in his mind.

It was in this world of ideas that Dostoevsky confronted religion. Faced with one intellectual world that reduced God and religious phenomena to purely human attributes; faced with another that boasted piety while reducing God and religious phenomena to national, folk attributes; and treasuring a world populated by monks, sectarians, and sufferers, all viewed from the innocent perspective of a young child, he set out to make religion if not *the* focus of his literary creation then one of a small group of focuses. No wonder, then, that the religious world for him is a world of warring systems, that it is the war more than the systems that captures our attention, and that it's impossible ever to discern in that world a set of beliefs we can honestly and unequivocally attribute to the author as his own.

For one thing, the phenomenon of belief itself and the struggle of conflicting beliefs interested him perhaps more than the content of any particular set of beliefs. For another, the beliefs he presents us with (leaving aside the question of whether or not he embraced them) are already structured in such a way as to make it impossible for anyone to embrace them fully.

Later on, I'll return to the question of the content of Dostoevsky's religion, such as it was. In the next two chapters, let's talk about the phenomenon of belief itself.

CHAPTER THREE

# Belief Is Contextual

A person can certainly be divided in two forever but
will just as certainly suffer from it.

—*From a letter to M. A. Polivanova*[1]

Sometime in April 1876, Dostoevsky is reported to have said, "I am a deist—a philosophical deist." He was actually quoting a character from *The Adolescent*, though he didn't say so. What on earth did he mean by this remark? It's one of the only places in his entire body of work where he applies to himself a term that describes his religious beliefs. His character used the remark to explain his previous statement that his faith was not particularly great. Dostoevsky used it in response to a question about an article he had written in the *Diary of a Writer* about a suicide. It's hardly the sort of thing we'd expect from the creator of Sonia Marmeladova. Though Dostoevsky didn't state what the word *deist* denoted to him, he could hardly have expected anyone to understand it as "faithful follower of Christ in the Russian Orthodox Church." In fact, when he applied the word to George Sand two months later in the *Diary of a Writer*, he explained that the French writer was a Christian but did not formally profess faith in Christ. Then again, he didn't qualify the word with "philosophical."[2]

So what do we mean when we say, "Dostoevsky believed such-and-such?" Of course, this is a question we can raise in connection with any author. Everyone can think of authors who change their minds about certain questions over time; who contradict themselves within a single piece of writing; or who profess one belief in their correspondence or in public life, while appearing to profess the opposite belief in their fictional writings. And of course everyone knows how tricky it is to attribute beliefs to any author on the strength of fictional writings alone.

But Dostoevsky's world of ideas, whether or not they have to do with religion, is truly dizzying. Let's say, for the sake of argument, that we were actually interested in what the "real" Dostoevsky was like and what he thought. Our first inclination would be to turn to his nonfiction writings, especially notes, diaries, personal letters, and printed articles. This is where we generally hope to avoid the pitfalls of looking for beliefs in any author's work of fiction. We might think that a passage scribbled in a diary not intended for publication could be expected to give us a direct, unfiltered view into the author's "true," private thoughts. The same thing should hold for a letter written to a close friend (though it is true that people express themselves differently depending on the correspondent). A public speech or a published article on a political or religious issue should give us a dependable sense of what an author officially believes, or at least what an author wishes to have on record as his or her official beliefs.

But we immediately run into problems with Dostoevsky. On any number of issues—not necessarily those directly connected with religion—he was capable of expressing sentiments that conflicted with one another. Moreover, he was capable of expressing such sentiments within a relatively brief period of his life, so that the conflicts can't necessarily be chalked up to any broad change in outlook. I'll talk about three of these issues: the "Jewish question," Slavophilism, and the Russian radical left. My idea here and in the next chapter is to show that Dostoevsky's failure to adopt a consistent set of beliefs on issues he considered significant means we end up looking at belief for him as a problem in its own right.

## HOW TO BE A PHILO-SEMITE AND AN ANTI-SEMITE AT (ROUGHLY) THE SAME TIME

"Philo-Semite" is probably too strong; a word that means "one sympathetic to the (or some) Jews" would be just right.

It seems to have become a received truth that Dostoevsky was a virulent anti-Semite. Had he lived only a few months longer (to judge from what many have said about him), one might almost have expected him to rush off to the south of Russia in April 1881, during the wave of pogroms that broke out there, so that he might experience the great thrill of joining the mobs that were beating Jews to death and burning Jewish business establishments to the ground.

Lord knows, there's plenty of evidence in his nonfictional writings, not just his letters, to support the view that he hated the Jews as a group. The references are far too numerous to list completely, and many are quite nasty—almost nasty enough to pass for the remarks of a *pogromchik*. The vast bulk of them date from the final decade of his life, suggesting to some a general change in convictions (though, as we'll see, even within the period in question we find conflicting sentiments). Here's our author in the *Diary of a Writer*, in 1873; he's been talking about drunkenness in Russia. How can we rid ourselves of this scourge? Through work and industry? But then we need a state budget (from the taxes on liquor), and the Jews will predictably step in.

> There will be nothing but beggars in general solidarity with each other, pawned and enslaved by the entire community, and then the Jews and the kulaks [wealthy, exploitative peasants] will provide the budget for them. Those petty, lowly *bourgeois* of the most depraved sort and an endless number of destitute slaves in bondage to them—there's a pretty picture! The Jews will drink the people's blood and feed themselves on the people's debauchery and degradation, but since these Jews will be providing the budget, we'll have to support them.[3]

There's no mistaking the tone of these comments, and there's no mistaking the use of the most time-worn images from the repertoire of anti-Semites in Russia and Western Europe. There's much more in the *Diary of a Writer*. The author repeatedly makes nasty comments about Benjamin Disraeli (who served as prime minister of Great Britain from 1874 to 1880), referring to him as a "tarantula." Another of Dostoevsky's obsessions was what he refers to as the Jewish *status in statu* (state within a state), that is, what he and others saw as the Jews' tendency to keep to themselves in semiautonomous societies. In a given host society, "they keep to themselves" is an age-old claim designed to blame the Jews for their exclusion from that society. Here's Dostoevsky at his sarcastic best in another *Diary of a Writer* entry, this one from 1876:

> So now the Jews are becoming landowners—and everywhere people are screaming and writing that the Jews are spoiling Russia's soil, that the Jew, having used up his capital on the purchase of an estate, immediately, in order

to recover his capital and his interest, exhausts all the strength and resources of the land he purchased. But just try to say something against this, and the first thing you know, people will start shouting about the destruction of the principle of economic freedom and equal civil rights. But what kind of equal rights are there if a manifest Talmudic Status in Statu exists above everything else, in top position, if what we have is not only the exhaustion of the land but also the future exhaustion of our peasant?

He goes on to complain that the Jews have already sucked the juice out of the Russian peasant and have begun buying off liberal opinion.[4]

These passages were written for publication—and, of course, the public read them. But could the venue have affected the views that Dostoevsky expressed? Is it possible he was merely tailoring his writing to a readership that, he assumed, would welcome such views? It's possible. But then again, we can find the same views in an even nastier form in writings Dostoevsky did not intend for publication. To be sure, many of the offending passages come from notebooks in which the author planned out his *Diary of a Writer* entries. Yet the impulse to defame is unmistakable. Consider, for example, the ugly comments that Dostoevsky wrote in the notebook for *Diary of a Writer* in 1875 and 1876. He is referring to a recently published report on the role of Jews in Russian industry.

Can't our Jews find defenders? They certainly have the means to do so. And what kind of arguments are these? That our kulaks and peasant extortionists are no worse? If there exists such a pestilence as the kulaks, does it follow from this that Jews are necessary? We need to restrict both. . . . We may and must restrict the rights of the Jews in many cases. Why, why support this Status in statu? Eighty million [Russians] exist only to support three million Jews. To hell with them [literal translation: "Spit on them"].[5]

Did Dostoevsky's views change over time? Are we simply looking at an attitude that he held for a short time and later abandoned? This is a difficult question to answer briefly, but we do know that, toward the very end of his life, some four years after he penned the remarks I've just quoted, he wrote a sarcastic entry in another planning notebook for *Diary of a Writer*:

*Jews.* And even if they were to rise over all Russia in a kahal [governing council of a Jewish community] and a conspiracy and suck the blood out of every Russian peasant—Oh, please, please let us not say a word. Otherwise some kind of *nonliberal calamity* will occur. Who knows—we might actually consider our religion superior to that of the Jews and oppress them out of religious intolerance, and what will happen then? Just think, what might happen then![6]

So if we're inclined to hope that Dostoevsky might have changed his views over time, in the sense that he *permanently abandoned* an aversion that he expressed in the mid-1870s, then we are bound to be disappointed, since this aversion turns up with renewed force till the end of his life.

In August 1879, Dostoevsky writes a letter to his friend Konstantin Pobedonostsev, the reactionary lay procurator of the Holy Synod (head of the Russian Orthodox Church). Perhaps unwittingly, he allies himself with the man who coined the term "anti-Semite." This is Wilhelm Marr, the German anarchist who founded the League of Anti-Semites in 1879, an organization founded on the belief that Jews are a *race* and that opposition to them must be conceived with race in mind (the use of the word *Semite* was purposeful: it suggested a tribal, rather than religious, characterization of the Jews). In the same year, Marr published the notorious *Victory of Judaism over Germandom Considered from a Non-Confessional* (that is, nonreligious) *Standpoint*, in which he warned of the increasing threat that Jews would come to dominate German society. Dostoevsky is writing from Ems, Germany, where he is taking a cure. He is miserable, in part because half the people he sees every day are Jews. A Russian journal has recently published an excerpt from a rebuttal by a German Jew to *The Victory of Judaism over Germandom* (though Dostoevsky names neither Marr nor the author of the rebuttal). "A certain German" (Marr) had dared to write "that Germany is being Judaized frightfully and in all respects," he writes. As he reads it, the rebuttal, distinguishing between a pejorative name for Jews (*zhid*, in Russian) and a more neutral one (*evrei*), claims that there is no such thing as a *zhid* but that one can see the pervasive influence of the *evrei* in Germany. "The Jewish (*evreiskii*) spirit and nationality," Dostoevsky says, sarcastically paraphrasing Marr's critic, "are superior to the German."[7]

There's no reason to suppose that Dostoevsky had actually read Marr's pamphlet, so it would be wrong to surmise that he expressly endorsed a racially grounded aversion to Jews. Still, the letter shows his willingness to refer approvingly to anti-Jewish sentiments of many sorts. On the other hand, we must take into account Dostoevsky's reader. Is there any possibility that Dostoevsky made these hateful remarks simply because he felt they would please his notoriously conservative friend?

But two brief personal relationships throw the entire matter of Dostoevsky's anti-Semitism into doubt. The first and more important involves Avraam (also called Arkady and Albert) Kovner, a Jewish Nihilist who had boldly embezzled a large sum of money from the bank that employed him.

He was quickly arrested, and in January 1877 he wrote a long letter to Dostoevsky from prison. Dostoevsky had never heard of him.

The letter is an amazing document in its own right, but there is no need to summarize the whole thing. The writer earnestly expresses his admiration for Dostoevsky and indicates that he modeled the justification for his crime on one that Raskolnikov uses for *his* crime in *Crime and Punishment*: Kovner would take the carefully calculated amount he stole from the bank, an amount he believed was completely insignificant to the bank (exactly 3 percent of its annual profits), and use it to help the poor, specifically his own family. After devoting a great deal of space (the letter is twenty-four pages long) to his crime and his personal story, Kovner gets to the point. "I'd like to know why you come out against the Jew [*zhid*] and not against the exploiter in general. I cannot tolerate the prejudices of my nation any more than you can—I've even suffered a good deal from them—but I can never agree that shameless exploitation flows in the very blood of this nation."[8] Kovner points out that, in condemning an entire people, Dostoevsky is condemning three million, of whom a good 2,900,000 are so desperately poor that simply staying alive is a daily struggle. Kovner also reminds his reader that within the same three million are quite a few very distinguished Jews with a university education and professional achievements to their name. Kovner now lays it on thick: "No, in the end, unfortunately you do not know the Jewish [*evreiskii*] people, not its life, not its spirit, not its forty-century history. I say 'unfortunately,' because you are in any case a sincere, absolutely honest man, yet you are unconsciously causing great harm to the masses of a destitute people."[9] Two days after sending this letter, Kovner sends another one (primarily in response to the new issue of *Diary of a Writer*, which he read immediately after sending his first letter), in which he refers to Dostoevsky's efforts to exalt the Russian folk as the true bearers of Russian Christianity. In truth, says Kovner, out of a total of eighty million, "sixty million live a literally animal life, having no rational conception of God, of Christ, of the soul, or of its immortality."[10]

Dostoevsky's response to these letters came in two forms: a personal reply to Kovner and an entire chapter of the March 1877 issue of *Diary of a Writer*, which he devoted to "The Jewish Question." Some might easily use the letter to Kovner to show that, deep down, Dostoevsky didn't really hate the Jews. Others might as easily use it to show that any claim he makes *not* to hate the Jews is at best disingenuous and at worst an out-and-out lie. But as I see it, of all Dostoevsky's writings this letter is one of the most astonishing examples of the author's capacity to present two reciprocally contradictory positions not on two occasions separated by at least a little bit of time but *in sequence and within the same short passage*—that is, at essentially the *same time*. After speaking of literary matters and saying he has rarely read anything more intelligent than his new correspondent's letter, Dostoevsky gets to *his* point. He politely uses the socially more acceptable of the two common Russian words for "Jew."

> Now as to the Jews. It's impossible to go on at length about such topics in a letter, *especially with you*, as I said before. You are so intelligent that we will not resolve a point of contention like this one even in a hundred letters but will only wear ourselves down. I'll tell you that I've received comments of this sort from other Jews, too. In particular, not long ago I received a perfect, very noble letter from a Jewish woman, who signed for herself, and also with bitter reproaches. . . . I'll tell you now that I'm not at all an enemy of the Jews and never have been one.

The next sentence is where the switch appears to come:

> But their forty-century (as you put it) existence proves that this tribe possesses an extraordinarily powerful vital force that has not, however, been able throughout history to avoid formulating itself in various *status in statu*. The most powerful *status in statu* is indisputable among our Russian Jews, too. And if this is true, then how can they not, at least in part, come to be in a state of dissension with the root of the nation, the Russian tribe? You point to a Jewish intelligentsia, but then you, too, are intelligentsia and just look how you hate Russians precisely *for the very reason that you are a Jew*, though a member of the intelligentsia. In your second letter, there are a few lines about the moral and religious consciousness of the sixty millions of Russian people. These are words of terrible hatred, yes hatred, because you yourself, as an intelligent man, must understand that in this sense (that is, on the question in what measure and with what force the Russian common man is a Christian), you are to the highest degree incompetent to judge. I would never have said of the Jews what you say of the Russians. I have seen for the fifty years of my life that Jews, both good and bad, do not wish even to sit at the same table with Russians, while the Russian is not squeamish about sitting with *them*. So who hates whom? Who is intolerant of whom? And what about the idea that the Jews are a nation that is debased and insulted? [Dostoevsky uses the words from the title of his early novel, usually translated into English as *The Insulted and Injured*.] On the contrary, it is the Russians who in everything are debased before the Jews, for the Jews, taking advantage of almost full equal rights . . . possess, apart from that, their own rights, their own law, and their own *status quo*, which Russian laws protect.

Dostoevsky repeats that he is no enemy of the Jews and that he has many Jewish acquaintances. He then moves to conclude:

> Your letter (the first one) is fascinatingly good. I want to believe, with all my soul, that you're completely sincere. But even if you're insincere, it's all the same: for in the present case, insincerity is an extremely complicated and profound matter in its own right. Please believe in the sincerity with which I shake the hand that you've extended me. But raise up your spirit, and formulate your ideal. No doubt you've been seeking it till now—or no?[11]

It's easy to see why people are so ready to find for the prosecution here, when Dostoevsky appears flagrantly to take back with one hand what he has first given with the other. David Goldstein, the author of a full-length and immoderately argued book on the subject of Dostoevsky's attitudes toward the Jews, hesitates not a moment to convict the Russian author of the most serious offense. The letter, or the passages in which Dostoevsky attempts to defend himself against the charge that he's an enemy of the Jews, is nothing but a lie. Dostoevsky uses the letter merely "to establish justification for his own lack of sincerity" in those passages. "Ambiguity," Goldstein continues, "is an unassailable stronghold, and Dostoyevsky finds comfort and safety inside it."[12]

But just a minute. Let's give the prosecution the benefit of all doubt about the author's intentions in the nasty passages. Let's say that Dostoevsky's claims about the Jews are incomplete, in the sense that each one is missing a necessarily attendant but tacit claim. If we put them in an ever-so-slightly-exaggerated form, they'll read like this (with the missing portion in italics):

> The Jews keep apart, *so now you can understand why I hate them and, by extension, you.*
> This is why there's strife between them and us, *but if there's strife, I'm necessarily a party to it and therefore hate them and, by extension, you.*
> The Jews hated us first, *so now you can understand why I hate them and, by extension, you.*

Even if these statements represented Dostoevsky's "true" feelings, who's to say that he was sincere when he made them and insincere both in his rejection of the charge of hating Jews and in the kind things he says to Kovner? Why is it impossible that he was sincere in both? What in the world prevents a person from *sincerely* saying something one minute and *sincerely* contradicting that same thing the next? Even with the full weight of the accumulated hostile

statements about Jews in his nonfictional writings of all types, why is Dostoevsky necessarily insincere when he extends his hand to a Jew, professes
admiration for that Jew, and claims not to be an enemy of the Jew's "nation"
(*nation* was a term commonly used in this era to denote the group to which
Jews belonged)?

If ambivalence—or to put it more accurately, expression of apparently
conflicting positions—is the problem, then the chapter Dostoevsky devoted
to "The Jewish Question" in *Diary of a Writer* can only make matters worse
for anyone who needs to know whether or not Dostoevsky really hated the
Jews. Remember that Dostoevsky is now writing for publication, not just for
himself or for a friend. Here are the highlights: "A Jew [*evrei*] without God is
somehow unthinkable; it is impossible to imagine a Jew without God. . . .
How is it that I have come to be classed among the haters of the Jew as a
people, as a nation?"[13] He defends his use of the word *zhid* on the grounds
that it's not really offensive and that it seems perfectly natural. Then, in a
subchapter titled "Pro and Contra," he raises tortured arguments like the
ones he presented in his letter to Kovner. In each instance, it's a matter of
giving with one hand and taking back with the other. To paraphrase: sure,
the Jews in Russia have lacked rights, *but then so have the common Russian
people*. In prison camp (Dostoevsky had spent four years in a Siberian camp
for a political crime), there was no hatred for Jews. In fact, no one found it
strange when the Jewish prisoners prayed, *even though Jews pray by scream-
ing and putting on special clothes*. Perhaps we might speak of a lack of sympathy for Jews (rather than of hatred for them), *but then this is the Jews' fault*.
If there were eighty million Jews and three million Russians (instead of the
other way around), *the Jews would certainly enslave the Russians*. The Jews
have survived *only by maintaining their status in statu*. I don't condemn this
institution, *whose aim is to keep the Jews separate and to allow them to exploit
others*. It's hardly surprising that they exploit others, since *the dominant characteristic of the Jews is their pitilessness*.[14] In his concluding subchapter, "But
Long Live Brotherhood!" Dostoevsky expresses his wholehearted support for
extending equal rights to the Jews (though he qualifies his statement a couple
of pages later by saying that Jews should enjoy full rights only if they can do
so without detriment to the "root" population).[15] After all, this is Christ's
law—*but let's not forget that brotherhood needs to come from both sides*.[16]

There's no need to perform a detailed analysis of this set of arguments.
Dostoevsky's detractors predictably find his sympathetic statements to be
lies. In the eyes of David Goldstein, the final subchapter contains nothing

more than cynicism and sophistry. "Dostoyevsky bears a heavy responsibility, and there is no reason why he should be exonerated," he says.[17] Once again, though, the sympathetic statements are lies only if we assume (1) that the unsympathetic statements *truly* represent Dostoevsky's beliefs and (2) that *only* these statements truly represent Dostoevsky's beliefs.

For those seeking to label Dostoevsky "pro" or "contra," the second personal relationship I spoke of complicates the issue even further. Sofia Lurye was a young Jewish woman who, starting in 1876, personally visited Dostoevsky and corresponded with him. Dostoevsky wrote a few pages about her in the June 1876 issue of *Diary of a Writer*. In February 1877, she wrote him a letter. As in the case of Kovner, Dostoevsky responded with both a personal letter and an entry in *Diary of a Writer*. In the entry, Dostoevsky quotes from his correspondent's letter a touching story about a German Protestant doctor in provincial Russia who was much beloved by all his patients, especially Jews. Lurye tells of an occasion when this Dr. Hindenburg treated a poor Jewish family, received in payment from them a goat, sold the goat to buy a cow (at a substantial loss to himself), and then, because he felt cow's milk was better than goat's milk, sent the cow to the family. At the graveside, a Protestant pastor and a rabbi gave eulogies.

Dostoevsky follows with a section that includes a fancifully embellished version of the graveside scene:

> The pastor, with tears in his eyes, gives his speech over the open grave. The rabbi stands to the side, waits, and, as the pastor finishes, takes the pastor's place and gives his speech, with tears in his eyes, too. And truly in this moment the entire 'Jewish question' is almost resolved! The pastor and the rabbi joined together in common love, and they practically embraced over this grave in plain sight of Christians and Jews.[18]

Dostoevsky even uses the word *evrei* (the more polite word for Jew) throughout this entry.

In the personal letter, we see the author as he directly addresses a Jew. Sofia's letter mentions a doctor that her mother has been strongly urging her to marry. The doctor loves Sofia, but she does not love him in return. What to do? A tender and fatherly Dostoevsky advises his young friend to give the matter careful thought, expressing the wish that she will come to like her suitor and accept his offer of marriage. Then he says this: "One thing you didn't write: of what confession is he? A Jew [*evrei*]? If he's a Jew, then how did he come to be a Court Counselor [a rank in the civil service]? It seems to me that

Jews have only recently won the right to occupy the ranks. In order to become a Court Counselor, one must have at least fifteen years of service."[19]

Here is Goldstein's judgment: "What is shocking here is precisely the fact that there is nothing at all shocking in the way in which Dostoyevsky broaches the question. . . . The question must, therefore, be asked whether Sofia Lurye was not for Dostoyevsky that classic 'Jewish friend' whom he needed to convince himself and to convince others of the preposterousness and groundlessness of the charge that he was an 'unconditional' anti-Semite."[20] Having raised this speculative conjecture, Goldstein then accepts it and goes on to draw inferences from it.

But this is completely absurd. How can it be beyond all possible doubt that Dostoevsky was insincere? How can his failure to say something on a given occasion imply that he really meant precisely that something? What kind of logic is that? Dostoevsky writes to someone he's enormously fond of. Why should he not be tender and even use the polite word for Jew both in his letter to her and in a *Diary* article about her? With Goldstein's assumptions, of course Dostoevsky can't "be exonerated." If he says nice things and nasty things, and if we decide arbitrarily that he meant only the nasty things, then of course he's an anti-Semite pure and simple. But he *did* say the nice things, and we need to acknowledge the possibility that he *meant* them, just as we need to acknowledge the possibility that he meant the nasty things when he said *them*.

There has been considerable debate about Dostoevsky's anti-Jewish sentiments. Sometime ago Gary Saul Morson wrote a review article about scholarly responses to these sentiments. He takes Goldstein severely to task for painting with too broad a brush and failing to make any distinctions between various types of anti-Jewish sentiment. He then moves on to speak about advocates of what he calls the "two Dostoevskys" theory. The theory proposes a distinction between "the subtle, compassionate novelist and the neurotic, chauvinist ideologue," that is, between the author's fiction and his journalism. When proponents of this theory come across passages in Dostoevsky's fictional works that appear "journalistic," Morson says, they describe such passages as simply artistic flaws. A scene from *The Brothers Karamazov* that has disturbed many of Dostoevsky's readers is the one in which Liza Khokhlakova asks Alesha Karamazov if Jews steal children and kill them at Easter. Alesha, the all-forgiving man of God, instead of dismissing the notion as nonsense, says, "I don't know." Now this is hardly a journalistic passage, but many readers see Dostoevsky's failure to make Alesha say the "right" thing as further evidence of the anti-Jewish attitude he expresses in his nonfiction. Yet because it appears in a fictional work, the claim is that the author simply made an artistic mistake, either by admitting ugly sentiments into a category of writing from which he normally excludes them or by making his character internally inconsistent.

One version of the two-Dostoevskys theory that Morson mentions is worth looking at. In a book titled *Ideology and Imagination*, Geoffrey C. Kabat distinguishes between Dostoevsky's journalistic writing, which he characterizes as "ideological," and his fiction, which he characterizes as "imaginative." The difference between the ideological and the imaginative is that the first represents a "tendency to resort to simple oppositions between absolutes in order to resolve complex problems," while the second represents a tendency "to explore the deeper connections between the terms of a contradiction and to mediate between contraries."[21]

Dostoevsky's anti-Semitism belongs largely to the first tendency, as do his nationalism and xenophobia. But Kabat recognizes that something different is going on with the Dr. Hindenburg story. His explanation is quite ingenious. When Dostoevsky speaks of Jews in the *Diary of a Writer*, he is fairly consistent in hewing to a position founded on opposition and absolutes. The passages in which he claims to be no enemy of the Jews present no challenge to this position because, immediately after those passages, he introduces his stock repertoire of anti-Jewish comments and thus "unconsciously reveals his hostility and prejudice against the Jews." But when he writes of a possible solution to the Jewish question (the pastor and the rabbi embrace over the good doctor's grave), it is because he has slipped into a fictional mode—the story, after all, is a fantasy. In that mode, Dostoevsky allows himself to mediate between the terms of contradiction and to imagine solutions.[22]

The problem with this explanation is that it ignores sympathetic statements that Dostoevsky made in his letters. Elsewhere in his book, Kabat describes the letters as a kind of transitional genre, in which the author expresses himself and begins to give form to deeply held beliefs.[23] This may well be true, but it would be difficult to take Dostoevsky's letter to Sofia Lurye and classify its sympathetic language as imaginative fiction. Nor can we take Dostoevsky's claim, in the *Diary of a Writer*, that he is no enemy of the Jews and completely discount it by saying he follows it with hostile remarks. It may be true that Dostoevsky gave freer reign to the play of contradictions in his fiction than in his nonfiction, but this does not alter the fact that he adopts pairs of reciprocally contradictory positions in both styles of writing.

Morson rejects all theories of this sort and concludes by saying we have no choice but to recognize that Dostoevsky did in fact entertain ugly thoughts about the Jews; that the passage in *The Brothers Karamazov* is, unhappily, all too consistent with Dostoevsky's thinking on the Jewish question; and that the author cannot be excused for expressing this thinking in fiction *or* in nonfiction.[24]

But once again, distinguishing between Dostoevsky the novelist and Dostoevsky the journalist is different from distinguishing between Dostoevsky the anti-Semitic journalist and Dostoevsky the philo-Semitic journalist (or correspondent or diary writer). He *did* entertain ugly thoughts about the Jews in his nonfiction writings and certainly should not be excused for doing so. But he also entertained sympathetic thoughts about Jews in the same body of writings, and we must take this into account before we simply label him an anti-Semite without qualification. For that matter, we need not explicitly speak of *two* Dostoevskys. They were the same man (Kabat, too, believes this). The same man entertained both sets of sentiments, even though the two sets contradicted each other. At one moment, he felt that Jews should never be offered equal rights; at another, he felt they should. At one moment, he felt that at least some individual Jews were worthy of respect and tender affection; at another he felt all Jews were entitled to nothing more than hostility and contempt. His sympathetic statements are not confined to personal dealings with individual Jews (haven't we all met someone who in the abstract expresses hatred toward a group of people but is incapable of bringing that hateful attitude to a personal encounter with an actual member of the group?). But Dostoevsky, in the same published forum where he expended so much energy in spitting on the Jews, urged equal rights for them, claimed (implicitly) not to be their enemy, and dreamed of a fanciful solution to the problem associated with them, all in the abstract.[25]

What does it matter that the solution was presented in a fictional passage, if the diarist concluded by saying that the Jewish question was resolved in it? He means the *real* Jewish question, just as he means the *real* Russian nationality question and the *real* Russian religious question when, in his many journalistic rantings on the subject, he proposes equally fanciful solutions to *them*.

## HOW TO BE A SLAVOPHILE AND A SLAVOPHOBE AT (ROUGHLY) THE SAME TIME

"Slavophobe" is probably too strong a word. Perhaps "person showing a skeptical attitude toward Slavophilism" would be more accurate. In any case, Dostoevsky gave this piece of bipolarism perfect fictional expression in the scene from *The Devils* that I spoke of in the last chapter. I mentioned there too that he expressed support for Slavophile ideas in his nonfiction writings. But even this is not so simple. As in the case of Dostoevsky's attitude toward the Jews (his especially shrill statements come only in the last decade of his life), we can find, over time, certain changes in his attitude toward the Slavophiles. But in both cases, it is equally possible to find conflicting views in the nonfiction writings within a short period.

A biographer might be inclined to dismiss, for example, the sarcastic remark that a very young Dostoevsky makes in a letter to his brother in 1845. As the aspiring writer surveys the current intellectual scene, he refers to "the last meeting of the *Slavophiles*, where it will be triumphantly proved that Adam was a Slav and lived in Russia."[26] Everyone knows, of course, that Dostoevsky's convictions underwent a substantial change in the early 1860s, after he returned from his decade-long imprisonment and exile. But the problem is that even in the period when Dostoevsky's views were presumably changing, his views toward the Slavophiles were sharply divided yet most often (when he was actually speaking of Slavophiles and not speaking their language without naming them) harshly unfavorable. In a series of articles on Russian literature that he published in his postexile literary venture, the magazine *Time* (*Vremia*), Dostoevsky develops a view of Russia that sounds for all the world like something we might have read in Kireevsky or Khomiakov. "We believe that the Russian nation is an extraordinary phenomenon in the history of all humankind," he says. He takes the Western Europeans to task for lacking all the unifying forces that Russia seems to have in her very soil: "The idea of common-to-all-humankind-ness [*obshchechelovech-nost'*] grows ever more dim among [Western Europeans]," he claims as he proceeds to use dozens of typically Slavophile words beginning with *vse* ("all," "pan-"), *obshche* ("common," "general"), and the prefix *so-* ("together," "con-").[27] Strictly speaking, Dostoevsky's outlook at this moment is classified as *pochvennichestvo*, an early 1860s nationalist movement—difficult to distinguish from Slavophilism—to celebrate Russia's native virtues and to urge a return to the Russian "soil" (*pochva*). Joseph Frank mentions that Dostoevsky at this point had little direct knowledge of Slavophile doctrine and, besides, wished at least to appear to be giving his readers something original and new.[28]

The remarks I just quoted appear in the first issue of *Time*, early in 1861. By the time he writes for the eleventh issue, later that same year, Dostoevsky has read the journal *Day* (*Den'*), edited by the prominent Slavophile brothers Konstantin and Ivan Aksakov, and now has sufficient confidence in his acquaintance with Slavophilism to launch a spirited assault on the doctrine. At this point, Dostoevsky appears to be upset as much by the tone he finds in Slavophile writers as by their ideology. He doesn't like the Slavophiles' haughtiness and intolerance. Using "terror of thought" and "domestic terrorism" (not in the modern sense of these terms but in the sense of "intolerance and intimidation," as in the Jacobin Reign of Terror during the French Revolution), the Slavophiles fight among themselves. They are completely intolerant of any views that diverge from their own. Dostoevsky finds Slavophile thought tainted with idealism, by contrast with the salubrious "realism" of their opponents, the Westerners (*zapadniki*, traditionally thought of as Dostoevsky's enemies).[29] The following year, again in *Time*, Dostoevsky, having acknowledged the merits of Slavophile doctrine, once again goes on the offensive. By fighting so strenuously for their archaic ideals and by attacking all contemporary Russian learned society, the Slavophiles are guilty of a fanaticism that taints their movement. In an amusing though rather tortured simile, Dostoevsky likens the Slavophile to a man picking through a pile of trash that is known to contain treasures, forcefully casting aside refuse in order to find the true object of his search: not treasures for his own use, but an old, worn-out shoe! Lest the reader not grasp the analogy, Dostoevsky explains: "The *Day* rejects contemporary life in the name of Moscow theory" (because of the Slavophiles' dream of restoring Muscovite Russia as it existed before the Westernizing reforms of Peter the Great).[30]

One might easily argue here that Dostoevsky is drawing fine distinctions within a movement for which he might possibly show some enduring sympathy, that in his eyes Slavophiles so named have simply taken to an unreasonable level views that he himself espouses. But even so, the record is mixed on the issue for the remainder of the author's life. In April 1866, he sends a letter to the conservative critic Mikhail Katkov, who has been publishing the first serial edition of *Crime and Punishment* in the *Russian Messenger*. "I'll tell you frankly," Dostoevsky writes, "that I have been and, it seems to me, always will remain in my convictions a real Slavophile, apart from minor differences of opinion."[31] Five years later, in a letter to Strakhov, he writes this: "In one of your brochures, there was a magnificent thought . . . that every slightly significant and true talent has always ended up turning to national sentiment, has become of-the-people [*narodnyi*], Slavophilic. So the 'whistler' Pushkin suddenly, before all the Kireevskys and Khomiakovs . . . that is, before all the Slavophiles, expresses their [the Slavophiles'] very essence and, what is more, expresses it incomparably more profoundly than they have done till now."[32] This mention of Pushkin is a reference to the polemic in which Dostoevsky engaged ten years earlier with the Slavophiles, to whom, Dostoevsky charges, Pushkin was a *svistun*, a mere whistler.

Here is a notebook entry for the 1876 *Diary of a Writer*, after Dostoevsky publishes *The Adolescent* (*Podrostok*) in a noted liberal journal and anticipates criticism:

> And how do you know my tendencies . . . ? You know, Mr. Liberal, that I'm more liberal than you. Or do you think that Slavophiles are not liberal?. . . . But I have in no way changed my ideals, and I do believe, only not in the commune but in the Kingdom of God. You can't understand me, so I won't explain myself more precisely, but you should know all the same that I am "more liberal than you," even a good deal more. . . . I belong in part not so much to Slavophile convictions, but rather to Orthodox, that is, to peasant convictions, that is, to Christian ones. I don't share their [the Slavophiles'] views entirely—their prejudices, and I don't care for their ignorance, but I love their heart and everything that they love. Already in prison camp.[33]

Here he is in *Diary of a Writer*, 1877, from a chapter titled "Confessions of a Slavophile": "I am in many respects of purely Slavophile convictions, though perhaps I'm not entirely a Slavophile." Slavophilism, Dostoevsky explains, falls into three types: the sort that signifies *kvas* (a fermented drink viewed as typically Russian) and radishes, that is, common peasant life; the sort that signifies "the aspiration to free and unite all Slavs under the supreme authority of Russia"; and the sort that shares the aspiration of the second sort but adds to it "the spiritual union of all those who believe that our great Russia, at the head of the united Slavs, will speak to the whole world, to all European mankind and its civilization, its new, powerful word not yet heard by the world." It is to this third type of believer that Dostoevsky belongs, he says.[34]

Here he is in the notebook to the same issue of *Diary of a Writer*: "I'm a Slavophile. What is a 'Slavophile'?"[35]

Here he is in a brief biographical sketch (in the third person) that he dictated to his second wife sometime in 1877 and that was published in an early edition of the author's works: "By conviction he is openly a Slavophile; his earlier socialist convictions have very powerfully changed."[36]

Finally there is the speech on Pushkin that Dostoevsky gave in June 1880, less than a year before his death. The circumstances were extraordinary. He gave the speech, significantly, not in his long-since-adopted Petersburg but in Moscow, the ancestral "Russian" capital favored by the Slavophiles. Speaking there to the Society of Lovers of Russian Literature, the much celebrated author of *The Brothers Karamazov* praises the beloved poet as a prophet and as the embodiment of Russia's national ideals. To Dostoevsky, Pushkin is about nothing if not his (Dostoevsky's) own favorite ideas. If you've ever read any of Pushkin's works, you'll have trouble recognizing him in what Dostoevsky says. But that hardly matters. The Pushkin speech was not really about Pushkin; it was about Russia—and Dostoevsky.

By the end of his speech, Dostoevsky has launched into a rhapsody on familiar themes from the Slavophile writers I mentioned in the last chapter, but with a most important difference: "Becoming a true Russian will mean just this: striving definitively to bring reconciliation to European contradictions, showing European anguish a way out in our own all-humankind [*vsechelovechnoi*] and all-unifying Russian soul, joining all our brothers to that soul with brotherly love, and, finally, perhaps speaking the definitive word of the great, general harmony, the brotherly, definitive concord of all tribes under Christ's evangelical law!"[37]

What's new in the remarks Dostoevsky makes in his speech is his confidence in the possibility of *reconciliation* with the West, or to put it more precisely, a reconciliation *within* the West to be shown to the West by Russia. In the next-to-last issue of *Diary of a Writer*, he printed a text of the speech and, in an introductory chapter, took his idea a step farther. Here, instead of speaking about a reconciliation between Russia and the West, he speaks about a reconciliation between Slavophilism and Westernism. By *Westernism* he means, of course, the tendency among his educated compatriots to prefer Western European culture to Russian, sometimes even to prefer residence in Western Europe to residence in the mother country. The Russian literary theme of the uprooted man, torn from the Russian soil by the corrupt and seductive influence of Western European rationalism and godlessness—a theme, Dostoevsky has claimed in his speech, to which Pushkin gave the first powerful expression—demonstrates how profoundly Westernism has

penetrated (and some say damaged) Russian culture. By all traditional accounts, Westernism is the tendency against which Dostoevsky consistently
railed since shortly after his return from exile. Contemporary Westerners
for whom he is said to have felt antipathy include a great many of the giant
literary and intellectual figures of the nineteenth century: Belinsky, Turgenev, Alexander Herzen, and many others. One need think only of such
characters as Raskolnikov, Stavrogin, and Ivan Karamazov, with all their logical syllogisms, to be persuaded that Westerners, in this sense, were on the
author's mind for a good part of his mature life (whatever he "truly" believed
about them).

Now, with only a short time to live, Dostoevsky finally declares victory
by claiming a reconciliation that was manifested at (he dares not say "caused
by") his speech. If the Pushkin speech were an "event," as Ivan Aksakov has
recently announced (and Dostoevsky himself describes how, at the end of
his speech, former sworn enemies threw themselves into each others' arms),
in what did this event consist? "Precisely in this," Dostoevsky writes, "that
an enormous and perhaps definitive step was made by the Slavophiles, or
the so-called Russian party (good Lord, we have a Russian party!), toward
reconciliation with the Westerners; for the Slavophiles declared the complete
legitimacy of the Westerners' striving for Europe, the complete legitimacy of
the Westerners' most extreme passions and conclusions, explaining this legitimacy as purely a striving of our Russian people, one that accords with
the very spirit of the people."[38]

What to make of Dostoevsky and Slavophilism? Throughout the introductory article, he speaks of the Slavophiles as of a group he doesn't belong
to. He stands back in wonder as the Slavophiles and Westerners behave differently from what we might expect. He never says "we," except to refer to
all Russians. Did he simply change his mind over time? Did he always consider himself separate from Slavophilism *as a movement*, in order to distance
himself from some of its more obnoxious views? If so, did he simply not
bother to say this every time he declared himself a Slavophile? When he has
Nikolai Stavrogin so successfully obliterate Shatov's Slavophile theories, is he
dramatizing nothing more than the struggle between Stavrogin's rational
mind and a *simple-minded, fanatical* Slavophilism?

But even at a given moment, Dostoevsky's position on this and related doctrines is so fraught with conflict that he's able to say, for example, that he's
more liberal than the liberals, that Slavophiles can be liberal (suggesting he
himself is one), that he's not so much a Slavophile, and that he's never changed

his ideals. He dictates to his wife that he is a Slavophile and that he *has* changed his liberal convictions. He stands back from Slavophilism and praises it for accepting the West, a position that appears self-contradictory on its face.

## HOW TO BE A LIBERAL AND A CONSERVATIVE AT (ROUGHLY) THE SAME TIME

Here I'll be brief and limit myself to just a few examples, especially because the connection between politics and religion is a bit indirect. Anyone who's read even an editor's introduction to *Notes from Underground, Crime and Punishment,* or *The Devils* knows the familiar story. Dostoevsky started out as a sentimental liberal in the 1840s, embracing a utopian socialist philosophy founded on a struggle to provide rights for the Russian common folk and on recognition of the worth of all individuals, regardless of social class. He was associated with the socialist Petrashevsky circle in the late 1840s. He was arrested, tried, and convicted for his alleged participation in a revolutionary conspiracy. He served ten years in prison and exile. He returned to public life and within a few years, in response to the new Nihilist revolutionary culture, swung sharply to the right. *Notes from Underground* (1864) is a direct response to the revolutionary Gospel of the day, Nikolai Chernyshevsky's didactic and hugely influential novel *What Is to Be Done?* (1863). From then till the end of his life, he remained a staunch conservative (though he became increasingly shrill in his last years while at the same time softening his attitude toward liberals who showed sympathy for the peasantry).

Of course, this is a simplistic version of the story, one that ignores the complexity of Dostoevsky's style of believing. Still, there's no need to rehearse the case for Dostoevsky's conservatism, that is, his expression or dramatization of conservative views. To take only *The Devils,* we can use any number of personal letters and notebook entries to prove that the author's purpose in this novel was to take aim at the increasingly anarchistic and violent revolutionary movement as it stood in the late 1860s. One of the most disturbing events of the day finds an echo in this novel. Sergei Nechaev, an associate of world-famous anarchist Mikhail Bakunin, organized a small radical movement in Russia in the late 1860s, requiring from his followers iron discipline and strict obedience to himself, their ruthless leader. The shockingly radical pamphlet *Catechism of a Revolutionary* (1869), which Nechaev composed either by himself or with the collaboration of Bakunin, was designed as a guidebook for members of the movement.[39] It is notable for its utter cynicism and its complete insistence that each member entirely subordinate his individual status to the cause. Late in 1869, Nechaev arranged for the execution of one I. I. Ivanov, a member of his circle, most likely because Ivanov had not shown adequate commitment to the cause (and its leader). The demonic Peter Verkhovensky in *The Devils* bears a distinct resemblance to Nechaev, and the murder of Shatov late in the novel bears a distinct resemblance to the murder of Ivanov.

Simple enough. Even on the left, who would rush to the defense of such a monster as Nechaev? But consider what Dostoevsky himself wrote in his *Diary of a Writer* during the first year of its publication (1873). The name of the article is "One of the Contemporary Falsehoods." First, he says, it's important to realize that his Nechaev was not *the* Nechaev. Second, *The Devils* has to do not with Nechaev but with *Nechaevs* plural and with how such people are possible. So far, no problem: the author is merely stating that his novel operates at a higher level of generality than if it were simple a *roman à clef* about contemporary politics. But how to explain what he says a short while later in the same article?

> And why do you suppose that Nechaevs must necessarily be fanatics? Quite often they are simply scoundrels. . . . Can you possibly be right in thinking that the proselytes that some Nechaev in our midst might recruit must necessarily be good-for-nothings? I don't believe it, not all of them; I myself am an old "Nechaevist," I too stood on the scaffold, sentenced to death, and I assure you that I stood in the company of educated people. Almost all this company had completed a course of studies at the very highest educational institutions. . . . Some subsequently, *after everything had already happened,* distinguished themselves through remarkable work in special fields of knowledge and through their writings. No, Nechaevists are not always slackers who have never studied a thing.[40]

This is very confusing, to be sure. Dostoevsky declares himself an old Nechaevist. He then goes on to elaborate further on his own political past, speaking warmly about the Petrashevsky circle: "How can you know that the Petrashevskyites could not have become Nechaevists, that is, set off down the Nechaevist path, *if matters had turned out this way?* . . . But allow me to say this of myself alone: a *Nechaev*, probably, I could never have become, but as to a *Nechaevist*, I can't be certain of anything, yet perhaps I could have . . . in the days of my youth."[41] What's the distinction between Nechaev, Nechaevs, and a Nechaevist? Dostoevsky's language initially suggests that Nechaevs are simply people like Sergei Nechaev, that is, people willing to go to extremes in support of their cause. Elsewhere in this article, he says that in *The Devils* his aim was "to represent the highly varied and diverse motives by which even the most simple- and pure-hearted people can be attracted to the commission of such monstrous villainy."[42] As to Nechaevists, Dostoevsky at first identifies himself as one and then says only that he *might* have become one in his youth.

Maybe the most we can say is that Dostoevsky is speaking of people who believe ardently in a cause, some of whom are prepared to go to the lengths that Nechaev himself did, others of whom simply believe very strongly in the need for change and are willing to risk a great deal for the sake of that change. But what truly matters is that Dostoevsky is willing to recognize the worth of someone previously involved in a revolutionary movement that he has ostensibly devoted considerable effort to savaging for more than a decade. After all, isn't it a widely accepted truth that *Notes from Underground* was Dostoevsky's squib against Chernyshevsky (in part one) and against Dostoevsky's own radical past of the 1840s (in part two)? Isn't *Crime and Punishment* generally and uncritically accepted as Dostoevsky's assault on several of the ideologies of the contemporary left? Mustn't we regard the group of Nihilists that abruptly enters the scene relatively late in *The Idiot* as a pack of laughable fools? Doesn't it go without saying that *The Devils* was originally conceived as simply a diatribe against the radical movement of the late 1860s? Weren't dozens and dozens of pages of the *Diary of a Writer* devoted to blistering attacks on the left?

In the last year of his life, Dostoevsky penned a curious little remark in his notebook: "*All nihilists*. Nihilism made its appearance in our midst because we're *all nihilists*. All that has frightened us is the new, original form of its manifestation. (All without exception Fedor Pavloviches.)."[43] It's hard to say exactly what he was thinking when he wrote this. "Nihilist" might refer merely to the elder Karamazov's cynicism, or it might refer broadly to the radical movement of recent times. But there can be little doubt that, at least during the moment when he expressed this thought, he aligned himself with a force that, in many other places, he clearly had in his gun sights.

Another fascinating case is Dostoevsky's relations with Populist thinking in the final decade of his life. Populism (*narodnichestvo*) was a progressive movement that garnered particular attention in the 1870s with its emphasis on directing political activity toward the "people" (*narod*) or actually incit-ing revolutionary activity among them. The movement comprised many groups espousing various tactics, some very violent indeed. But when Dos-toevsky returned from an extended stay in Europe in 1871, he suddenly found that to the extent Populism now dominated the left in his home country, his attitude toward radical politics would necessarily grow even more complicated than it was before.

No one tells this story better than Joseph Frank, who has made it a ma-jor theme of the final volume of his Dostoevsky biography. As Frank sees it, Dostoevsky was bound to feel at least some sympathy for the new move-ment simply because of its focus on the well-being of the peasantry. Perhaps because of an incapacity to blame anyone completely who embraced the in-terests of the common folk; perhaps because of his residual, tempered sym-pathy for the entire revolutionary movement's commitment to reforming Russia, he now found himself adopting positions almost impossible to rec-oncile with the intemperate language he used so often to lambaste the left.

One stunning example of Dostoevsky's conflict-ridden attitude is his re-sponse to the sensational Vera Zasulich affair. Zasulich, a committed mem-ber of the revolutionary movement, had boldly but unsuccessfully attempted to assassinate the governor of Saint Petersburg because of the role he played in the flogging of a Populist prisoner. When the case came to trial, Dosto-evsky was firmly opposed to convicting Zasulich, preferring instead some-how to admonish the young woman not to sin again. In a diary entry, he went even farther. Quoting Zasulich's statement that "it is difficult to raise your hand [against another] in order to shed blood," Dostoevsky comments: "This hesitation was more moral than the shedding of blood itself."[44] It's a striking remark since, whether or not the author means to suggest that shed-ding blood *is* moral, he shows at least a willingness to accept the existence of moral scruples in someone who represented a cause to which he so often ex-pressed hostility.

Frank gives many more examples of Dostoevsky's sympathetic attitude toward the latest radical movement and even toward earlier, more extreme phases of the revolutionary movement. In the last years of his life, Dosto-evsky became a sort of mentor and prophet to the progressive youth of Rus-sia, who, despite the novelist's sometime conservatism, regarded his *Diary of a Writer* as a source of truth about their country's future.[45] *The Adolescent*, the novel that Dostoevsky published between *The Devils* and *The Brothers Karamazov*, contains an important character that, in Frank's view, shows a connection between Populism and the author's version of Christian faith.[46] It's also worth noting that Dostoevsky, who normally published his fictional work in a conservative journal, shocked his friends by choosing to publish this novel in *Notes of the Fatherland*, a liberal journal with Populist leanings.

One of the most surprising examples that Frank gives of Dostoevsky's conciliatory attitude toward Russian radicals concerns two figures who are not Populists at all. The first is Dostoevsky's own fictional character Kirillov, and the second is Dmitry Karakozov, who attempted to assassinate Alexander II in 1866. Dostoevsky speaks of both in some notes for a planned epilogue to *The Devils*: "In Kirillov there is an idea that belongs to the people— to sacrifice oneself at once for the truth. Even the unhappy, blind suicide of April 4 [Karakozov, who did not literally commit suicide but was executed for his crime] at that time believed in his truth."[47] The remark about Kirillov is odd, because it scarcely seems to fit him. Kirillov doesn't really come across as a Populist or a man of the people. His plan, to be sure, is placed in the service of an idea, that one may become God by killing oneself, and killing oneself certainly represents a sacrifice. But the Kirillov we meet in the pages of *The Devils* does not appear to regard his deed as a sacrifice to the truth, because he shows little concern for what he is about to lose. Dostoevsky seems to be offering us a revisionist reading of his own novel expressly to convey a feeling of sympathy with radicals who *did* regard what the martyrs in their movement were doing as sacrificing everything for their version of the truth. The remark about Karakozov is even more remarkable, given the numerous occasions on which Dostoevsky spoke with effusive praise of Alexander II, the great Emancipator. Here as in his correspondence with Kovner, sincerity—in the sense of loyalty to one's own version of the truth, no matter what that truth might be—is the criterion by which we judge the actions and attitudes of others. But using this criterion necessarily implies a degree of moral relativism, willingness on some level to accept truths that contradict each other. To complicate matters further, Dostoevsky contradicts even *this* belief, in a diary entry from the last month of his life: "I cannot admit that one who burns heretics is a moral person, for I do not admit your thesis that morality consists in concord with one's inner convictions. That is merely *honesty* . . . but not morality. I have a moral model and ideal, it's given: Christ. I ask: would he have burned heretics? No. So burning heretics is an immoral action."[48]

Who, then, was Dostoevsky, and what did he believe? In the way we usually understand it, this question misses the point, as I'll further explain next.

## CHAPTER FOUR

# Belief Is Expressed in Antinomies

In the fifth volume of his biography of Dostoevsky, Joseph Frank tells a weirdly funny and somehow unsurprising story about Dostoevsky. After the death of his son Aleksei in 1877, the grief-stricken novelist, with Vladimir Solov'ev at his side, went to visit the famous Optina Pustyn' monastery, located about a hundred fifty miles from Moscow. At the monastery there resided a religious man whom Dostoevsky was eager to engage in conversation for the purpose of deriving comfort over his recent loss. No sooner did the two men start talking, however, than Dostoevsky showed himself to be anything but a passive recipient of fatherly advice; he constantly interrupted the venerable old man with arguments and objections.[1] Anyone with the slightest knowledge of Dostoevsky's personality would expect arguments and objections in conversations on a range of subjects. The subject here was religion, and as we've seen Dostoevsky was able to persuade a great many people, when it came to this subject, that he believed one thing and a great many others that he believed the opposite. In fact, of course, his behavior was completely typical. It's easy to imagine that if he had been somehow able to sit down to dinner with *himself* and heard himself proclaim the virtues of Orthodox Christianity, he would have argued and objected. Each Dostoevsky would have been expressing himself with the utmost sincerity.

## BELIEF, DOUBT, AND "PARADOXALISM"

The evidence I've shown so far might simply point to a man who was confused, who changed his mind repeatedly, or who was not a very rigorous thinker. But it's another story when we realize how much Dostoevsky was interested in belief as a topic in its own right, how particularly fascinated he was by the notion of asserting different things at different moments. If we leave aside, for the moment, his fictional writings (especially since that would require us to consider the complicating factors of irony and authorial distance), we find in his nonfiction plenty of evidence of his fascination. Belinsky was a figure who generally excited a host of complicated sentiments in Dostoevsky, so it is not surprising to read in *The Diary of a Writer* and elsewhere thoughts of blame and thoughts of praise. But as we can see in an article that Dostoevsky published in *Time* in 1863, Belinsky aroused interest also because of an issue he raised in connection with the topic of belief.

It's apt that the article was in response to a published letter accusing the *Time* editors of making conflicting claims, in this case about the progressive literary critic Nikolai Aleksandrovich Dobroliubov (1836–61). One article in *Time*, the letter charges, praised Dobroliubov while another accused him essentially of muddled thinking. Dostoevsky's response is not long on logic. The point of the rhetorical exercise of responding to published criticism appears to have been to score points by whatever means necessary. He first defends his journal by claiming that Dobroliubov merely made mistakes and that one must make allowance for them. He then defends Dobroliubov on the grounds that the late critic, despite his flaws, acted nobly and always "strove unswervingly for the truth." His mistakes, no doubt, arose from "an excess of passion in the stirrings of his soul." Dobroliubov might have changed his view of things, but "he could never betray his noble, truthful goal." To support this view, Dostoevsky cites the example of Belinsky, who, like Dobroliubov, always acted with the noblest of motives yet who three times in his life "fundamentally changed his convictions." "But one thing he never betrayed," Dostoevsky writes, "and that was the truth."[2]

But if Belinsky fundamentally changed his convictions, then the truth must have changed with those convictions. To be sure, with reference to

Dobroliubov and any possible errors or inconsistencies in the critic's thought, Dostoevsky has just defined the truth as "the emancipation of society from darkness, from filth, from inward and outward slavery."[3] Even if this is what he has in mind when he speaks of Belinsky (and he doesn't say it is), a fundamental change in convictions (not just a change in tactics) suggests a change in the larger truth of which those convictions are a part. In sum, the message seems to be that, provided one is committed to *some* truth (in other words, provided one is sincere), there is nothing wrong with fundamentally altering on Tuesday what one believed on Monday. Remember that sincerity was the golden quality Dostoevsky would attribute to Kovner years later, even though on some level he felt he did not share his correspondent's views.

This, then, is one peculiar way in which belief can work: one can believe something for a period, and then change and believe something else for another period. One's commitment to the truth can remain unchanged, either in the sense (Dostoevsky does not spell this out) that something from the first period persists in the second or in the sense that one's new sense of what *is* true carries as much conviction as one's old sense of what *was* true. There's nothing dazzling about this observation; it happens all the time that people undergo conversion or otherwise change their mind. But what is remarkable is that Dostoevsky is prepared to *sanction* the change, when commitment to the truth (which he does not describe in detail) persists from one state to the next. This implies a level of detachment from the content of the views. Let there always be sincerity, and I'll give my blessing to any change in views, he appears to be saying.

A much more interesting case, however, is the coexistence of conflicting beliefs. We might name this "duality" or "doubt." No one needs to be reminded that duality and doubt are major themes in Dostoevsky's fiction. But Dostoevsky comments on both in his nonfiction writings. Two passages from the last months of the author's life stand out.

The first occurs in a letter that Dostoevsky wrote to an artist and writer, Ekaterina Fedorovna Iunge, who had written the novelist about the duality in her own personality and the consequent "varied feelings" that tormented her. His response:

> What are you writing about duality? But this is the most common trait in people . . . those, of course, who are not entirely ordinary. The trait is characteristic of human nature in general, but by far not encountered with so much force in every [individual] human nature as in you. You're related to me, as it were, because this *division-in-two* in you is exactly like the one that

exists and always has existed in me. It's a great torment but at the same time a great delight. It indicates a powerful consciousness, a need for self-aware-ness, and the presence in your nature of a need for moral duty to yourself and to humankind. That's what this duality means.[4]

He encourages her to believe in Christ as a cure for her affliction, but if believing in Christ signals the end of duality, how can duality continue to be the valued and mandatory trait of extraordinary people that it is?

The second passage is part of a notebook entry in which Dostoevsky sketched out a response to a liberal critic of his *Diary of a Writer*. The re-sponse was to appear in that journal in the months following what turned out to be the final number (for January 1881, when Dostoevsky died). At is-sue is precisely the notion of sincerity, though the author does not use this word. He assails his opponent for suggesting that Jesuits can very well be true to their own convictions, though we know these convictions to be false. To Dostoevsky, Jesuits intentionally lie for practical purposes, and lying is bad. He insists that there is such a thing as moral ideas, which come from feeling and from Christ. Having established this concise, authoritarian moral system, he concludes by paraphrasing a passage of his own, from *The Brothers Karamazov*. It's come to be one of the more often-quoted passages in all Dostoevsky. Ivan and his hallucinated devil are speaking about belief. What the devil says is hugely funny in its layers of irony (the devil speaking as a creation of Ivan, who in turn is speaking as a creation of Dostoevsky):

> By some sort of premature designation, which I've never been able to grasp, I've been assigned the role of "denier," while in reality I am sincerely good and completely incapable of denying. No, go ahead and deny, for without denial there would be no criticism, and what kind of journal would it be without a criticism section? Without criticism, there would be only "hosanna." But for life, you need more than just "hosanna"; you need this "hosanna" to pass through the crucible of doubts, and so on.[5]

Now, toward the end of his life, Dostoevsky resurrects the final sentence of this passage: "The Inquisitor and the chapter about the children . . . It is not like a child that I believe in Christ and confess [his faith], but my *hosanna* has passed through the great *crucible of doubts*, as my devil says in the same novel."[6] As in the passage to Iunge, Dostoevsky suggests there comes a point when all doubt is removed, a point at which the hosanna, having withstood the passage through duality and doubt, gains its eligibility to stand as an absolute. Dostoevsky suggests that he himself has made this passage, presumably so that he can safely dispense with the sincerity argument and declare Jesuits absolutely to be liars.

Does this mean that in his final days Dostoevsky finally found his way to absolute faith, having satisfactorily passed through the requisite period of doubt and duality? Did the duality of which he spoke to Iunge cease to be an inveterate characteristic? Of course it's impossible to know for certain what the author had in mind when he sketched out ideas for an article that he would never get to write. But there are several reasons to be skeptical of the suggestion that he had finally reached a state of absolute belief. The letter to Iunge contained essentially the same thoughts as this notebook entry. In the letter, Dostoevsky spoke of a way out of duality (accepting Christ) but insisted that duality was a condition from which he suffered and had always suffered. Accepting Christ thus appears as a purely theoretical and ideal—but not practical—solution to the problem. As I'll explain in detail later on, for Dostoevsky if there's one truth claim we can feel confident in making, it's that the absolute embracing of *any metaphysical* truth claim (there is a God, there is no God) is an unattainable ideal, something "not of this world," as Ivan Karamazov (quoting Jesus) would put it.

There is a curious little character Dostoevsky created for the *Diary of a Writer* and who from time to time shows his face in that work. He's called the Paradoxalist, and his role is to do exactly what his name suggests. He puts in his first appearance in the April 1876 issue, where the author presents him to us as an acquaintance. Not unexpectedly, the Paradoxalist introduces his ideas in a dialogue. His partner is apparently a fictionalized version of the author. The topic of conversation is war (rumors were already in the air, and a year later Russia would be at war with the Ottoman Empire). The Paradoxalist asserts that war is beneficial to humanity: it is the expression of magnanimous ideas, it leads to periods of cultural productivity, and it unites nations by forcing them to respect each other. Prolonged peace, by contrast, leads to low spirits, loss of magnanimous ideas, and enfeeblement of the arts and sciences. The narrator asks leading questions that appear to suggest he doesn't agree with the Paradoxalist. He's concerned, for example, that his friend's ideas violate essential principles of Christianity.

What might have passed originally for an amusing trifle, however, sinks a year later into a morass of further paradox and contradiction. With Russia's declaration of war on Turkey in April 1877, Dostoevsky launches into one of his jingoistic rants in the *Diary of a Writer*. A reader of the first article about the Paradoxalist would be astonished to see that the prophetic author, now ostensibly speaking in his own voice, has composed what at first glance appears to be the same treatise on war as what the Paradoxalist delivered the previous year. But there is one essential difference. The Paradoxalist spoke of the virtues of war *in general*, advocating it as a salubrious activity for any nation. He spoke of an idea, that of "sacrificing one's own life while defending one's brothers and one's fatherland or even simply defending the interests of one's fatherland." He told us that humankind cannot live without "magnanimous ideas."[7] The author of the *Diary of a Writer*, by contrast, while repeating many of the Paradoxalist's ideas about war in general, imposes a condition on his own endorsement of military conflict, one that entirely changes the tenor of his article from that of the Paradoxalist's remarks. He speaks contemptuously of wars designed merely to promote market interests and then contrasts this type of war with what he is urging: "A war conducted for a magnanimous goal, for the liberation of the oppressed, for the sake of a disinterested and holy idea—such a war only purifies the infected air of accumulated miasma, heals the soul, drives away shameful cowardice and indolence, declares and establishes a firm goal, offers and clarifies an idea to whose realization a given nation is summoned."[8] Toward the end of the article, he appears to contradict this sentiment by stating that "war is necessary for anything, it is wholesome, it relieves humankind." But he immediately follows this remark with this statement: "Only that war is beneficial that is undertaken for an idea, for a higher and magnanimous principle."[9] In the Paradoxalist's view, *war itself* is the idea; in the view of the "author" a year later, a war must be fought only *in the name of* an idea.

Will the real Dostoevsky please stand up? The Paradoxalist presents the charmingly paradoxical and subversive (but hardly original) idea that war in general is beneficial, while his interlocutor, speaking fictitiously as the author, challenges him with simple, "commonsense" ideas. Why does Dostoevsky present the same ideas a year later, modifying them significantly (not to mention momentarily contradicting his own modifications *in the same article*)?[10]

The Paradoxalist shows up later in 1876. Dostoevsky recounts meeting him at Bad Ems, Germany, where the two were taking the waters. The dialogue between the author and his "friend" occupies almost an entire chapter of the July-August issue, covering such topics as the social scene at Ems, the woman question, how many children women should have, and "the earth and children," including an amusing little theory of history. Here are the views the Paradoxalist expresses: in connection with Russian women and our (that is, Russian men's) relations with them, "the greatest happiness is to know at least why one is unhappy." In connection with the position of women: women should marry and have as many children as possible, though they should have the right to higher education and should exercise that right (before they settle down and start having children). In connection with history, humankind moves in stages from the era of castles, barons, and vassals to the era brought about by the revolution of the bourgeoisie (complete with crystal palaces and universal expositions), to the era when the bourgeoisie comes to an end and a Renewed Humankind arises, dividing the land into communes and living in the Garden of Eden.[11]

Dostoevsky himself elsewhere vigorously defends women's right to an education, but I can think of no occasion on which he announced that women should be child-bearing machines. Nor is it possible to imagine his proposing this idiotic and simplistic theory of history borrowed either from Marx or from some popularized socialist theory of the day (though in its basic structure, the Paradoxalist's theory resembles Dostoevsky's three-stage model of history, which I've mentioned previously).

But the key point is that a character of Dostoevsky's creation *gets to take these positions*. He gets to take positions that are themselves implicitly contradictory or that at least partly conflict with claims the author is making elsewhere in the same journal. There can be little doubt that the very act of creating the Paradoxalist shows a high level of interest in the notion of asserting claims that one does not believe at all or that one does not *consistently* believe. It shows the assertion of such claims as a kind of temptation, as if to say, "What would it feel like to make *this* claim and *really mean it?*"

## AN IMPURE ANTINOMY OF REASON

But Dostoevsky had a much more compelling way of handling the assertion of conflicting claims: creating something very much like an antinomy and presenting it in dramatic form. He did this best in his fictional writings.

What is an antinomy? Put simply, it's merely an example of paradoxical thinking. The Paradoxalist's claim that war is beneficial is a simple antinomy since it contradicts our everyday sense that war is associated with destruction and that destruction is not at all beneficial. But for more than two hundred years the term has suggested something a bit more specific, with a formal structure all its own. This is because Immanuel Kant used a set of four antinomies in the *Critique of Pure Reason* (1781, 1787) to support his case against the claim that our faculty of reason is omnipotent.

I should say right away that the question of whether Dostoevsky studied Kant's antinomies is at best unsettled. During the Soviet era, a Russian scholar by the name of Golosovker wrote an entire book on the subject of Dostoevsky and Kant. Golosovker spent most of his book explaining close analogies between Dostoevsky's and Kant's thought, which is all to the good. But when it came time to answer the question, "Was Dostoevsky really acquainted with the work of Immanuel Kant?" Golosovker simply said that, despite the complete lack of biographical evidence, the texts of the *Critique of Pure Reason* and *The Brothers Karamazov* are sufficient evidence to prove Dostoevsky was indeed acquainted with the philosopher's work.[12]

I suspect this is not true, if by "was acquainted with" we mean "sat down and carefully read." But this isn't really the question anyway. Rather, did Dostoevsky come up with a structure similar to Kant's? If so, does the structure tell us something important about Dostoevsky's conception of belief? I think Dostoevsky did come up with such a structure and that it does tell us something important. But the structure was not identical to Kant's, and the difference between Dostoevsky's and Kant's antinomies is precisely the most important feature in Dostoevsky's conception of belief.

Let's have a quick look at the first of Kant's antinomies. Each one consists of a thesis followed by a proof, and an antithesis followed by *its* proof. The aim is to show that thesis and antithesis are equally plausible and that the corresponding proofs are equally persuasive. The thesis and its proof are generally printed opposite the antithesis and its proof, either in adjacent columns or on facing pages (depending on the edition). The first antinomy looks like this (I have quoted the thesis and antithesis and only summarized the proofs; the "underlying conditions" at the end are mine):

| THESIS | ANTITHESIS |
|---|---|
| *The world has a beginning in time and is also, with respect to space, confined within limits.* | *The world has no beginning and no limits in space but is, with respect to both time and space, infinite.* |

PROOF

*As to time, if the world did not have a beginning, we must assume that an infinite succession of states of things in the world preceded the world, but this is impossible. As to space, the only way we can imagine infinity is through a synthesis of the individual parts of the world. But this implies that the synthesis has been completed, which is impossible if it is infinite.*

PROOF

*As to time, if the world has a beginning, then there must have been a preceding, empty time when the world did not exist. But nothing can come to exist in an empty time. As to space, if the world had a beginning, then it would be limited while existing in an empty space that is unlimited. But things must not only exist in relation to each other in space but also exist in relation to space. Things would thus ultimately exist in relation to nothing, or empty space, which is impossible.*

UNDERLYING CONDITION FOR
ACCEPTING THE THESIS

*Capacity to submit the cosmological concepts of finitude and infinity to reasoning.*

UNDERLYING CONDITION FOR
ACCEPTING THE ANTITHESIS

*Capacity to submit the cosmological concepts of finitude and infinity to reasoning*

The standard account of the antinomies, their form, and their function, goes something like this: Kant's entire purpose in the *Critique of Pure Reason* was to remove the faculty of reason from the exalted position that the Enlightenment had assigned to it. In order to do this, he needed to show reason's limitations, that is, show the realms into which it is not entitled to venture. One of these realms is cosmology, understood as a system of knowledge whose aim is to understand the world, or universe, as a whole. A cosmology built on reason would be a "rationalist cosmology," and it would attempt, *by reason*, to answer questions about the beginning and end of the universe (the first antinomy), the existence of composite and simple parts (the second antinomy), causality and freedom (the third antinomy), and the existence or nonexistence of a first principle, or God (fourth antinomy). But the instant reason sets foot in this realm, it finds itself tripped up, because when it attempts to deal with concepts such as the ones I've just listed, it can do nothing better than generate pairs of reciprocally contradictory propositions.

The final solution to the antinomies requires recognizing that *some faculty other than reason* must step in when it's time to speak of infinity, composite substances, freedom, and God. Thus Kant's antinomies, at least as *he* envisioned them, are perfectly symmetrical, because thesis and antithesis have the exact same origin, namely the supposition that reason is capable of speaking the truth in connection with the questions that these antinomies raise. So it's not by choosing between thesis and antithesis that we escape the impasse to which Kant's antinomies lead, but by refusing to play at all, by opting out of the entire system.

It works out differently in Dostoevsky. Let's go back to a scene I described earlier, the one in which Stavrogin speaks with his former disciple Shatov. With (admittedly) some violence to Dostoevsky's text, let's frame the discussion as an antinomy, like this:

| THESIS (SHATOV) | ANTITHESIS (STAVROGIN) |
|---|---|
| *One who is not Russian Orthodox cannot be Russian.* | *One who is not Russian Orthodox may very well be Russian.* |
| PROOF | PROOF |
| *The goal of the whole movement of a people* [narod] *is the pursuit of that people's very own God. God is thus the synthetic personality of the entire people. The people is thus the body of God. In order to be a member of a people, one must profess the religion of that people, in this case Russian Orthodoxy. In order to profess the religion, one must believe in God.* | *God cannot be reduced to a simple attribute of the people* [narodnost']. *The goal of the whole movement of a people thus cannot be the pursuit of that people's very own God. The people can in no way be viewed as the body of God. It makes no sense, therefore, to say that in order to be a member of a people one must profess the religion of that people. There is thus no need to believe in God.* |
| UNDERLYING CONDITION FOR ACCEPTING THE THESIS | UNDERLYING CONDITION FOR ACCEPTING THE ANTITHESIS |
| *Belief in God, specifically a national God.* | *No belief in any god, let alone a specifically national god.* |

Of course I realize that I'm reordering what Shatov says and putting into Stavrogin's mouth words that he never says. I realize, too, that what Stavrogin himself does say is more complicated than the position I've just attributed to him. In fact, by himself he serves as a good example of the point I was making a moment ago. In response to the charge that Stavrogin once believed in what Shatov is now saying, Stavrogin says, "If I believed, then, without a doubt, I would repeat this even now; I wasn't lying, speaking as a believer."[13] In other words, if one is able to adopt the persona of a believer (though Stavrogin, in his insistence on having been an atheist at the time he taught Shatov Slavophile beliefs, was consequently not capable of adopting such a persona), one may say what Shatov says and still be sincere.

But, at least for the purpose of understanding his dialogue with Shatov, let's take seriously Stavrogin's professed commitment to atheism or, at the very least, his claim to be an atheist right now and to have been one at the time he indoctrinated his pupil. Then Stavrogin is taking the rationalist's side against the believer's propositions on Shatov's side. Thesis and antithesis are thus based on two distinct faculties: faith and reason, respectively. If this is to be an antinomy, we need at some moment to think that the two sides are argued in an equally compelling way. On their face they are, provided that we accept the underlying condition for each. Shatov's argument, once reordered and removed from its dramatic setting, is reasonably consistent from a logical standpoint, as is Stavrogin's. If we were presented simply with the two arguments in this form and if we were hypothetically to accept the two conditions, we would have trouble deciding which one had the upper hand. This would be bad enough, since we would be left without a clue about which side to accept.

But Dostoevsky complicates the matter even more than this. In the actual dramatic scene, Stavrogin appears to have the upper hand. It's much more difficult to argue with his taunting attacks on Shatov than to argue with Shatov's wild and undisciplined ranting. More important, Shatov shows comically that he doesn't believe, which means that, strain as he might to mean what he says, he can't. Though he shows plenty of earnestness, the critical element of sincerity (truly meaning what you say, at least at the moment you say it) for him is unhappily missing. Of course, if Stavrogin's "argument" is more compelling, it's no doubt because it is a logical argument founded on an empirical underlying condition. If Shatov's views—based, as they should be, on faith and not on reason as applied exclusively to empirical observation—are to be compelling, it will have to be that they simply compel us, beyond reason, to believe. Then we would have something like a dialogue between an empirical scientist and a theologian: both use logic and reason to structure their arguments, but the theologian uses as a point of departure a claim that must be accepted purely on faith.

This might well have been so—except for the circumstance that Shatov plays into his antagonist's hand by undermining his own credibility. A reader familiar with Dostoevsky's publicist writings on nation and religion might easily have derived the idea that the author, despite the tangle of conflicting remarks he made on the issue, at times embraced the views that sound so ridiculous when Shatov expresses them. A deeply nationalist reader in Dostoevsky's day might have found Shatov's views, had they been expressed by a more respectable character, to be compelling at the level of religious belief, if not at the level of logic. Yet for a representative of the Slavophilism that he himself professed elsewhere, Dostoevsky chose a ridiculous and pitiful character who says things he cannot possibly believe. Thus if we accept Shatov's *position* in and for itself (whether or not he is capable of embracing this position), then we end up with a thesis based in faith and an antithesis based in faithlessness. But if we accept what Shatov himself really believes (or fails to believe—that there is a God), then we end up oddly with a thesis and an antithesis both based in faithlessness. To state it simply, the antinomy first pits faith against reason, leaving us no hope of a solution (like the one we find in Kant), and then undermines the faith argument by destroying the credibility of its proponent.

Let's take another fictional example, this one from *The Brothers Karamazov*. You'll remember that book five of that novel, "Pro and Contra," contains Ivan's famous "rebellion" against Christianity, in addition to his "poem," the Legend of the Grand Inquisitor. You'll remember too that book six, "The Russian Monk," contains a "saint's life" of Father Zosima, Alesha Karamazov's mentor, in addition to numerous sayings of the elder monk.

From Dostoevsky's correspondence, it's easy to tell that he viewed these two books as paired with each other, the second of them answering claims and ideas appearing in the first. On May 10, 1879, he writes to Nikolai Alekseevich Liubimov, editor of the journal *Russian Herald*, which is publishing the novel serially. The letter announces that a portion of book five is in the mail. Here's how Dostoevsky characterizes his current work (in an extraordinarily rambling sentence):

> This fifth book, in my view, is the culminating point of the novel, and it has to be completed with particular care. Its meaning, as you will see in the text I've sent, is the portrayal of the extreme blasphemy, the kernel of the idea of destruction in our time in Russia among our youth, which has torn itself away from reality, and, together with the blasphemy and anarchism, their repudiation, which is now in preparation, in the final words of the dying Elder Zosima (one of the characters in the novel).

A bit farther on, he explains to Liubimov the gist of Ivan's argument: "My hero chooses a theme that, *to my mind*, is incontrovertible, [namely] the senselessness of children's suffering, and deduces from it the absurdity of all historical reality."[14] On August 7 of the same year, Dostoevsky writes another letter to Liubimov, this one accompanying book six. He wonders whether he has succeeded in his portrayal of the character Zosima. "I regard this *sixth book*, however," he says, "as the culminating point of the novel" (apart from different case endings, these are the exact same words he used in his previous letter). He then goes on to announce that he entirely shares Zosima's views (though he says that Zosima expresses those views differently from how he, Dostoevsky, would express them).[15]

Nor is it hard to see in the text itself how the two chapters are paired. I'll give only two examples. Ivan's Grand Inquisitor uses his personal encounter with Jesus to harangue the Savior with an account of Christianity's failures and fallacies. The burden of the argument is that Jesus gave us more freedom than we could tolerate and consequently expected too much from us. As a representative of the Catholic Church, complete with its hierarchical power structure, the Inquisitor offers Jesus the famous trinity of ideas on which Christianity ought to have been founded if it had ever cherished any hope of success in the real world: miracle, mystery, and authority. The Inquisitor's use of "miracle" and "mystery" raises an obvious question: Does he actually believe in miracles (divine truths revealed to humankind) and mysteries (divine truths concealed from humankind)? Does he believe in the (partial) divinity of the creature sitting in front of him and the power of that creature to work miracles? In the end, it hardly matters, since his lesson for Jesus, *even under the assumption that Jesus is (partly) divine*, is that the Savior should have performed miracles for the purpose of facilitating humankind's choice to follow the Son of God. Let the miracle be a fake magic trick, or let it be the real thing; what counts is simply that people believe and then follow.

Zosima has his own trinity of ideas, though he does not present them all at once as a list. The first two are the same as Ivan's: miracle and mystery. Zosima has not exactly redefined these terms; rather, he has reoriented our understanding of them. For Zosima, a miracle is a gracious act by which God favors humanity with a material truth of his own existence (or Jesus' divinity). Alesha conceives the full truth of this understanding in the scene where he prays by Zosima's dead body. As another monk in the room reads aloud the Gospel story of turning water to wine at the wedding in Cana, Alesha realizes that Jesus performed this miracle not to convert nonbelievers but to bring joy to those who already believed.

As to mystery, Zosima offers his understanding of the term by giving an example. The story of Job at first glance is incomprehensible. How could God send his most devoted servant such terrible suffering and then raise him to good fortune in the end? "What is great about it is precisely that it is a mystery."[16] Ivan would no doubt deduce from the story "the absurdity of all historical reality." Zosima instead remains with the mystery and celebrates it. Finally, Zosima replaces authority with a concept that suits his own worldview. The aim of authority is to bind people together. Zosima has in mind another force that will accomplish the same purpose. There is a thought, he tells his listener, "before which you must stand in bewilderment, especially considering people's sins, and ask yourself, 'Should I use force or humble love?' Always decide thus: 'I'll use humble love.' You will thus have decided once and for all, and you will be able to conquer the whole world. Loving humility [humility of the loving sort] is a frightful force, the strongest of all, one that knows no equal."[17]

The story of Job and the questions about justice it raises are the second example of the pairing of books five and six. Ivan does not speak of Job, but he certainly speaks of inexplicable suffering. The suffering of children is the most charged instance of inexplicable suffering he can think of, first because it's secular and second because in his view "innocence" is built into the very definition of *child*, just as are "youth" and "human being." For Ivan, it's a matter of justice. The occurrence of inexplicable suffering is inconsistent with the claim that we live in a world created by a just god. Ivan recognizes the possibility that some might consider God's justice to be simply inscrutable, but he himself cannot accept the idea of a justice whose workings are not perceptible to the human mind. So he rejects any suffering that appears undeserved.

Zosima does not speak of justice in the abstract. But the story of Job is his Scriptural equivalent to Ivan's children, since "undeserving of suffering" is built into the concept of "Job" (which is to say, in the Book of Job, it's established at the outset that the hero is a righteous man who does not deserve the fate God sends him). Zosima has two messages for us. The first I have already mentioned: it's the mystery of the story that makes it great, and thus, by extension, we should celebrate a justice we limited human beings cannot truly grasp. The second has to do with suffering itself. Like Sonia, the mystically inclined prostitute in *Crime and Punishment*, Zosima urges us to accept it. In fact, when he urges this, Zosima is speaking not of justice but of being the judge of others. None of us can be such a judge, he tells us. If the evildoing of our fellows arouses our anger, we must seek suffering for ourselves: "And accept this suffering and endure it, and your heart will be soothed, and you will come to understand that you yourself are guilty."[18]

We can now formulate the opposed positions in books five and six as an antinomy. Let justice be the subject of the antinomy (though we could equally well use Christianity, faith, love for neighbors, or suffering). To maintain consistency with the Shatov-Stavrogin dialogue, I'll put Zosima's position on the left, as the thesis. With due allowance here again for simplification, reorganization, and attribution to both characters of statements that those characters never make in precisely this form, our antinomy looks like this:

| THESIS (ZOSIMA) | ANTITHESIS (IVAN) |
|---|---|
| *There is justice in the world, but it is imperceptible to us.* | *There is no justice in the world, for if there were, it would be perceptible to us.* |
| PROOF | PROOF |
| *The events of the world do not always conform to our conception of God's justice. If we believe that there is a God, that he is not directly accessible to our senses, and that he is just, then his justice must be "not of this world," which is to say inaccessible to our senses. If it is inaccessible to our senses, then I must simply accept it—even celebrate it— as God's way.* | *The events of the world do not always conform to our conception of God's justice. Only if we believe that there is a God, that he is not directly accessible to our senses, that he is just, and that his justice must thus be "not of this world," which is to say inaccessible to our senses, may we accept God's justice. But there is neither God nor immortality. There can thus be neither justice that is "not of this world" nor justice of any sort in the world.* |
| UNDERLYING CONDITION FOR ACCEPTING THE THESIS | UNDERLYING CONDITION FOR ACCEPTING THE ANTITHESIS |
| *Belief in God.* | *Absence of belief in God.* |

As in the case of the Shatov-Stavrogin exchange (where Shatov's *position*, not his personal belief, or absence of belief, is the thesis), we find that thesis and antithesis are based on two faculties of mind. The thesis and antithesis in each of Kant's antinomies *both* made sense in the realm of "reason." Here, however, the thesis makes sense only if it comes from a position of faith, while the antithesis makes sense only if it comes from an absence of faith. Once again, we cannot resolve the antinomy by stepping out of the game and appealing to a faculty of mind that can promise not to give antinomies.

Once again, the antinomy first pits faith against reason, leaving us no hope of a solution.

We find, however, a complication in both antinomies that is more pronounced in the Zosima-Ivan one. Belief in God is no doubt a condition for accepting Father Zosima's thesis, but—as he and any other self-respecting man of religion in a work by Dostoevsky will be the first to point out—belief is never perfect. It can't be. Perfect belief is an ideal unrealizable on earth. As Ivan too is aware, the unattainability of perfect Christian brotherhood on earth is an affirmation of the distance that, until the end time, will always separate each of us not only from our fellows but from God too. Father Zosima tells the story of a "mysterious visitor" who helped show him the way to certain Christian truths. One thing he said was this: "Until you have made yourself in actual fact a brother to everyone, brotherhood will not come." First there must be a period of terrible personal isolation, when people are disunited.

> But it is certain that this terrible isolation will come to an end, and everyone will understand at once how unnatural it is for us to separate ourselves from one another. Such will be the spirit of the times, and people will be astonished at how long they have sat in the darkness and not seen the light. And then shall appear the sign of the Son of man in heaven.[19]

Surely perfect brotherhood will come, but not before the Apocalypse, which is to say, not in history. The final sentence in the quote here is Matthew 24:30, where Jesus speaks to his disciples about how they will know of his coming at the end of the world.

Similarly, nonbelief in God is no doubt a condition for accepting Ivan's antithesis, but his nonbelief is not perfect. Like Zosima's belief, it can't be. Perfect nonbelief is an ideal unrealizable on earth (think of Stavrogin's incapacity to live in accordance with the principle that there is neither good nor evil). Why else would Ivan conduct himself as he does in the cell of Father Zosima? There, remember, he delivers an impromptu lecture on the proper roles of church and state, a lecture whose content meets with the approval of Father Zosima. When the old monk tells him he (Ivan) probably doesn't believe anything he says, Ivan simply answers, "Perhaps you are right! Still, I was not entirely joking."[20] Not believing is consistent with what he will shortly tell his father about the existence of God and immortality. But "not entirely joking" indicates a position somewhere in between belief and nonbelief. Now that I've mentioned the conversation (in the chapter called

"Over a Glass of Cognac") in which Fedor Pavlovich interrogates Ivan and Alesha on the existence of God and immortality, why else would Ivan tell his father unhesitatingly and unequivocally that there is neither God nor immortality,[21] only to tell Alesha later on, before he recounts the tale of the Grand Inquisitor, that he "accepts" God but merely wishes to return his entrance ticket?[22] Accepts God how? Accepts him for the sake of argument, so that he can say why God's world would be unacceptable even if he really accepted God (though he can't)? Accepts him right now, and sincerely, maybe because he is speaking with his devout younger brother? Accepts the idea of, but doesn't believe in, God? No matter what the explanation, we see Ivan, like the author who created him, straddle the line between belief and nonbelief.

I'll give one more, much simpler example of an antinomy, without bothering this time to draw a diagram. It is in the pair of famous scenes in *Crime and Punishment* in which Raskolnikov first explains himself and then confesses to Sonia. As in the Shatov-Stavrogin scene, the man of intellect appears to have the upper hand, at least as far as logic goes. Raskolnikov tauntingly asks Sonia if she often prays to God. When she answers with the question, "What would I be without God?" her new friend asks what God does for *her*.[23] Since she extols the virtues of her consumptive but vain and ill-tempered stepmother, Raskolnikov poses the ultimate moral question of how Sonia would choose if, knowing in advance that Luzhin planned to commit evil deeds that would cause the stepmother and her children to perish, she (Sonia) were given the power to let either the stepmother or Luzhin go on living.[24]

To all of Raskolnikov's wicked, goading questions, Sonia can do little more than issue disjointed exclamations and nonverbal sounds. To his confession of guilt in the murder of the pawnbroker and the pawnbroker's half-sister (Sonia's best friend), she responds more articulately (after immediately showing sympathy for Raskolnikov), but in a series of somewhat disordered, ecstatic imperatives: rise up; go to the crossroads; bow down and kiss the earth; proclaim to the world that you have committed murder, so that God will send you new life; accept your suffering.[25] For the purpose of showing that this is an antinomy, we could say (1) Sonia has the "truth" of religious revelation on her side, while Raskolnikov has logic on his side; (2) the thesis (Sonia's position) is thus compelling within its own system, while the antithesis (Raskolnikov's position) is compelling within *its* system; and finally (3) religious revelation rests on faith, which is independent of reason, and the absence of logical coherence is in its very nature, while logical coherence is in the nature of Raskolnikov's "reasoned" arguments.

As in the case of the Shatov-Stavrogin dialogue, we can say that the two positions *in their own terms* (Sonia's based in unreasoned faith, Raskolnikov's based in reason and logic) enjoy an equal or almost equal status. Once again, we can look elsewhere in Dostoevsky's writings for apparent confirmation that the position based on faith is the one for which he has greater sympathy. But again, if this is the case, we have to wonder why he chooses to put the expression of this position in the mouth of a defenseless half-wit. Why does he endow the arrogant intellectual with qualities that make him, on occasion, similar to Sonia (his impulsively leaving all his money for Sonia's family, his rushing to the defense of the molested girl, his recoiling in horror from his own murder plans, all in part one of the novel)? Is it because if an arrogant intellectual, with logic and reason on his side, is "defeated" by a defenseless half-wit with the truth about religion on hers, the defeat is all the more humiliating for the intellectual? Or because if the same intellectual, deep down, is just like the defenseless half-wit with respect to religious sentiment, then the case for the righteousness of her side is all the more compelling? Quite possibly. But the fact remains that even in their simple form (even when we don't take into account the dramatic circumstances, even when we don't consider the personal character of each participant in the dialogue), thesis and antithesis offer no clever Kantian solution, since they remain on opposite sides of the faith-reason divide.

Of course, it wasn't Dostoevsky's idea to frame any of these interactions as a Kantian antinomy; it was mine. Dostoevsky never intimated that pairs of his ideas would conform to a model set by Kant almost a century earlier. But the point is not to show that Dostoevsky failed to meet the standard Kant set; it is to use Kant as a basis of comparison, to show why the conflict in a pair of ideas, or a pair of points of view, is more intractable for Dostoevsky than it is for Kant in *his* antinomies. Kant gives us an easy way out, one that accords with the statement in the preface to the second, revised edition of the *Critique of Pure Reason* (1787), that his aim in writing the work was "to get rid of knowledge in order to make room for faith."[26] Once we quit the game of submitting cosmological concepts to rational analysis, we're home free. To put it simply, Kant's antinomies demonstrate the divide between reason and faith and thus lead us to recognition of that divide; Dostoevsky's antinomies, by contrast, even in their simplest form, start with the divide as a *premise* and lead nowhere. But then, as we've seen, Dostoevsky doesn't give them in their simplest form; instead, he presents them in a dramatic form that confuses the issues even more than would an insoluble antinomy.

## THE TEMPTATION OF MAKING
## CONFLICTING TRUTH CLAIMS

To take what man says, promises, concludes in the heat of passion and advocate it later, in a moment of cool sobriety—this requirement belongs to the
heaviest burdens that oppress mankind. . . . Simply because one has sworn
loyalty, even if only to a purely fictitious being, like a god, simply because
one has given over one's heart to a prince, a [political] party, a woman, a
priestly order, an artist, a thinker, in a state of blind madness that enchants us
and makes us consider these beings worthy of any veneration, any sacrifice—
is one now inescapably and inextricably bound? Haven't we then in such a
case deceived ourselves? Was it not a hypothetical promise, under the presupposition (admittedly never expressed aloud) that these beings to whom
we have devoted ourselves are actually as they appear in our conception? Are
we duty-bound to be loyal to our mistakes even with the insight that by this
loyalty we are inflicting harm on our higher self? No, there is no law, no
obligation of the sort; we *must* become traitors, practice disloyalty, always re-
linquish our ideals. . . . Why do we marvel at someone who remains loyal to
his conviction and disdain someone who changes it? . . . If for once we were
to examine how it is that convictions arise, we would see whether they are
not greatly overvalued: in any case, it would then follow that even a *change* in
convictions is measured by a false standard and that till now we have suffered
too much from such change.

This is Nietzsche in the first volume of *Human, All Too Human* (1878).[27]
Here he's initially speaking about people who, presumably for the sake of
appearing consistent, rigidly defend convictions arising in the heat of the
moment. But Nietzsche also advocates something more radical than just
abandoning a view because we did not give it adequate reflection. He's advocating, in the name of "our higher self," the betrayal of our own views and
the relinquishment of our own ideals. Presumably our higher self is not a
realm of fixed and unchanging ideas that we merely need to discover; it
must be a realm of ideas that we truly embrace *at a given moment.*

In the paragraph following the one from which I have just quoted, Nietzsche expresses profound mistrust for convictions in general, setting up an
invidious distinction between "the man of convictions" and "the man of science."[28] But there's no doubt that he prizes the act of changing convictions,
if only by comparison with an unbending and unreasoned adherence to
them. In the second volume of *Human, All Too Human* (1886), under the
heading "Miscellaneous Opinions and Sayings," Nietzsche pays tribute to
Laurence Sterne, whom he calls "the freest writer." What's so wonderful

about the creator of *Tristram Shandy* is that he's "the great master of ambiguity" (the word for which in German is literally "two-meaningedness").

> The reader who wants to know at every moment precisely what Sterne truly thinks about a given matter, wants to know whether his face is serious or smiling, will be lost: for Sterne is at home with both [the serious and the smiling] in a single wrinkle of his face; he understands this, too, and wants to be right and wrong at the same time, to tangle up profundity with clownishness.[29]

Maybe all those writers who felt Nietzsche and Dostoevsky were the same person were on to something. Though Nietzsche has not yet discovered the great Russian "psychologist," we have here virtually the same ideas as we find in Dostoevsky (with a slightly different purpose and set of emphases): we can change our convictions while remaining true to our higher self, and we can, in a single moment, be at home in two conflicting meanings. Nietzsche does not speak specifically about changing our convictions *back and forth*; Dostoevsky and his characters attach more gravity to what Nietzsche calls "ambiguity," since the opinions on which an ambiguous or (for Dostoevsky) *doubtful* attitude splits are generally more serious than profundity versus clownishness.

A half-century or so after Nietzsche penned the scattered sayings that he collected in the second volume of *Human, All Too Human*, the Viennese philosopher Ludwig Wittgenstein (1889–1951) began to write a series of paragraphs that would be collected, in two parts, under the name *Philosophical Investigations*. With almost no formal training in philosophy, Wittgenstein spent much of his life pondering the nature of logic, language, and meaning. He puzzled over the limitations of language and wondered about our ability to use it for representing states of affairs in the world. An essential part of meaning is *intention*, that is, what we "mean to say," what object, concept, or state of affairs we "have in mind," what serves as our target and what we wish our listener or reader to understand, when we say a certain thing. I'm not going to summarize everything that Wittgenstein said on this subject. One paragraph in *Philosophical Investigations*, however, stands out in connection with the topic of changing beliefs. Wittgenstein is wondering whether, as we are about to utter a sentence, we intend from the outset the entire sentence, word for word, as it comes out. This would mean that a speaker of German and a speaker of French, both "intending" the same thought, would in the event intend differing things in their construction of the sentence designed to express that thought, because German and French use different words and rules of syntax. Here's what Wittgenstein says:

But have I not already intended the entire form of the sentence, e.g., from its beginning? Thus it was already in my mind even before it was pronounced! If it was already in my mind, then, generally speaking, it would not be there with a different word-order. But we are creating here another erroneous image of "intending," that is, of the use of this word. *The intention is embedded in the situation*, in human customs and institutions. If there were no technique of playing chess, I could not intend to play a chess game. To the extent that I can intend the form of the sentence in advance, this is made possible by the circumstance that I speak German.[30]

Of course, Wittgenstein is speaking here about the rules of language, specifically how the rules of a particular language help frame the way a speaker of that language formulates sentences in order to express thoughts. This is hardly the sort of problem Dostoevsky cared about. But when Wittgenstein says that every intention is "embedded in the situation," referring specifically to two possible elements of a situation (customs and institutions), he has suggested a conception of the individual quite unlike any conception assuming a store of thoughts and ideas that remain fixed despite movement in space and the passage of time. If, as Wittgenstein maintains (even though his topic in this paragraph is how the rules of language affect the formulation of thoughts), what a person *intends* by a certain utterance, what the person has in mind in speaking of something, is wholly dependent on a situation; if it is bound up inextricably with the historical moment and the circumstances in which the utterance occurs, then (1) it is impossible to assure the speaker can "intend" the same thing in the same utterance fifteen minutes later, and (2) there is nothing to stop a speaker from "intending" reciprocally contradictory things in *different* utterances fifteen minutes apart. Each utterance, after all, is "embedded in the situation." Though Wittgenstein appears to use the word *situation* to refer to a set of external circumstances, there is nothing in his paragraph that would forbid a person from forming an intention now and, fifteen minutes later, an intention that contradicts the first intention. Whether the reason for the contradiction lies in the speaker or in the external circumstances is immaterial; in either case, the circumstances will be new fifteen minutes from now.

The views I've described—Nietzsche's and Wittgenstein's—show an implicit theory of intention and of the individual person, whether or not it is the chief aim of each author. What emerges, again, is that the individual person is not an aggregate of fixed, eternal truths, even though the person may sometimes express truths he or she regards (at the moment of expression) as fixed and eternal. The important factor is the correspondence of intention with utterance and the dependence of both on a specific situation at the moment when the situation existed. We can call the correspondence of intention and utterance "sincerity." The important factor about *it* is that it is defined only in relation to the moment of utterance.

I'm not trying to show that there is any sort of historical connection between these two writers and Dostoevsky, at least as regards the question of intention and sincerity. What I'm trying to show is that the two writers, specifically directing their attention to this question, explicitly or implicitly described the same phenomenon Dostoevsky did. In revealing roughly the same conception of individual, intention, utterance, and correspondence between intention and utterance as we find in Dostoevsky, they can help us describe something that the Russian novelist never formally elaborated.

So what *does* it mean for an author to take two sets of ideas, present them as antithetical to each other, and then, in two places, submit both sets to ridicule and also lend credibility to both sets? Or, to ask a slightly different question, what does it mean for an author to take two sets of ideas and present them as an antinomy that, even in its simplest form, offers no plausible solution?

What I'm speaking of here is the dramatization of a tendency we've seen in Dostoevsky's nonfiction writings. There we saw the author repeatedly adopt a position one day only to adopt a position later that calls into question or flatly contradicts the first position. The fictional equivalent of this tendency is to create characters who enact conflicts of the sort we see played out in the world of Dostoevsky's personal ideas (at least as expressed in letters, diaries, notebooks, and the *Diary of a Writer*). What it means in any of these cases is that beliefs are things of limited duration. We inhabit them, so to speak, for a time—maybe as an experiment, maybe for the thrill of it, or maybe because at a given moment we truly embrace them—but there is nothing to keep us from inhabiting others later in the same day.

Some readers may be familiar with the theories of the brilliant Russian critic and philosopher Mikhail Bakhtin (1895–1975). He made his entry into the literary world in 1929, with the publication of a book titled *Problems of Dostoevsky's Creative Art*. He first gained a significant reputation in his own country after the publication of an expanded version of this book in 1963 (with a modified title, *Problems of Dostoevsky's Poetics*). He became widely known in the West only in the 1970s, with the publication of the first

French (1970), German (1971), and English (1973) translations of the 1963 version. Since then, but especially in the 1980s and 1990s, he's become something of an obsession in Russian and Western literary studies. What concerns us here is the insight that appears not only to have stimulated so much interest but also to have propelled Bakhtin's theoretical speculations after the first version of his Dostoevsky book. It has to do with the related concepts of polyphony and dialogue (or "dialogism," to give it the status of an abstract, theoretically investigated phenomenon). Bakhtin noticed that Dostoevsky's central characters rarely exist in "monological" form, which is to say that they each seem to speak in several voices (thus they are "polyphonic") and to exist only in connection with a dialogue.

Raskolnikov, for example, has many clashing "voices." To justify his crime, he employs not one but two theories. The first is utilitarian. This is the one we read about in the flashback scene in which he overhears a young student expressing the exact thoughts that he, Raskolnikov, has been pondering. The student is speaking of the pawnbroker that Raskolnikov has been plotting to murder. "Kill her," the student exclaims to his friend, "and take her money, so that with its help you may then devote yourself to the service of all humanity and the common good. What do you say? Won't one tiny transgression pale before thousands of good deeds? In exchange for one life, thousands of lives saved from decay and decomposition. In exchange for one life, hundreds—why, it's just plain arithmetic!"[31]

The other theory is the "extraordinary man" theory, which Raskolnikov has presented in the article "On Crime." In his article, written some six months before the action of the novel begins, he argues that humanity is divided into a majority of ordinary people and a tiny minority of extraordinary people. We never get to see the text of the article, but Raskolnikov presents its ideas orally in conversation with the police inspector Porfiry Petrovich, who gleefully goads his prey by distorting and exaggerating what appeared in the published text. "The 'extraordinary' man," a defensive Raskolnikov disjointedly explains, "has the right . . . that is, not the official right, but he himself has the right to permit his conscience to step over . . . certain obstacles, and solely in the case where the fulfillment of his idea (sometimes salutary, maybe, for all humankind) requires it." He elaborates:

> Of course, the transgressions of these people are relative and highly varied; for the most part they require, in completely diverse manifestations, the destruction of the present in the name of something better. But if, for the

fulfillment of his idea, [an extraordinary man] must even step over corpses or through blood, then, in my opinion, he may give himself permission, within himself and by his own conscience, to step through blood—but in accordance with his idea and its dimensions—note that well.[32]

Two phrases, the one in parentheses ("sometimes salutary, maybe, for all humankind") and the one set off in dashes, are what distinguish this theory from the utilitarian theory. In translating these two phrases, I've sacrificed any stylistic elegance in order to stick as closely as possible to the original text. Here, the grand idea *need* not be salutary for all humankind; it simply *may* be—and then again it may *not* be. Here, the only condition for committing a great crime is that it be in the service of an idea, that it accord with the idea, and that it be of an appropriate magnitude for the idea. It thus completely rejects the absolute requirement of the first theory: that a crime ultimately have in view the benefit of humanity. Under this "superman" theory, the benefit of humanity *might* qualify as an idea, and one *might* very well find an act appropriate and adequately big for realizing that idea, but the benefit of humanity is only one of an infinite number of ideas. This theory sets absolutely no requirements for the content of the idea. Though it appears the idea ought to be *big*, by implication it can be anything at all.

Raskolnikov is also something of a self-sacrificing Christian. In part one of the novel, he impulsively leaves money for the impoverished Marmeladov family, unthinkingly comes to the aid of a molested girl, and continually recoils in horror from his own criminal plans. Later he kisses Sonia's foot, telling her that he is bowing down "to all human suffering," and then asks her to read the New Testament story of the raising of Lazarus.[33]

He thus speaks the language of the utilitarian ethicist, the language of the "extraordinary man" theorist, and (through word and deed) the language of pious Christianity. Dostoevsky handles the character's polyphony not only by having him give expression to ideas associated with each system of thought but also by creating other characters with whom the central character interacts and each of whom embodies *one* of the many voices in which the central character speaks. Thus in his guise as the utilitarian ethicist Raskolnikov encounters Luzhin, who *is* a utilitarian ethicist (or at least wishes to be taken for one). In his guise as the proponent of the extraordinary man theory, he encounters Svidrigailov, who *lives* by this theory. In his guise as the unreflectingly good Christian, he encounters Sonia, who *is* consistently an unreflectingly good Christian. Similarly Dostoevsky handles the "dialogic" nature of human interaction by almost never giving us any character's voice in isolation. Thus when it comes time for the author to present Raskolnikov's theory of crime, Dostoevsky does not do the natural thing and "reprint" it for us. Instead he allows us to see it only as it emerges from a heated dialogue between someone attempting to distort its meaning (Porfiry) and someone attempting to fend off the distortion (Raskolnikov himself). Polyphony and dialogism give Dostoevsky's characters and ideas an unfinished quality, since characters and ideas are constantly interacting in dialogue.[34]

Bakhtin would eventually come to generalize his findings on Dostoevsky and construct from them a broad theory of speech (Russian *rech'*, usually translated into English as the much overused "discourse"). Predictably, a dominant feature of the theory is that "the word" does not exist except in dialogue, which means that, like Wittgenstein's intention, it exists uniquely in every utterance. A word (or any speech) occurring only at *this* moment in *this* dialogue cannot possibly mean the same thing at any other moment in this or any other dialogue. So this word or speech is "embedded," just as Wittgenstein's intention is in its situation, and cannot exist apart from that situation.

Bakhtin's theory is primarily social; he's interested more in speech as a social phenomenon than in the content of beliefs to which speech might give expression.[35] So he is interested not in the fact that Raskolnikov can mean two conflicting things at two moments, not in the general issue of sincerity, and not in a general notion of belief, but rather in the fact that Raskolnikov, like all social beings, betrays a kind of "uncompletedness" and is thus perpetually, dynamically in progress.[36] But even if Bakhtin is not primarily interested in Dostoevsky's notion of belief, his observations on polyphony and dialogue show a close connection with this notion. Bakhtin's theory and Dostoevsky's notion both rest on the assumption that an individual can speak in different voices and that utterances are somehow peculiar to the moment in which they occur.

A somewhat less controversial way of putting Dostoevsky's inconsistencies is what we find in James Scanlan's *Dostoevsky the Thinker*. Scanlan regards Dostoevsky as a man of beliefs that, though they might have changed over time, remained consistent within individual periods. His explanation for the contradictions we find is "the dialectical method of his philosophizing." "Dostoevsky," Scanlan says, "always kept his sights on the opposite of what he believed and sought to establish his own positions by demonstrating the failure of their antitheses."[37] His work is thus inherently polyphonic and dialogical.

If Bakhtin's comments throw any light on Dostoevsky and the issue of belief, we must recognize that an implicit feature of dramatizing a clash in views, whether the clash happens between two characters or within one, is irony. Let's accept a crude definition of this term: it is a rhetorical device that consists in the speaker's presenting two levels of meaning, one superior to the other. The lower level carries the literal "surface" meaning, while the higher level carries the winking glance of the speaker, who tacitly shares with the listener or reader the view that the surface meaning is somehow to be mistrusted (because, for example, it is disingenuous, foolish, wrong, or insane). Thus when Socrates claims not to be wise, he knows *we* know that he *is* wise, even though he may honestly claim not to know (or not yet to know) the truth.

Of course, irony need not exist within a single statement by a single speaker. When the hero of *Notes from Underground* "quotes" his imaginary antagonists, he has created what these antagonists say; he is ironically heaping ridicule on what they say, yet he is speaking in an adopted voice. When Dostoevsky as author constructs a tirade for one of his characters, of course he's the author of the words his character speaks, but the character's voice is not Dostoevsky's. He is winking at us to let us know we mustn't take seriously (or at least, not completely seriously) what we are reading. There is nothing in this alone that is peculiar to Dostoevsky.

But two observations: first, Dostoevsky the author's irony is thus frequently directed at points of view that he himself represents seriously in other places. Both Prince Myshkin and Shatov express sentiments very close to what the author would publish in the *Diary of a Writer*. If the ironic attitude tells us not to take seriously what Shatov and Myshkin have to say on the subject of Russia and Christianity, then what are we to make of virtually the same sentiments when they appear in a publicist article? Second, the treatment of an idea alternately with and without irony shows a considerable measure of discomfort with the consistent embracing of the idea and thus reinforces the notion of belief as a temptation. Any belief is impossible to embrace absolutely. The alternately serious and ironic expression of the belief shows that something holds us back from the consistent maintenance of the belief, especially in its extreme form.

But this is the subject of the next chapter, where we finally return fully to the subject of religion. For now, I propose this conclusion: if, when we say "Dostoevsky believed such-and-such" we mean "Dostoevsky at least for an extended time consistently and exclusively believed such-and-such," then we must recognize that it's impossible to identify a belief or set of beliefs—about religion or almost anything else—that we can safely call Dostoevsky's own. If, on the other hand, when we say "Dostoevsky believed such-and-such" we mean "Dostoevsky *at times* believed such-and-such," then we are on much safer ground.

I don't at all mean to suggest that Dostoevsky believed *nothing*. Critics and biographers who claim, for example, that he advocated beliefs similar to those of the Slavophiles are not wrong, unless they claim that he *exclusively* embraced these beliefs (even if only for a certain period in his life). He also subjected those beliefs to ridicule. He *did* express, no doubt sincerely, Judeophobic views, and to those who find the expression of such views inexcusable his behavior *was* inexcusable. But he also expressed views sympathetic to the Jews, and at least as far as the expression of these views goes, he deserves credit for it. One might argue that giving Dostoevsky credit for expressing views sympathetic to the Jews is like giving a murderer credit for all the occasions on which he or she did *not* commit murder. But I'm inclined to think this argument is not entirely fair. I'm inclined to think that, even though the act of publicly expressing Judeophobic views is one that caused great hurt to many people (and not just Jews), it's worth knowing that the man who committed this act also committed the act of expressing sympathetic views.

But this is a moral issue, and I'll leave it to the professional ethicists to figure out what it all adds up to. The essential point, for the moment, is to show that Dostoevsky was always prepared to succumb to the temptation of holding conflicting views, especially when it came to religion, and that as a phenomenon this was of enormous interest to him.

## CHAPTER FIVE

# Belief Is Ideal

So, what can we say about Dostoevsky's religion? If it's true that we can never pin him down to a consistent set of beliefs on this and many other topics, then is it also true that he has nothing to teach us about it?

Of course, there is no reason why this *must* be true. If we stick with the simplistic notion that an author—or anyone else, for that matter—has an obligation to be consistent in adhering to a set of beliefs that are themselves internally consistent, and if we think Dostoevsky has failed us in this obligation, it does not follow that he has nothing valid to say on a given subject. If, on the other hand, we accept the less simplistic notion that an author— or anyone else, for that matter—has the right to make conflicting truth claims at various moments, and if we think Dostoevsky has asserted this right, then it is easy to suppose that the author may have something quite illuminating to say on the subject. In either case, despite what the author's beliefs might be—whether or not they're constant and consistent, whether or not the author consistently holds them—there's nothing to prevent an author from formulating a conception about religion (or any other subject) that's worth taking seriously.

In fact, Dostoevsky has plenty to say. It's quite possible to speak about a conception of religion that he formulated; regardless of what beliefs he personally may have embraced (on any given day), it's possible to speak about what his thoughts were when he turned his attention to the topic of religion. As it turns out, not surprisingly, his not consistently embracing beliefs is inextricably linked with his conception of religion.

Let's not forget that the intellectual milieu in which Dostoevsky grew up and worked was alive with ideas such as the ones I described in Chapter Two. Received wisdom about religion tended to point a Russian intellectual of Dostoevsky's generation in the direction of either the humanistic line of thought that produced Feuerbach and the many "Lives of Jesus" or a Slavophilic, nationalist view of Russian Orthodoxy as the lone true system of religious belief on earth. Yet there are places where he offers a conception of religion that is entirely free of the nationalistic content of Slavophilic belief. Religious nationalism was something to which Dostoevsky reverted almost instinctively when he thought about religion in general and Christianity in particular, but it's not at all entirely consistent with the other conception. In fact, religious nationalism isn't much about religion at all; it's much more about nationalism. When Dostoevsky thought about religion as such, he thought idealistically.

## KEEPING VIGIL OVER MASHA

I think we can say without too much exaggeration that the kernel of this religious conception lies in an extraordinary piece of writing that precedes all the "big" novels for which Dostoevsky is best known. I don't know whether Dostoevsky had earlier, in his own mind, formulated the thoughts he expresses in this piece of writing or whether he formulated them on the spot.

The setting is worth knowing, if only because of the high drama it suggests. The date is April 16, 1864. Dostoevsky has finished part one of *Notes from Underground*. He was married in 1857, and the marriage was what one might expect from Dostoevsky's novels: tumultuous and unhappy. His wife, Maria Dmitrievna (Masha), has just died of consumption, the day before. As Dostoevsky keeps vigil over her body, he writes down his thoughts in a notebook. Since this entry is so crucial, I will quote it at some length. Here is what he wrote:

*16 April.* Masha is lying on the table. Will Masha and I see one another again?

To love a person *as oneself*, according to Christ's commandment, is impossible. The law on earth that there must be such a thing as an individual person is binding. The *I* is an obstacle. Only Christ was able to do it, but Christ was an eternal ideal toward which man strives and, by a law of nature, must strive. After the appearance of Christ as the *ideal of man in the flesh*, however, it became as clear as day that the highest, the ultimate development [*razvitie*] of the individual person must reach the point (at the very end of the development, at the very point of attainment of the goal) where man can find out, recognize [*soznal*], and, with all the force of his nature, be convinced that the highest use he can make of his individual person, of the fullness of the development of his *I*, is, as it were, to annihilate this *I*, to give it over completely to each and to all, undividedly and selflessly. And this is the greatest happiness. In this way, the law of the *I* fuses with the law of humanness, and in the fusion both, that is, both the *I* and the *all* (to all appearances, two extreme opposites), being reciprocally annihilated for one another, attain at the same time, each by itself, the highest goal of their individual development.

This is Christ's heaven. All history, both of mankind and partly of each person taken separately, is nothing more than development, struggle, striving, and the attainment of this goal.

But if this is the final goal of mankind (and mankind, if it attained it, would not need to develop, that is, would not need to strive for attainment, to struggle, to begin to see, through all its falls, the ideal and eternally strive toward it, consequently would not need to live)—then as a result, man, attaining it, will finish his earthly existence. Thus man on earth is a being that is merely developing and consequently not finished but transitional.

But in my judgment, reaching such a lofty goal is completely senseless, if at the attainment of the goal everything is extinguished and disappears, that is, if through the attainment of the goal man will no longer have life. Consequently there is a future, heavenly life.

What sort of life would this be, where, on what planet, in what center? In a definitive center, that is, in the bosom of the general synthesis, that is, of God?—this we don't know. We know only one feature of the future nature of the future being, who can hardly be called "man" (consequently we have no conception of what sort of beings we will be). This feature was foretold and guessed by Christ—the great and final ideal of the development of all mankind—who appeared to us, by the law of our history, in the flesh;

This law:

"They neither marry nor are given in marriage, but are like angels of God."[1] This is a deeply significant feature.

(1) Neither *marry* nor *are given in marriage*—for there is no reason; developing and attaining the goal, by means of the changing of generations is no longer necessary, and

(2) Marriage and the giving of a woman in marriage are the highest act of pushing humanness away, the complete isolation of the pair from *all* (little remains for all). The family, that is, a law of nature, is nonetheless an abnormal and, in the full sense, egoistic state of man. The family is the greatest sacred object of man on earth, for by means of this law of nature, man attains the development (that is, by means of the changing of generations) of the goal. But at the same time, man must, by a law of nature, in the name of the final ideal of his goal, uninterruptedly deny the family. (Duality.)

NB. The anti-Christians are mistaken when they attempt to refute Christianity with the following chief point of refutation: (1) "Why does Christianity not reign on earth if it [Christianity] is true; why have men suffered till now and not become brothers to one another?"

Well, it's quite understandable why: because this is the ideal of the future, final life of man, while on earth man is in a transitional state. This will be, but it will be after the attainment of the goal, when man will be reborn definitively, by the laws of nature, into another nature—one that neither marries nor gives in marriage. And (2) Christ Himself preached his doctrine only as an ideal, he himself foretold that till the end of the world there would be struggle and development (the doctrine of the sword),[2] for this is a law of nature, because on earth life is developing, while over beyond, there is being that is full synthetically, eternally taking delight and eternally filled, being for which, as a result, "there will no longer be time."[3]

NB2. Atheists, denying God and a future life, are terribly inclined to present all this in a human form, and thus they sin. The nature of God is directly opposite to the nature of man. Man, according to the great results of science, goes from manifold to Synthesis, from the facts to the generalization of those facts and to cognition. But the nature of God is different. It is the full synthesis of all being, regarding itself in the manifold, in Analysis.

But if man is not man, then what kind of nature does he have?

It's impossible to understand on earth, but all mankind and every individual person may have a presentiment of the law of this nature in direct emanations (Proudhon, the origin of God).[4]

This is the fusion of the full *I*, that is, knowledge and a synthesis *with everything.* "*Love everything as yourself.*" This is impossible on earth, for it contradicts the law of the development of the individual person and the attainment of the final goal, by which law man is bound. Consequently this is not an ideal law, as the anti-Christians say, but rather the law of our ideal.

NB. And so everything depends on this: Is Christ taken for the final ideal on earth, that is, from Christian faith? If you believe in Christ, then you believe that you will live forever.

In this case, is there a future life for every "I?" They say that man goes to ruin and dies *entirely.*

We already know that it is not entirely, because man, as someone physically begetting a son, transmits to that son a part of his own individual person, thus morally leaving his memory to people (NB. *The desire for eternal memory* at funerals is significant), that is, through a part of his prior individual personality that lived on earth, enters the future development of mankind. We can see very clearly that the memory of the great developers of humanity lives among people (just as does the development of evildoers), and even for humanity the greatest happiness bears a resemblance to those great developers. That is to say, a part of these natures, in the form of both flesh and soul, enters other people. Christ entirely entered humanity, and man strives to become transfigured into the *I* of Christ as into his (man's) own ideal. Having attained this, he will clearly see that all those who have attained this goal on earth have, like him, entered into the composition of his ultimate nature, that is, into Christ. (The synthetic nature of Christ is astonishing. In fact, this is the nature of God, that is, Christ is the reflection of God on earth.) Just how each *I* will be reborn at that time—in the general Synthesis—is difficult to represent. But that which lives, that which has not died all the way up to the very attainment, that which is reflected in the ultimate ideal must enter into a life that is ultimate, synthetic, infinite. We shall then be persons who never cease to fuse with the "all," persons who neither are given in marriage nor marry, persons of various sorts ("In my Father's house are many dwelling places").[5] Everything at that time will feel and know itself forever. But how this will occur, in what form, in what nature—this is hard for humanity to imagine in any definite way.

And so man strives on earth for an ideal, one that is *opposite* to his own nature. When man has not fulfilled the law of striving for an ideal, that is, when he has not sacrificed, *through love*, his *I* to people or to another being (I and Masha), he feels suffering and has called this condition "sin." And so man uninterruptedly must feel suffering that is balanced out by the heavenly delight in the fulfillment of the law, that is, by sacrifice. This is earthly balance. Otherwise the earth would be senseless.

The teaching of the materialists, the general inertia and mechanism of matter, means death. The teaching of true philosophy is the annihilation of inertia, that is, thought, that is, the center and the Synthesis of the universe and its external form, matter, that is, God, that is, life without end.[6]

It's astonishing to think that someone might write these thoughts in these circumstances. If we take a close look, we can see that Dostoevsky has presented a remarkably profound and coherent religious worldview. One thing that's remarkable about this religious worldview is how very little it has to do with the nationalistic Christianity that Dostoevsky has spoken of and will speak of in so many other places. In fact, when it comes right down to it, this worldview is a form of philosophical idealism that could describe virtually any religion featuring an afterlife and an invisible deity. Let's examine the implicit and explicit claims the bereaved author makes in his entry.

SELF, LOVE, AND FUSION

Any reader of *The Brothers Karamazov* will immediately recognize Dostoevsky's opening thought (after he comments on Masha), since it serves as the
point of departure for Ivan's rebellion. It is impossible in this world to love
one's neighbor as oneself, and thus it is impossible in this world to fulfill one
of Christ's principal commandments (quoted from Leviticus 19:18). But
whereas Ivan offers a practical reason for the impossibility of loving one's
neighbor as oneself (proximity to our neighbors makes them repulsive to us;
we cannot truly feel the suffering of another), Dostoevsky in his diary offers
a reason that has to do with the very nature of the self and love. Why is the
*I* an obstacle to fulfillment of the commandment to love our neighbor? Dostoevsky simply leaves out a few steps in his argument (understandably, given
the state he was in). In the sense in which Dostoevsky interprets Christ's
commandment, love consists in the complete fusion of the individual with
the "all." It represents an absolute. For the individual *I* to enter into such a
fusion, it must be annihilated. Why? Because it is implicit in the concept of
the *I* that it be separate, or bounded, so to speak, by a shell. An *I* is not an *I*
without this shell. Hence the moment the *I* enters into a fusion with the *all*,
it must burst the shell asunder and cease to be an *I*. To put it in more concrete terms: once I have joined in the ultimate fusion, I will no longer be an
*I* who can say, "I have joined in the ultimate fusion."

Ivan will use the impossibility of Christ's love as evidence of a primary
failure of Christianity—or at least as evidence of an important paradox in it:
first ask people to fulfill an obligation that their very nature makes impossible, and then make the fulfillment of that obligation a condition for mem-
bership in the religious community. For Ivan's literary creation, the Grand
Inquisitor, this is what Christianity is all about. The insupportable obligation is the obligation to bear the burden of freedom to believe, which is by
nature beyond the capacity of human beings. Dostoevsky the diarist shows
right away that he has in mind something rather different. Impossibility is
no sign of a fundamental flaw. On the contrary, it is the very essence of the
thing. Christ, as the Son of God, can; we, as fleshly beings, cannot. Christ,
as the Son of God, dwells in a world to which we, as fleshly beings, have no
access. But it is not enough to describe Dostoevsky's conception as a two-
worlds model, if by that phrase we mean static, unchanging worlds separated from one another by an impenetrable barrier. This is because of the
concepts of development and the ideal.

## DEVELOPMENT AND IDEAL

We ran into these concepts in Chapter Two. Owing to Hegel and his followers, the word *development* (and its related forms) became ubiquitous in discussions of history and human society in the nineteenth century. Of course, not everyone understood the word as referring specifically to the dialectical, stagewise movement of human Spirit and its several manifestations (history, art, philosophy), but many certainly understood it as suggesting a spiritual movement toward a higher state. There's no good reason to suppose that Dostoevsky had in mind anything fancier than this.

He uses *develop* and its related forms a total of sixteen times in this entry. At first glance, the words have a Hegelian (or popularized Hegelian) meaning. They refer to a process of exaltation that has as its final point an absolute state, just as Hegel's development always ended in something either called "the absolute" or qualified by the adjective "absolute." So Dostoevsky describes mankind's earthly condition as a development leading to a point where the *I* is annihilated. Man is bound by "the law of the development of the individual person and the attainment of the final goal."

The final goal is the *ideal*. What does it mean? The best definitions I know of—definitions that seem entirely consistent with Dostoevsky's use of the term—are the one that Kant gives in the *Critique of Pure Reason* and the one that Hegel gives in the *History of Philosophy* for the purpose of explaining Kant's use of the term. Kant distinguishes the *ideal* from the *idea*. The idea, he says, is something so removed from reality that no concrete representation can be made of it; the ideal, by contrast, is "the idea, not merely *in concreto*, but *in individuo*, i.e. as an individual thing that may be determined, or actually is determined, by the idea alone."[7] Hegel explains Kant's term by saying that his predecessor used it with reference to God. For Kant, God is "the most real being of all," one "that not merely is a thought but has reality, being." God may thus be named "the ideal, by distinction with the idea; it is the idea as existing."[8] The important elements in the ideal are, first, its intimate relation with the entirely immaterial and invisible *idea* and, second, its concretization.

The word *ideal* occurs as a noun thirteen times in the Masha entry. In every instance, the author employs it to designate either Christ or "Christ's heaven"—the state of fusion and synthesis where the *I* is annihilated. He never uses it to designate God himself. This is completely appropriate and completely consistent with the definitions I gave a moment ago (though in Hegel's account, Kant uses the word *ideal* to name God). Christ is a being who already, by his very nature, is partially concretized. Dostoevsky acknowledges this when he says, "Christ entirely entered humanity, and man strives to become transfigured into the 'I' of Christ as into his (man's) own ideal." Who better to embody the concept of the ideal than a being who is part immaterial divinity and part material man? Similarly, the ultimate fusion, Christ's heaven, is defined as the fusion of the individual *I* with the collective *all* and thus represents a wedding of the contingent and concrete with the eternal and absolute.

If development is a process that leads to higher states, then its natural end is the ideal. Since the ideal embodies the absolute *idea*, this end is not something material and attainable. To be sure, it is concretizable; we are capable of representing it to ourselves, as Dostoevsky has done in this diary entry. Representing it to ourselves means using phrases such as "Christ's heaven." It appears to stand at the "end" of an endless path, and when we concretize it, it appears continuous with that path. But it remains invisible and unattainable, which means that at the end we will need to take a "leap" to cross the gap between it and the path leading to it.

This is because there is a categorical difference between the state that the *true* end represents and all the states preceding it. This difference is essential to the model Dostoevsky presents in his diary entry. "All history, both of mankind and partly of each person taken separately," he says, "is nothing more than development, struggle, striving, and the attainment of this goal." "Man on earth is a being that is merely developing and consequently not finished but transitional," he adds. Christ himself sees the premillennial state as "struggle and development," because "on earth life is developing, while over beyond, there is being that is full synthetically, eternally taking delight and eternally filled, being for which, as a result, 'there will no longer be time.'"

Development happens in time; it is the condition of earthly existence and history. The realm "over beyond" is characterized by synthesis and timelessness. There has been some debate among scholars about the meaning of the passage from Revelation (10:6) whose literal translation is "there will no longer be time [*khronos* in Greek]." Some say the true meaning is that there will be no further *delay* before "the mystery of God is fulfilled" (10:7), and many modern translators reflect this view by using the word *delay* to translate the Greek *khronos*. Dostoevsky, however, interprets the phrase to mean that, at the end of days, historical time will have been abolished. No matter; he wishes to tell us that Christ's heaven is beyond history and development (Dostoevsky was so fond of the passage that, amusingly, he had the materialist Kirillov use it in *The Devils*).[9]

This way of envisioning the relation between earth and heaven allows Dostoevsky to explain a puzzle in the New Testament. Why, if marriage is a sacred state, does Jesus promise that in the resurrection there shall be none? Didn't he, on the subject of "putting away" one's wife, answer the Pharisees by citing Torah to demonstrate the permanence of marriage? "Have you not read that the one who made them at the beginning 'made them male and female,' and said, 'For this reason a man shall leave his father and mother and be joined to his wife, and the two shall become one flesh'? So they are no longer two, but one flesh. Therefore what God has joined together, let no one separate."[10] As Dostoevsky sees it, marriage is precisely the engine of *development* (he associates it with "the changing of generations") on earth and is consequently a condition belonging to this world. Striving for the "final ideal," he reminds us, requires us to deny the family.

As in Hegel's various processes of development and as in Marx's theory of history, all contradictions are resolved in the final, absolute state. If we call this state "God" in Hegel, then we can return to a sentence I quoted in Chapter Two: "God is God only in so far as he knows himself; his self-knowing, furthermore, is [both] his self-consciousness in man and man's knowing *of* God, which leads to the self-knowing of man *in* God."[11] Whether or not this adds up to an assertion of the existence of God, one thing is certain: essential to the nature of God is the connection with man that Hegel attempts to describe when he refers to God's "self-consciousness in man," "man's knowing *of* God," and "the self-knowing of man *in* God." The nature of the Hegelian dialectic is such that the final stage is inconceivable without the presence in it of sublimated elements from lower stages. In Dostoevsky's conception, as I indicated a moment ago, there is a break between the limiting, next-to-last stage and the ultimate fusion. The self is annihilated and enters into a state categorically distinct from and inaccessible to its earlier state. This is not the process of *Aufhebung* (defined in Chapter Two) that Hegel conceived; this is a rupture.

So Dostoevsky's two-worlds model is peculiar. On *this* side, it is dynamic, since the dynamic process of "development, struggle, striving" is integral to *this* side. On *that* side, it is static, since time is abolished on *that* side. One might say the very same thing about Hegel, since the absolute stage for him represents the absence of contradictions that could lead to yet higher stages in the dialectical process. But Dostoevsky insists on the qualitative difference between *this* side and *that* side. For him, there can be no talk of God's self-consciousness in man or the self-knowing of man in God. The divide is absolute; only a son of God has ever been able to bridge it. As I'll show in detail shortly, it's like Prince Myshkin and his epileptic seizures: once he reaches the limiting moment beyond which all is synthesis and harmony, "he" (the Prince who can say *I*) is simply not there anymore to say, "I am now in a state of synthesis and harmony." No, all is now darkness, as his consciousness is extinguished.

The model can mean at least two slightly different things, depending on our perspective. It can describe me, an individual, and my experience in this world from *my* perspective. This experience then consists in the path of development that, by a law of nature, I follow. The path takes me ever closer to the ideal that lies at its end, though *I* can never touch that ideal. The minute I've bridged the gap between my path and the ideal, *I* cease to exist, though the *I* that I used to be has now joined in a blissful synthesis with the *all*. The model can also describe, from a hypothetical outsider's perspective, the earthly world and the eternal world. The earthly world is characterized by time, movement, and fragmentation, while the eternal world is timeless, static, and synthetic.

It would be quite a challenge to represent this model graphically, especially given the several perspectives from which to examine it. If the idea is to describe *me* as an individual and my experience as I make the journey, then we need a graphic representation that illustrates the infinity of the line of development—or perhaps more accurately a ray or a line extending infinitely in just one direction and having a starting point—together with a divide separating the limiting "next-to-last" point from the end. The starting point of the ray would correspond to a hypothetical base level of earthly physicality. Or we can use a graphic representation showing the line of development as an *asymptotic* function, a curve stretching to infinity and growing ever closer to its asymptote, a straight axis (representing the ultimate fusion), without ever touching the axis. If the idea is to describe the two worlds, then we'll need a graphic representation that somehow shows a process of development leading up to, but not wholly continuous with, a static realm of timelessness and synthesis.

A DOSTOEVSKIAN DIALECTIC:
EPILEPSY AND MAYHEM, GOOD
AND EVIL, FAITH AND ATHEISM

The more common perspective in Dostoevsky is that of the individual mak-ing the journey. Where we best see the dynamics of the limit-development model at play from this perspective is in *The Idiot* and *The Devils*. By con-trast with *The Brothers Karamazov*, in neither of these novels does Dosto-evsky devote a tremendous amount of space to religion as an explicit topic. Apart from a few key passages, these novels treat religion symbolically more than they do directly. Still, the key passages are enormously important, and even apart from them no reader can possibly mistake the presence of reli-gious meaning in either novel, especially *The Idiot*.

### The Imperfect Delights of Epilepsy

Almost everyone seems certain, especially in the West, that Prince Myshkin is some sort of saint, but an odd one; either he fails for reasons connected with his own saintliness, or Dostoevsky has failed in his construction of the character. Some, like de Vogüé and Krieger, have claimed that the novel it-self is deeply flawed.[12] In either case, readers seem persuaded that something about Myshkin represents *failure*.

Yet on one level the character of the prince is pretty simple. He represents a kind of conundrum, and a truly ingenious one. Say what you like about *The Idiot*—it's poorly organized (maybe), it's sloppily written (maybe), Dos-toevsky had no idea where he was going with it as he wrote it (that's a fact)—the hero presents an excellent illustration of the concepts I've just de-scribed, with all their paradoxical features. This is not to say that I've found a way to reduce Prince Myshkin to a formula. Naturally there's much more to be said about him than his status as a conundrum. But for a discussion of development and the ideal, the function of this character can be described rather briefly.

I'd imagine that very few people have read the Masha entry before read-ing *The Idiot*. For that matter, it's probably safe to assume very few readers of *The Idiot* have read the Masha entry at all. But if you were to read the di-ary entry first (knowing it was written first) and *The Idiot* immediately af-ter, you couldn't help noticing the remarkable number of parallels between the entry and one passage in the novel. It comes in the scene (in part two) that ends with Myshkin's first epileptic fit. Myshkin has been walking the city with an eerie sense of dread, aware that a pair of eyes seems to be following him around. Because of the darkness of his mood, his thoughts turn to the subject of the illness that is shortly to attack him. Let me quote selectively from the fairly long passage containing these thoughts.

> He fell into thought about how, in his epileptic condition, there was one stage almost right before the fit itself (if only the fit were to strike one when one is in a waking state) when all of a sudden, amidst the sadness, the darkness of the soul, the stress, for moments his brain would catch fire, as it were, and in an extraordinary upsurge his vital forces would all at once become strained to the utmost. The sensation of life, of self-consciousness was magnified almost tenfold in these moments, which lasted about as long as flashes of lightning. His mind, his heart would be illuminated with an extraordinary light; all his agitation, all his doubts, all his anxieties would at once grow calm, would be resolved into some sort of higher tranquility, filled with clear, harmonious joy and hope, filled with reason and the final cause. But these moments, these flashes were still only the foretaste of that final second (never more than a second), with which the fit itself would begin. This second, of course, was unendurable. Thinking over this moment afterwards, when he was again in a healthy state, he would often say to himself that all this lightning and all these flashes of higher self-sensation and self-consciousness, consequently of "higher being," are nothing more than disease, the destruction of the normal condition, and that if so, then this is not higher being at all but, on the contrary, must be reckoned among the lowest. And yet he would nonetheless finally arrive at an extraordinarily paradoxical conclusion: "So what if it is a disease?" he decided finally. "What difference does it make that this strain is abnormal if the very result, the minute of sensation, recalled and observed from a healthy state, turns out to be, in the highest degree, harmony, beauty, turns out to give a hitherto unheard-of and undivined feeling of fullness, measure, reconciliation, and rapturous, prayerful fusion with the very highest synthesis of life?" These foggy expressions seemed to him quite comprehensible, though perhaps too weak. That this was truly "beauty and prayer," that it was truly "the very highest synthesis of life" he had no doubt—indeed he could permit no doubts at all.

After another page or so, Dostoevsky turns once again to the final moment before a fit:

> "In that moment," as he was saying to Rogozhin one day in Moscow, at the time when they used to get together there, "the extraordinary saying that 'there will no longer be time' somehow becomes comprehensible to me.

Probably," he added, smiling, "it's the very same second in which the epileptic Mohammed's overturned jug of water did not have time to spill, though during the same second Mohammed had time to survey all the dwellings of Allah." Yes, in Moscow he and Rogozhin often got together and talked about more than just this. "Rogozhin said recently that back then I was a brother to him; he said that for the first time today," the prince thought to himself.[13]

Shortly after, in a scene borrowed from the horror fiction Dostoevsky was so fond of, Rogozhin surprises his "brother" in a darkened staircase and attempts to assault him with a knife. Not surprisingly, the prince enters the preseizure moment he was thinking about earlier, and we read, "then his consciousness was extinguished completely and total darkness set in."[14] Reporting this, the narrator necessarily switches point of view from inside to outside the prince, since there is no longer any inside to report: "He suffered a fit of epilepsy, an illness that had left him in peace for quite some time now. It is well known that fits of epilepsy, properly speaking the *falling sickness*, come instantaneously. In this instant, the face, especially its expression, suddenly grows extraordinarily distorted."[15]

It's easy to see the parallel between the Masha entry and the long passage about epileptic auras. The path to the actual seizure is exactly like the path that earthly beings follow as they approach "Christ's heaven." In the Masha entry, down here all is history and development. For Myshkin, down here all is physicality and disease. In the Masha entry, the goal may be reached only at the cost of the self, which then becomes lost in a higher fusion. For Myshkin, the goal may be reached only at the cost of consciousness (essentially the same thing as "the self"), which then becomes lost in a higher fusion. In both instances, whether we're speaking of the *I* or of consciousness, the being that knows it's approaching the goal will never know it has reached the goal (if it does), since exactly the properties that allow it to know it's approaching must disappear once it gets there. In the Masha entry, it's a law of nature that down here we're condemned to the limitations of our individuality, even though through our individual consciousness we enjoy the sensations our physical nature allows us. For Myshkin, it's a law of nature that down here an epileptic is condemned to yet more pronounced limitations than healthy people, even though the illness affords an approach to something very much like the absolute. For the grieving Dostoevsky, the limitations of the *I* were a sign of the impossibility of perfect Christian love. For Myshkin, the limitations of the individual consciousness are not necessarily a *sign* of the impossibility of brotherly love, but they are closely associated with an illustration of this impossibility: it's precisely Myshkin's "brother" who assaults him and precipitates the epileptic seizure. Assault and seizure both demonstrate the unattainability of the ideal.

The prince's other epileptic fit occurs, of course, in the vase-smashing scene. The first fit occurred in connection with an attempted assault that served as a reminder of the fleshly world and the failure of brotherly love. The second one occurs in connection with two reminders of the fleshly world and its pitfalls. The first reminder is the dramatic smashing of the ornamental Chinese vase, a visual image equaled in strength perhaps only by that of Nastasia Filippovna's flinging a hundred thousand rubles into the fire early in the novel. The prince's human weakness causes him to wave his arm "incautiously."[16] The second reminder is the prince's delivery of his maniacal tirade on Slavophilism. Critics who find this tirade out of place may well be right. It arises apropos of just about nothing. If anything has characterized Myshkin as a religious being up to this scene, it has been the relative lack of explicit attention he gives the subject of religion. *We* can think all we want about how saintly he is, about how much he suffers, about his humility; but outside this scene and one or two others, *he* seems not to be conscious of any of this and certainly seems not to be conscious of any of his own virtues. Now, out of the blue, he finds himself raving specifically and historically about a particular version of Christianity and forcefully urging it upon his listeners. But the version he speaks of, as I've mentioned before, is as earthly as they come. What's the supreme principle here? God and Christ, or the Russian nation? He mentions God and Christ negatively, in order to describe how the Catholic Church has distorted and rejected both; when he mentions them positively, however, it is only to claim that belief in the "Russian God and Christ" must go hand in hand with belief in *Russia*.

In fact, the fit occurs as the Prince is speaking not of God but of God's world in all its physical details:

> Oh, what do my sorrows and troubles matter, so long as I have the strength to be happy? You know, I cannot understand how you can pass by a tree and not be happy that you're seeing it, how you can talk to someone and not be happy that you love him! Oh, I simply can't express it—but imagine how many things there are at every step that are so beautiful, things that even the most unprepossessing man finds beautiful! Look at the child, look at God's sunset, look at the grass and how it grows, look at the eyes that look at you and love you.[17]

What is he talking about here? Earthly happiness and earthly love. The fit immediately follows the word "love." Once again epilepsy serves as a reminder that absolute, other-worldly bliss comes at the end of a path that is simply human.

Seen in this light, Prince Myshkin is a human version of the conundrum that Dostoevsky set out to explore as he gazed upon the body of his late wife. Let's bring back Dostoevsky's Paradoxalist and let him try to explain things to us. We, in italics, will be the straight man.

*How can brotherly love be the dominant requirement in a religion that presupposes the impossibility of that requirement's complete fulfillment?*

Remember that complete fulfillment is something purely ideal, something from a realm to which we have no access.

*So what should I do?*

Strive toward that ideal, with the knowledge that you'll never reach it.

*Only to be cast back into utter baseness, owing to a property (my physicality) that is ineluctable?*

Yes, I'm afraid so.

*So what's the point?*

The point is that the goal, by its nature and yours, is inconceivable to you and that, if you reach it, you will no longer be "you."

*So I won't know it?*

Exactly.

*What kind of goal is that?*

Don't forget that the goal is well worth reaching. It's the absolute, after all. In fact, there's a "law of nature" that says you should try.

*And this is what Christianity adds up to?*

Again, I'm afraid so. Look at Prince Myshkin: he's the closest they come to the Christian ideal, and he ends up losing his mind in the end. Talk about no longer being *you!*

*But doesn't he lose his mind because of an illness, which is to say a physical weakness?*

Absolutely (so to speak). It's the very same physical weakness that brings him close to the ideal in the first place.

*So I should try to catch some illness, and this will bring me closer to Christ?*

No, of course not. Prince Myshkin, you see, is only a model, a sort of, well . . . conundrum.

## The Imperfect Delights of Mayhem

Stavrogin as the foil to Myshkin: In Chapter Two, I quoted a conversation that Nikolai Stavrogin has with Bishop Tikhon, in a passage often omitted from a chapter that itself was omitted from all editions of the novel until 1922. It's a pity most readers never get to read this passage, because I can think of nothing else in *The Devils* that so clearly and succinctly expresses what Stavrogin is all about. Stavrogin is remembering the occasion in his life when he first grasped this "formula" of his life:

> . . . that I do not know or feel evil or good and that not only had I lost all sense of them, but that there is no such thing as evil or good (and this was pleasant for me), only prejudice; that I could be free from all prejudice, but that, if I should ever attain that freedom, I would perish. It was the first time I had been conscious of this in a formula.[18]

Let's start with *prejudice*, a word far from casually chosen in this passage. The Russian word *predrassudok* is formed, like "prejudice," from a prefix that means "before." Our Latin-based word contains a root that means "judgment"; the Russian word contains a root that means "reason," though not in the strict sense of the faculty of reason that philosophers speak of. But both words suggest a judgment or a determination that is made *in advance*. In advance of what?

*Predrassudok* was a favorite word of the Nihilists, who used it to heap scorn on worldviews that were corrupted by the presence of metaphysical elements: the soul, the spirit, absolute truths, in short, anything not susceptible to strictly scientific explanation. The idea is that claims about such elements always imply a judgment in advance of *the facts*. If we make the claim that killing another human being is absolutely wrong, we are doing so *in advance of* factually establishing the possibility of a killing that might be justified in practice. So "prejudice" means *a priori* judgments— in other words, judgments whose truth we know *before* we verify them empirically. In the Nihilists' system, such judgments are invalid on their face. There *are* no a priori judgments. Dostoevsky's underground man uses the word as frequently as he does in order to shred the naïve claims of his imaginary Nihilist opponents.

Stavrogin's use of *predrassudok* is largely consonant with that of the Nihilists. "Good" and "bad" are exactly the qualities about which we have little choice but to make a priori claims, since conventionally we can advance no empirical claims about them. Utilitarian ethics (the ethics that Russian Nihilists were fond of) attempted to purify claims about good and bad by replacing purely moral judgments with judgments of utility. An action can't be good or bad, but it can be shown empirically to be advantageous or disadvantageous to a particular person, to have or to lack utility for the person. So by 1870, when Dostoevsky was at work on *The Devils*, the sentiment that "there is no such thing as evil or good . . . only prejudice" was already timeworn in Russian intellectual circles.

But there's an important difference between Stavrogin and the Nihilists, one that almost perfectly replicates the difference between the two justifications for Raskolnikov's crimes. The Nihilists, like the student Raskolnikov overhears in the tavern, want empirical justification for their claims. We establish the truth of the claim "It is right to kill the pawnbroker" by pointing to measurable quantities, such as the profits that will surely accrue to a determinate group of people. Stavrogin, like the extraordinary man in Raskolnikov's article, seeks justification only in the self. A priori for him thus comes to mean "in advance of consideration of *my* interests and will." Absolute moral judgments as a class are implicitly a priori in this sense, because they take no account of Stavrogin's will.

The clause that follows the statement about prejudice is the one containing the conceptual core of Stavrogin's character: "that I could be free from all prejudice, but that, if I should ever attain that freedom, I would perish." To be free from all prejudice means to be free from all a priori judgments, at least as defined in connection with Stavrogin's self. Since judgments about moral absolutes certainly form a subclass of "all a priori judgments," to be free from all such judgments means to be free from all judgments that presuppose the existence of moral absolutes, or (what is the same thing) to be free from the presupposition that moral absolutes exist. I'm assuming here that the person making judgments presupposing the existence of moral absolutes *believes* those judgments.

In Stavrogin's eyes, to attain freedom from this presupposition is to perish. Both Myshkin and the just-widowed Dostoevsky had a realm to which finite, earthly beings could not obtain access. Stavrogin has one too. The path to Myshkin's and Dostoevsky's realm lay in the direction of increasing self-abnegation. The realm itself was characterized by pure brotherly love, but at the expense of the *individual* human self. The path to Stavrogin's realm lies in the direction of increasing self-assertion. The realm itself, presumably, is characterized by pure self, but once again at the expense of the individual *human* self. Myshkin's and Dostoevsky's absolute consists in the absorption of the individual self into the all. Stavrogin's consists in the absorption of the all into the individual self. Both realms violate the grieving Dostoevsky's "law on earth that there must be such a thing as an individual person" and therefore bring about the permanent or temporary extinction of that earthly individual person. Thus the absolute for Dostoevsky and Myshkin brings about the loss of self, while the absolute for Stavrogin *is* the self (which asserts "itself" over moral absolutes).

For the moment, we can form a picture of the relationship between Myshkin and the widowed Dostoevsky, on one side, and Stavrogin, on the other, by simply taking the ray I described earlier, establishing its starting point as a middle point, and extending it infinitely in the direction opposite to the one Dostoevsky hints at in his notebook. Here too, there would be some sort of break before the theoretical end point (at infinity). So the notion we would form is of a completely symmetrical scheme: travel down the path toward "the good" (defined here as perfect Christian brotherly love) and you'll find yourself unable, as a still fleshly being, to attain the good and absolute selflessness; travel down the opposite path toward absolute will and "the absence of good and evil" (but defined here only as evil, since it is through evil, not through good, that Stavrogin seeks *his* absolute) and you'll find yourself unable, as a still fleshly being, to attain evil and the absolute self. Myshkin ends up mad; Stavrogin ends up dead, by his own hand.

There's an additional complication in Stavrogin's idea. His path lies solely in the direction of evil. If he really thinks he's acting in accordance with a theory, and if that theory is about acting in the absence of knowledge of good and evil, what Stavrogin chooses to do in order to test the limits ought to include titanic acts of charity and goodness in addition to titanic acts of evil. Or he should behave as Raskolnikov's extraordinary man is meant to behave, in obedience to a principle that has nothing to do with good and evil. Stavrogin's plan, however, is simply to commit acts of evil and to do so *without remorse.* To show remorse, after all, is implicitly to judge an action evil. But then Stavrogin has already judged his actions evil so as to discover whether he can commit them as if he *hadn't* judged them evil. Of course, he has realized that to do so is to perish.

Perhaps the Paradoxalist can help us out once again.

*How can rape and mayhem without remorse be the dominant requirement in a worldview that presupposes the impossibility of that requirement's complete fulfillment?*

Remember that complete fulfillment is something purely ideal, something from a realm to which we have no access.

*So what should I do?*

Strive toward the ideal, with the knowledge that you'll never reach it.

*Only to be cast back into utter, bland, moral mediocrity, owing to a property (the impotence of my self) that is ineluctable?*

Yes, I'm afraid so.

*So what's the point?*

The point is that the goal, by its nature and yours, is inconceivable to you, and if you reach it you will be so much more than *you* that you will no longer be *you.*

*So I won't know it?*

Exactly.

*What kind of goal is that?*

Don't forget that the goal is well worth reaching. It's absolute evil, after all. In fact, there's a law of the self that says you should try.

*And this is what the quest for evil adds up to?*

Again, I'm afraid so. Look at Stavrogin: he's the closest they come to the evil ideal, and he ends up taking his life in the end. Talk about no longer being *you*!

*But doesn't he take his life because of the impotence of his will and his inability to ignore good and evil, which is to say because of human weakness?*

Absolutely (so to speak); it's the very same human weakness that makes him choose the evil ideal and that brings him close to it in the first place.

*So I should try to lose my will and focus hard on evil, and this will bring me closer to the ideal?*

No, of course not. Nikolai Stavrogin, you see, is only a model, a sort of, well . . . conundrum.

It begins to look as if Dostoevsky paired *The Idiot* and *The Devils* as thesis and antithesis.[19] Prince Myshkin travels the path toward ultimate goodness and, owing to his status as a mere fleshly being, fails to reach the end; Stavrogin travels the path toward ultimate remorseless evil and, owing to *his* status as a mere fleshly being, fails to reach the end. Human nature is categorically inadequate to the twin ideals consisting in selfless synthesis with the all at one end and complete ignorance of absolute moral truths at the other. Yet the inadequacy seems to be precisely what drives us to pursue the ideals. If we return to the visual image of a line extending in both directions, where both ends are either infinitely remote or separated by a gap from the realm they approach, we find ourselves at a perpetual impasse.

But the most remarkable thought in *The Devils* is one that the bishop himself expresses, again in a portion of the novel that was not published at first. Stavrogin and Tikhon have begun to speak about a question that will come up again and again in *The Brothers Karamazov*: whether or not it is legitimate to require as a basis for one's faith a material manifestation of God's existence, that is, a miracle. Stavrogin wonders, too, if it is possible to believe in the devil without believing in God. Tikhon answers that it is. Then Stavrogin asks if Tikhon considers it more respectable to believe in the devil without believing in God than not to believe at all. The answer: "On the contrary, perfect atheism is more respectable than worldly indifference." Stavrogin expresses surprise, and Tikhon then pronounces the all-important sentence: "The perfect atheist stands on the next-to-last rung before most perfect faith (whether he steps over it or not), while the indifferent man has no faith at all besides rank terror."[20] He cites the seventh letter from Revelation (3:15–16): "I know your works; you are neither cold nor hot. I wish that you were either cold or hot. So, because you are lukewarm, and neither cold nor hot, I am about to spit you out of my mouth." Once again we find ourselves confronting a duality of unattainable absolutes. Till now, we've seen polar absolutes that have to do with good and evil. But Tikhon and Stavrogin are speaking of faith and lack of faith. I've said little about faith so far in this chapter, so now it's time to see whether we can show (as we might easily expect) that the opposition faith-atheism lines up with the opposition good-evil.

Prince Myshkin and his epileptic auras strongly resemble the *I* in the Masha entry, since both approach an absolute goal. But this goal is nowhere explicitly described as "perfect faith." In fact, the word *faith* occurs relatively rarely in *The Idiot*. We find it in connection with Holbein's *The Corpse of Christ in the Tomb*, a copy of which hangs in Rogozhin's house, and we find it in Myshkin's Slavophilic tirade on Catholicism. The German master's grim, human representation of the Savior in the tomb inspires the prince to exclaim that some people, looking at it, might lose their faith.[21] Myshkin then gives a discourse on faith, consisting of four parables that lead him to conclude: "The essence of religious feeling has nothing to do with any type of argumentative reasoning, any crimes or misdemeanors, or any sorts of atheism. Something is wrong with this and will be wrong forever. There's something here that all the atheisms will forever just glide over, for they will forever talk about *the wrong thing*."[22]

If the four parables have anything in common, it's an illustration of the principle that there are countless *earthly* ways of expressing faith (and its opposite) but all are oblique and imperfect, no doubt precisely because they're earthly. There's the man who claims to be an atheist but seems always to be speaking not about that but about something else. There's the peasant who says a prayer before slitting his friend's throat in order to steal his watch. There's the soldier who cheats the prince by selling him a crucifix for much more than it's worth. There's the peasant woman who responds with great joy to her baby's first smile.[23] The very next chapter tells the story of the prince's first epileptic fit.

Toward the end of the Slavophilic rant, Myshkin, losing control of himself, blurts out, "I want to explain everything to you, everything, everything, everything! No, as God is my witness, I have such simple ideas . . . You don't believe me? You're smiling? You know, I'm sometimes truly base, because I lose my faith"—this in the middle of a speech ostensibly designed to explain to his audience what truth faith is all about. As in the case of the parables, the words the prince speaks (1) have as their subject the imperfection of earthly faith, (2) demonstrate through the prince's language and behavior the imperfection of earthly faith, and (3) lead to proof positive that the prince is doomed to failure, for a moment or two after he claims to lose his faith he issues "the feral cry of 'the spirit that threw down and convulsed' the unhappy man" and falls to the floor.[24] The faith the prince describes is in all instances earthly-all-too-earthly for the good and simple reason that he—*even* he—cannot possess perfect faith. Faith lies beyond the end of the line, just as does the divine synthesis.

Stavrogin, by contrast, explicitly mentions faith in a way that associates the term with the path he has followed. If one can, with sufficient faith, move a mountain (as it is said), why can't or won't Tikhon? Because he doesn't "perfectly" believe. How is this possible? If anyone can believe perfectly, it must be this saintly man. Alas, it's all too true. If anyone can reach the divine synthesis, it's Prince Myshkin. But he can't, no matter how hard he might try. If anyone can reach the absolute pinnacle of evil, it's Stavrogin. But he can't, no matter how hard he might try. It turns out that perfect belief—like its opposite, perfect atheism—is not humanly attainable. Perfect faith is as closely tied to Christ's heaven, or the divine synthesis, as perfect atheism is to absolute evil.

So in his statement about the perfect atheist and most perfect faith, Tikhon must mean "perfect" in a purely theoretical sense: there can be no such thing *on earth* as a perfect atheist or perfect faith. There's this, too: till now, it has appeared that good and evil, faith and faithlessness lie at opposite ends of a continuum. But now they are suddenly separated by a single "rung," and it's only a matter of stepping from one to the next. How does this accord with the model of the line extending in opposite directions and approaching but not reaching opposite ends? There actually is an almost plausible way to represent this visually. If we take our infinite line, wrap its ends around so that one (the one representing perfect faith) lies slightly higher than the other (the one representing perfect atheism) then (allowing for the impossibility of wrapping ends that are infinitely distant) we have a figure that looks like a single turn of a helix, a single coil of a Slinky toy. Let's say that the ends are in front, closest to us. Then the point on the coil directly behind these ends is the midpoint of the original line. In Tikhon's formulation, this midpoint represents "worldly indifference." The only problem with this visual representation, of course, is that if the ends represent perfect faith and perfect faithlessness and if it's true that no fleshly creature can ever reach either of these states, then we need to understand that the step up from atheism to faith is merely a step up from being very near perfect atheism to being very near perfect faith.

Still, if the visual model in some way describes Tikhon's characterization of faith and its opposite, it offers no true solution to the impasse I described a moment ago. It does, however, tell us a possibly surprising truth about extreme good and extreme evil, about great faith and great faithlessness, namely that we are capable of the one in proportion to being capable of the other (though, to be sure, Tikhon speaks only of stepping *up* from atheism to faith, not vice versa). Dostoevsky was fascinated with the idea of a great sinner who atones for his sins and then follows a worthy Christian path. The hero of *The Life of a Great Sinner*, a work that Dostoevsky was perennially planning but never wrote, was to be such a man. Raskolnikov presumably was the more capable of spiritual rebirth for having committed a grave sin. In the first plans for *The Idiot*, the prince was to be a proud and violent man, a rapist who is subsequently transformed into a sympathetic soul. Stavrogin, during his conversation with Tikhon, is apparently the closer to a good Christian life for having committed a sin at least as grave as (and quite possibly graver than) Raskolnikov's. Versilov, the father of the hero in *The Adolescent*, is a character in whom the qualities of a proud and faithless Russian gentry intellectual share space with the (at least professed) virtues of Christian meekness. And, as we learn in *The Brothers Karamazov*, Father Zosima in his life has followed the formulaic Dostoevskian trajectory from impetuous, proud sinner to humble man of God.

## THE PUZZLE OF THE INDIVIDUAL AND THE "ALL"

So the individual can never "get there." That's not all, because it turns out, to compound matters, there's a fatal paradox within Dostoevsky's very conception of the individual (or *I*, as Dostoevsky often likes to put it). The Masha entry introduces half of this paradox, but nowhere is it stronger than in *The Idiot* and *The Devils*. This is it:

1(A)  The dissolution of the individual is an ideal positive good.

1(B)  The integrity of the individual is an evil.

2(A)  The integrity of the individual is an ideal positive good.

2(B)  The dissolution of the individual is an evil.

The second paragraph of the Masha entry is where the grieving husband speaks of the *I* as an obstacle and refers to annihilating that *I*, "[giving] it over completely to each and to all, undividedly and selflessly."[25] Much of the remainder of the piece is devoted to developing this notion.

For the moment, let's set aside the question whether or not these statements are true and examine them from a purely logical standpoint. The two statements in each pair have a relation to each other similar to that of *obversion*. Technically, obversion applies where one can directly infer one proposition from another by refuting the negation of the original proposition. Here, of course, we can in no way directly infer 1(B) from 1(A) as bare statements until we have explained exactly what we mean by them; before that, we are simply asserting both. But 1(B) certainly shows the truth of 1(A) after its subject and predicate have both been negated. All four statements form a paradox; statements 1(A) and 1(B), taken together, form a paradox relative to statements 2(A) and 2(B), taken together. This is for the simple reason that the outside two statements, 1(A) and 2(B)—claiming together that the dissolution of the individual is both good and evil—directly contradict each other, as do the inside two statements, 1(B) and 2(A), claiming together that the integrity of the individual is both good and evil. So if, from a purely logical standpoint, 1(A) and 1(B) are consistent with one another and 2(A) and 2(B) are consistent with one another (as it would appear at first glance), then 1(A) and 1(B) as a pair contradict 2(A) and 2(B) as a pair.

Continuing to leave to one side the truth of the statements, let's take a step back and examine them not from a purely logical standpoint (where the paradoxes are completely obvious) but from the standpoint we adopt when we accept certain features of Dostoevsky's fictional world (for the sake of simplicity, let's speak as if there were only one such world). If we understand the statements as expressing *goals*—if we rephrase them as commands ("Seek your own dissolution, and escape the integrity of your person"; "seek the integrity of your person, and escape your own dissolution")—the members of each pair don't contradict each other, but taken together they contradict a practical feature of Dostoevsky's fictional world. Each pair rests on two assumptions that real experience will never bear out in that world: first, it's possible for an individual to attain absolute dissolution and still be around to experience it, and second, it's possible for an individual to attain absolute wholeness of personality. We already know about the impossibility of attaining absolute dissolution in this world. But what about absolute wholeness? Dissolution would appear at first glance to be a condition of the ideal world, "Christ's heaven," while wholeness would appear to be a condition of *this* world. We might then expect that dissolution is impossible, while wholeness is possible. But wholeness, understood in the absolute sense, that is, as a condition in which the individual displays no fractures and consequently no doubt (*doubt* in many Indo-European languages, including Russian, is rendered by a word that suggests *doubling*) cannot be anything but ideal and, practically speaking, unattainable. What's more, as we'll see, the path toward wholeness ends not in wholeness but in dissolution.

Let's now examine each claim and its implications.

## 1(A) The Dissolution of the Individual Is an Ideal Positive Good

This is the message of the Masha entry, where Dostoevsky presents the claim as paradoxical in and for itself—that is, paradoxical at the practical, not at the logical, level:

. . . the highest use he can make of his individual person, of the fullness of the development of his *I*, is, as it were, to annihilate this *I*, to give it over completely to each and to all, undividedly and selflessly. . . . But that which lives, that which has not died all the way up to the very attainment, that which is reflected in the ultimate ideal must enter into a life that is ultimate, synthetic, infinite. . . . And so man strives on earth for an ideal, one that is *opposite* to his own nature.

Of all Dostoevsky's characters, Myshkin is no doubt the clearest concretization of this belief; yet in one important respect the diary entry does not really describe the epileptic hero. It's not just that the prince *is* epileptic (whereas the bereaved husband does not appear to have any specific type of person in mind); it's also that the general "man" of the diary entry must make the ultimate dissolution his *goal*—must strive through an effort of will to attain that goal, while Myshkin is led to his moment of dissolution by his morbid condition, therefore *against* his will. In *The Idiot*, this circumstance, of course, serves its own purpose, as further evidence of the distance at which we all ultimately find ourselves from the ideal, since (to judge by *The Idiot*) the finest candidate for attaining the ideal will be the one who is the most imprisoned in the weaknesses of the flesh. Still, the simple message is the same in the world of the diary entry and in Prince Myshkin's world: the ideally good situation is that in which the *I* has completely dissolved and become at one with the all.

## 1(B) The Integrity of the Individual Is an Evil

This obverse claim too appears in the Masha entry: "The law on earth that there must be such a thing as an individual person is binding. The 'I' is an obstacle." If the ultimate goal is dissolution and dissolution is good, it must be true that anything standing in our path toward dissolution must be evil. In this case, it is the *I* in its wholeness that stands in our way, so it must be evil.

The Masha entry is not the only place in Dostoevsky's writings where this principle is explicitly or implicitly asserted. Think, for example, of the dream Raskolnikov has before the conversion experience in the epilogue to *Crime and Punishment*. In the apocalyptic scene that the author draws for us, people are suddenly infected with a dreadful pestilence.

There appeared some sort of new trichinae, microscopic creatures that moved into people's bodies. But these creatures were spirits, endowed with mind and will. People who took these creatures into themselves immediately became possessed, mad. But never, never had people considered themselves so smart and so unwavering in connection with the truth as the infected now considered themselves. . . . Everyone was anxious, and people did not understand one another. Each thought that the truth was contained in him alone, and each, looking upon others, tormented himself, beat his breast, wept, and wrung his hands.[26]

A passage in *The Brothers Karamazov* describes not only the problem but the opposite, salubrious condition. Father Zosima tells a story from his past about a mysterious older visitor who once committed a murder. The visitor began to appear frequently, and one day he abruptly tells his younger friend that life is a paradise. This view, of course, conflicts with the one the author presented years earlier in the Masha entry. The description the visitor gives of life-as-heaven and life-as-hell, however, is significant in a discussion of the individual:

But that every man is guilty before everyone for everything, apart from his own sins, you have judged completely right, and it is astonishing how you are able suddenly to embrace this thought in such fullness. And in truth it is correct that, when people grasp this thought, the heavenly kingdom comes for them not in a dream but in actual fact. . . . Until one has made himself in actual fact a brother to everyone, brotherhood will not come. People will never by any sort of science or self-interest be able to share their property and their rights without offense to others. There will always be too little for everyone, and people will constantly grumble, will envy and destroy each other. You ask when this will come to pass. It will come to pass, but first the period of human *individual isolation* must end. . . . For now everyone attempts to cut himself off as much as possible, to experience within himself the fullness of life, and yet what emerges from all his efforts is, instead of the fullness of life, nothing but full suicide, for instead of attaining the fullness of the determination of their being, people will fall into complete individual isolation. For in our era, all have separated themselves into units, everyone isolates himself in his own hole, everyone alienates himself from others, hides. . . . But it will happen without fail that the end of even this frightful individual isolation will come, and people will at once understand how unnaturally they have separated themselves from one another. Such will be the spirit of the times, and people will be astonished that they have sat so long in the darkness and have not seen the light. "Then the sign of the Son of Man will appear in heaven."[27] But until that time, we will have to guard the banner, and even if it must be individually, man will suddenly have to demonstrate by example and bring his soul out of individual isolation into the great exploit of brother-loving community.[28]

You'll notice that the speaker refers to a heaven that we appear to reach in this life, on this earth. I'll return to this in the next chapter. For now, what matters is the description of the opposition between a state in which individuals exist in isolation and one in which they exist in solidarity (though there is no talk here of abandoning one's individuality and dissipating into the all).

### 2(A) The Integrity of the Individual Is an Ideal Positive Good

This statement is true especially after the resolution of a crisis of doubt, since doubt necessarily means a split. In the improbable conversion scene in the Epilogue to *Crime and Punishment*, Raskolnikov finds himself restored to wholeness—paradoxically, soon after the dream in which the wholeness of individual personality appeared as an evil. Raskolnikov's "resurrection" appears to remove the division in his personality that has plagued him till this moment: "But he was resurrected, and he knew this, felt it completely with his entire renewed being, and she [Sonia]—she lived only through his life! . . . Instead of dialectics, life had stepped in, and in his consciousness something completely different had to be produced."[29]

Even more explicit is the scene in which Alesha, having undergone his own spiritual crisis, finds the truth and is restored to wholeness. He has prayed by the body of Father Zosima and, hearing Father Paissy read the Gospel story of the wedding at Cana of Galilee, has resolved for himself the problem of miracles. He now throws himself down and kisses the earth. He is seized with a desire to forgive everyone for everything and to beg forgiveness for everyone.

> But with each moment, he felt clearly and as if palpably that something steadfast and unshakable, like this heavenly vault, had entered his soul. Some sort of idea had come to rule in his mind—and for his whole life and for ever and ever. He had fallen to the earth a weak youth and had arisen a warrior steadfast for his whole life, and he was aware of this and felt it suddenly, in just this minute of his rapture."[30]

### 2(B) The Dissolution of the Individual Is an Evil

A passage I quoted earlier comes to mind here: "What are you writing about duality? But this is the most common trait in people . . . those, of course, who are not entirely ordinary. . . . You're related to me, as it were, because this *division-in-two* in you is exactly like the one that exists and always has existed in me. It's a great torment but at the same time a great delight."[31] This is what Dostoevsky wrote to Ekaterina Fedorovna Iunge in April 1880. But the torment of splits and duality is not always offset by great delight. The two most dramatic manifestations of splits in Dostoevsky's fictional world are madness and suicide.

This statement should not require much documentation, and it applies to characters both good and evil. Myshkin's descent into madness at the end of *The Idiot* shows the ultimate failure of his nature to unite behind either the earthly or the heavenly. Rogozhin's shows the ultimate failure of *his* nature to unite behind the ambition to bend another human being entirely to his own will. Ivan Karamazov's madness is expressed through his creation of a double, something hardly surprising in a man who is at war with himself from the beginning. The dissolution of the individual is thus either the ultimate outcome of an evil personality or the ultimate evil outcome of a good personality. In either case, it is evil.

As to suicide, in Dostoevsky's world some of those who take their own lives do so purely out of despair, but others do so as a result of the same sort of deep split that leads to madness. Anyone who wants to have a sense of the larger cultural meaning of suicide in nineteenth-century Russia (and, for that matter, in Western Europe, too) should read Irina Paperno's excellent book, *Suicide as a Cultural Institution in Dostoevsky's Russia*. Paperno rightly suggests early on that the act of suicide intrinsically indicates a split, because, as legal philosophers see it, suicide is "a crime in which the perpetrator and the victim are the same person," and as psychologists see it suicide represents a case where self as subject and self as object are confused. From both perspectives, the individual is split.[32] In Dostoevsky's characters, naturally, the split involves more than just the existence, in one person, of an active and a passive element. The grand suicides in Dostoevsky's works are committed by men who are unable to see their way out of a metaphysical or specifically moral dilemma. Think of Svidrigailov, in *Crime and Punishment*, who kills himself after a haunting dream in which (apparently) one of his young sexual victims taunts and defies him. Think of Kirillov, the inventor of the man-God, who kills himself in an effort to demonstrate that man can become God. Finally, of course, think of Stavrogin, who kills himself after having unsuccessfully sought redemption in the cell of Bishop Tikhon.

Statements 2(A) and 2(B) point to a peculiar feature of individual personality in Dostoevsky's world. *Wholeness* may be correlated with *will*. The breakdown of the individual is frequently a failure of will. Shortly before Myshkin's first epileptic fit, as he is being drawn irresistibly to his fateful encounter with Rogozhin, we read this: "An extraordinary, inexpressible desire, almost a temptation, suddenly overpowered his entire will."[33] We see the connection particularly vividly in some of Dostoevsky's titanically evil characters, since for such characters individual will and its unconditional imposition on others is the supreme goal. Svidrigailov, for example, represents the perfect living correlate to Raskolnikov's extraordinary-man theory. The extraordinary man is the one who may, with raw force and at any cost, assert his will over others. Svidrigailov, as the "living" exemplar of that theory, is of course no Napoleon; he is a vice-ridden petty landowner with a hankering for younger women, and especially little girls. But his "program," if it is proper to speak of one, consists of imposing his will completely on others and attempting to negate their will by requiring them to surrender it *voluntarily* to him. When Dunia refuses to give herself to him of her own accord, demonstrating the practical impossibility of her assailant's program, Svidrigailov has no choice but to commit the ultimate self-splitting act.

Much the same may be said of Stavrogin, who in some ways is merely a socially grander and more deep-thinking version of Svidrigailov. The simple fact that Stavrogin is intentionally indifferent to the content of the teachings by which he submits others to his will suggests that it is the submitting of others to his will that is important, not the Slavophilism he preaches to Shatov on Tuesday or the atheistic humanism he preaches to Kirillov on Wednesday. Will those who surround him allow themselves to be buried in his will? That is the driving question. Convert Shatov, convert Kirillov, marry Marie Lebiadkin, molest a little girl and let her hang herself—we don't need to be persuaded that it's all an experiment. The aim is to demonstrate, through the subjugating power of one's own despotic will, the wholeness of one's personality, for without wholeness the individual cannot rid himself of the "prejudicial" belief in good and evil in order to commit acts designed precisely to test the limits of the human power to do evil.

But as we know too well, such experiments invariably end in disaster, in fact, precisely in the dissolution of the individual. Svidrigailov doubts his ability to conquer and repents of his actions, so he shoots himself; Stavrogin doubts his ability to remain free of prejudice and repents of his actions, so he hangs himself. Kirillov has a peculiarly apt way of putting this paradox, in a nutty, presuicide comment to Peter Verkhovensky (who is itching to get the philosophizing over with so that Kirillov can finally keep his promise to blow his brains out): "If God exists, then all will is his, and I can't escape from his will. If not, then all will is mine, and I'm obliged to proclaim my self-will [*svoevolie*]. . . . I'm obliged to shoot myself, because the fullest point of my self-will is to kill myself."[34]

The thought is funny when it's expressed in this ridiculous way, but it's actually one more expression of the idealism that takes us ordinary earthlings toward a necessary goal that will dissolve us. This idealism operates not only for the earth-bound path that Svidrigailov, Stavrogin, and Kirillov attempt to follow, but also for the heaven-bound path that other characters attempt to follow. Prince Myshkin is the best example, since the division in him between the earthly and heavenly, in particular the weakness of his earthly side, robs his will of the ability to follow a heaven-bound path. *The Brothers Karamazov* contains a curious reference to a related phenomenon, one in which we exercise our will in order ultimately to renounce it. The reference occurs early in the book, in the chapter titled "Elders." "What is an elder [*starets*]?" asks the narrator. He continues:

> An elder is someone who takes your soul, your will into his own soul and his own will. Once you've chosen an elder, you renounce your own will and give it over to him in full obedience, with full self-renunciation. This novitiate, this frightful school of life—the man who has thus condemned himself accepts it of his own free will, in the hope that after the long novitiate he will conquer himself, master himself to the point where he may finally attain, through an entire life's worth of obedience, perfect freedom, that is, attain freedom from himself and thus avoid the fate of those who have lived their whole lives without discovering themselves within themselves.[35]

The Russian word *volia* can be variously translated as "will" and "freedom." Russian has another word for "freedom": *svoboda*. To a certain extent, the meanings of the two words overlap, but one uses only *volia* to signify freedom of will and generally *svoboda* to signify freedom *from* something. The latter word is the one I have translated as "freedom" in the previous passage. So the will eliminates the will, and this produces freedom from self.

It turns out that the narrator is following a train of thought Dostoevsky took up a few years earlier in *The Adolescent*, where we see a real preoccupation with the same paradoxical act. Early in the novel, for example, Arkady Dolgoruky, the hero, is explaining his "idea," namely, to become a Rothschild. The whole aim of the idea, he says, is isolation (*uedinenie*), in addition to power. "Yes," he exclaims, "my 'idea' is the fortress in which I may always, on any occasion, hide myself away from everyone. . . . And you should know that what I need is my vice-ridden will, *all* of it, solely in order to prove to myself that I have the strength to give it up."[36] Thus an assertion of both the will and the integrity of the person (isolation) leads to renunciation of the will.

Later we read about a period in the life of Versilov (the hero's biological father), during which he gives himself over to the project of tormenting himself through discipline, "the very same that monks employ." "Gradually and through methodical practice," Versilov explains, "you overcome your will, beginning with the silliest and pettiest things, and you finish by completely overcoming your will and becoming free."[37]

Versilov embodies another type of assault on the integrity of personality, the one caused by the phenomenon of doubling. It's hardly worth saying that the theme of the double preoccupied Dostoevsky from his earliest days. We have *The Double*, his youthful, not entirely successful salute to a tradition to which E.T.A. Hoffmann, Ludwig Tieck, and Edgar Allan Poe had already contributed. The narrator-hero of *Notes from Underground* doubles himself in order to give voice to a wholly imaginary group of antagonists. Raskolnikov, as Bakhtin shows, doubles himself in the various incarnations of himself that I mentioned in Chapter Four. Apart from this, he continually carries on dialogues with himself in which one tendency debates with another. The list goes on and on. But in *The Adolescent*, we read a kind of philosophical description of doubling, one that includes a reference to the will. The description appears in the final chapter of the novel, where the narrator offers some final reflections on his father. How to account for Versilov's conduct? It would be wrong, Dolgoruky explains, to declare him completely insane but permissible to say that he has a double (*dvoinik*, the title of the earlier short novel). What exactly is a double? "A double, at least according to a certain medical book by a certain expert (a book that I subsequently made a point of reading), is nothing other than a first step in a particular, fairly serious disorder of the soul that can lead to a rather unhappy outcome." Versilov refers to his own disorder as a "division-in-two of his feelings and will."[38] "Division-in-two" (*razdvoenie*) is the same word Dostoevsky used in his response to Iunge.[39] To be sure, the separation of the will from feelings (I'm assuming Versilov means this, rather than that his feelings are divided in two and his will is divided in two) is not the same thing as the will's own efforts to deny itself, but it certainly suggests a division in the individual, suggests that the will is involved, and indicates that the division is bad.

Thus the end of the path along which the will takes us when it asserts itself is division, dissolution. This is true whether the will takes us in the direction of "Christ's heaven" or the opposite. Svidrigailov ends up losing the integrity of his self, just as do those characters who seek to employ their will to achieve the ultimate freedom from self. Application of the will leads to its own negation, which means to negation of the individual person.

So, what precisely is the place of religion and belief in all this? At first glance, our two pairs of statements appear to display a simple division as regards religious issues. Statements 1(A) and 1(B) are both conceived in connection with what Dostoevsky presents in several works as the ultimate religious experience, and both appear to refer to the heavenly "end" of the path I've described. If "Christ's heaven," as the author calls it in his Masha entry, is characterized as a state in which individuality has been exploded into a grand synthesis with the all, then from the perspective of that state the dissolution of individuality is clearly good, while the integrity of individuality is clearly bad. Similarly, statements 2(A) and 2(B) appear to be conceived in connection with what Dostoevsky presents as the earthly end of the path. If the material world is characterized as a state in which some degree of individual separateness is an unavoidable fact, then from the perspective of that state the dissolution of individuality is clearly bad, while the integrity of individuality is clearly good. If we decide to take our description of 2(A) and 2(B) a step farther and declare the material world at its limit to be ultimately evil (the state in which men of gigantic will can force others into complete subjugation), then our model becomes neatly symmetrical: heaven versus earthly hell, the godly versus the godless, the dissolved individual versus the ultimately self-asserting individual.

But things are not so simple. The pilgrim who journeys toward Christ's heaven is a Christian and therefore knowingly and gladly accepts the dissolution that waits at the end. The man of will who journeys toward the hell at the opposite end, however, does not accept or necessarily expect the dissolution that awaits him. The whole model, in other words, is constructed from the perspective of religious belief in Christ's heaven. One who adopts this perspective knowingly accepts the existence of both the heavenly end and the earthly end, while one who does not adopt it knowingly accepts only the existence of the earthly end.

As in so many other aspects of Dostoevsky's religion, we are dealing here with an issue that is clearly fundamental to religion (the nature of the individual self) but that betrays no peculiar connection with Dostoevsky's own native religious tradition. Despite any similarities his conception might bear to that of any other writer, this seems to be the area where we find Dostoevsky at his most idiosyncratic. To be sure, it is in the most general sense a Jewish-Christian notion that inspires his musings on the subject of the individual in the Masha entry, and we might connect the idea of dissolution with one or another Christian eschatology (belief about the end of time), but the structure of this thinking is, once again, essentially idealist. If the self lives between two states of dissolution, this is because it lives between two ideals, as we saw earlier. Of course, "idealist" does not exclude Christian or religious, but it also does not *imply* Christian or religious. With Dostoevsky, the tendency to think ideals appears logically to precede the tendency to think religion.

But in fact, the model I'm speaking of takes us only through the end of *The Devils*. *The Idiot* and *The Devils* are the two novels that look at the two sides of the paradox of faith and lead us to the view that the two sides are almost symmetrical. As we've seen, though, both sides of the paradox are constructed from a perspective founded in at least an awareness of religion and religious faith. Stavrogin pursues an earthly path not out of ignorance of the heavenly path but, quite the contrary, out of an impulse to reject this path and defy the ideal that lies at its end. But we cannot make the correlative claim of Myshkin. It's *not* true that for Myshkin the existence of the earthly is in question; instead, it's true that for Myshkin the earthly needs to be overcome through the dissolution I've been speaking about. This is because, when it comes right down to it, in this system the heavenly lies higher than the earthly. *The Brothers Karamazov* addresses this imbalance by reasserting the earthly *within* religion—but at a huge price.

## SO WHERE DOES THIS LEAVE US?

Things don't look too hopeful at this point. We've sought a set of beliefs we might attribute to Dostoevsky and discovered that, when it comes to purely religious issues (fundamental questions of belief, not those mixed up with nationalism), the most we can say is that Dostoevsky *sometimes* embraced a particular set of beliefs. As we've discovered, when it comes to issues that are not purely religious (those not strictly tied up with theological concepts and fundamental questions of belief), the religious element practically disappears in a sea of earthly notions, like nationalism. Now we discover that as Dostoevsky addresses (in dramatic form) fundamental questions of belief, he leaves us at an impasse from which there appears to be no escape. The reciprocally heterogeneous natures of earthly beings and absolutes of any sort render unrealizable any ambition to believe perfectly or disbelieve perfectly. What's more, the unstable nature of the individual renders suspect the status of the thing that's doing the believing or disbelieving.

These facts must certainly bear an intimate connection with an outlook that forbids a consistent and prolonged commitment to a given set of beliefs. Let's overlook, for the moment, the problematic status of the individual. If the attempt to believe *anything* perfectly is irrevocably doomed to failure, then any attempt to assert a belief is always going to look like little more than a "try on" of a sensation that merely approximates what we might experience if we ever could fully embrace the belief. Since our natures condemn us to be "neither [perfectly] hot nor [perfectly] cold" but only lukewarm, we're free to experiment, to test but never to reach limits. This is essentially the story of Stavrogin. A lukewarm man immersed in the filth of earthly existence is free to teach Slavophilism to one friend, teach atheistic humanism to another, and pursue a course of atheistic negation on his own.

Many have spoken of how both *The Idiot* and *The Devils* are failures artistically. Maybe they're right. But there is no doubt that both books *describe* failures, and not only the failures of the heroes. They also describe our necessarily unsuccessful attempt to reach what are presented to us not only as mutually antithetical goals but also as ultimately the *only* two possible goals. Shatov's Slavophilism and Kirillov's atheistic humanism hardly qualify as directed toward these goals. Even though the question of belief is at least ostensibly integral to both of them, they are filled with all the silliness and triviality of stubbornly small minds. These are "impure" systems of belief because they are corrupted—in Shatov's case, with so much specific historical reality, and in Kirillov's with so much foolish religion. Shatov and Kirillov are as lukewarm as they come, because neither can begin even to *envision* an absolute that is (as absolutes are by definition) free of impurity. Stavrogin, by contrast, though he served as master to these two petty apostles, possesses the breadth of mind to envision this sort of absolute. And Myshkin, of course, possesses the illness to experience a presentiment of this sort of absolute.

Where this leaves us is with the notion that Dostoevsky's mode of thought is idealist through and through, but in his own peculiar sense. In one version of idealism, there is an ideal realm that is unattainable because it lies on the other side of an impenetrable wall. In Dostoevsky's system, there is an ideal realm, and I am obliged to stand on a path that leads to it. The realm is unattainable here because the path is separated from it by a gap. The gap is what distinguishes Dostoevsky's view from Hegel's. In Hegel's system, at whatever stage of spiritual development I find myself, I can take comfort from the fact that I am joined with the absolute by the continuum on which I stand. Dostoevsky's continuum never reaches the absolute, yet it is still a continuum that takes me ever and ever closer to the absolutes lying at either end—and no one can escape being on the continuum. So in his world I can at least take comfort from the fact that I am joined with a point *very close* to the absolute. But then I remember this *I* is something that forever hesitates between an unattainable wholeness and an equally unattainable dissolution. This something is what never stands more than very close to the absolute.

## CHAPTER SIX

# "Bathe the Earth with the Tears of Thy Joy"

Earlier I mentioned the Russian kenotic tradition and suggested that Dostoevsky may have had more than a little to do with its creation. Characters such as Sonia Marmeladova and Prince Myshkin, with their natural humility and their attraction to suffering, appear to exemplify a tradition in which these qualities bespeak a spiritual proximity to the Son of God. In the eyes of George Fedotov, who introduced Russian kenoticism to the Western world, the kenosis, or "emptying," by which Christ became a man is a lowering or humiliation (Russian translations of the New Testament render "to empty" with a word that means or suggests humiliation). The kenotic character is thus humble, for humility imitates both Christ's descent from divinity and his comportment on earth. Because Christ, as a corporeal being, suffered in the flesh, we can imitate him by voluntarily accepting suffering.

This is essentially the message of Fedotov's treatment of Russian kenoticism in *The Russian Religious Mind*. He tells the story of Russia's first canonized saints, the princes Boris and Gleb, who, shortly after the Christianization of Russia in the late tenth century, heard that their older brother was plotting against them, inexplicably stopped in their tracks, and without fighting let him murder them. For Fedotov, such voluntary suffering, like humility, is a fundamental feature of kenoticism. In an attempt to show that there is a close link between kenotic comportment and the Russian national character, Fedotov oddly identifies first one, then the other as enjoying priority. "The act of nonresistance is a national Russian feature, an authentic religious discovery of the newly-converted Russian Christians," he says, as if, at the time of Russia's conversion in the late tenth century C.E., an innate tendency toward nonresistance in the people was just waiting for kenoticism to come along and validate it as a Christian virtue. A moment later, he says this: "Through the lives of the holy sufferers as through the Gospels, the image of the meek and suffering Savior entered the heart of the Russian nation as the most holy of its spiritual treasures," as if the kenotic character, like the devils who enter the herd of swine in the Gospel story, abruptly took possession of an otherwise indifferent populace.[1]

Any way we look at it, not long after the baptism of Russia the kenotic virtues, either because they were there in the first place or because Christianity introduced them, were inseparable from the Russian character. In fact, the way Fedotov sees it, popular belief rather than the church was responsible for the canonization of Boris and Gleb, since the two voluntary sufferers were canonized over the initial resistance of the highest ecclesiastical authority in Eastern Orthodoxy, the Greek Metropolitan.[2] The same is true of the prime exemplar of Russian kenoticism, the eleventh-century saint Theodosius, who founded the Monastery of the Caves in Kiev; the virtues of "social humiliation and degradation" were innate in him, but they also represented "the most national of his characteristics."[3]

To Fedotov, Theodosius's style of kenoticism signals a true focus on both the earthly ministry and the earthly nature of Jesus. The Christology of this saint thus represents a genuine departure from the prevailing Byzantine one that we find in a fifth-century Alexandrian bishop by the name of Cyril. Here's how Fedotov puts the contrast between the two men: "Theodosius draws his main religious inspiration from the contemplation of the human nature of Christ (Cyril [draws his from] the divine), of His descent to earth (not His ascension, as with Cyril). In the light of this Christology, one is fully entitled to term the spirituality of Theodosius as 'kenotic,' using the Pauline word of 'kenosis' or 'emptying' of Christ." Even so, as Fedotov explains a page later, the kenotic virtues are a path back to Christ: "Obedience is not an exercise for eradicating self-will and shaping another higher self. It is a direct way to Christ." Kenotic behavior signifies "following Christ";

"Boris and Gleb followed Christ in their sacrificial deaths—the climax of His kenosis—as Theodosius did in His poverty and humiliation."[4]

But Fedotov has clearly forgotten to explain something here. The story of Boris and Gleb, which is the story of voluntarily accepted "sacrificial deaths," is in no way the same as the story of Theodosius, which is the story of a life lived in poverty and humiliation. For Fedotov, the whole point of the canonization of Boris and Gleb is that, because there was nothing heroic about their deaths and nothing heroic about *them*, the Russian people must certainly have set a great deal of stock by *voluntary suffering* if they favored this canonization despite the brothers' lack of heroism or other admirable qualities. There *was*, however, something exemplary about Theodosius: his *humility* and his engagement in this world. He made a point, for example, of building his monastery right next to the city, so as to bring it "into close relationship with the lay society."[5]

There are so many problems with Fedotov's explanation of the cult of voluntary suffering in the legends of Boris and Gleb that it's impossible to list them all without wandering quite some distance from the subject of Dostoevsky. But I'll mention a few. Medievalist Gail Lenhoff has devoted a book-length study to the cult of Russia's two "martyred princes," examining the various versions of the legends and the sources of those versions. Her book is in no way intended as an attack on Fedotov, whom she mentions very few times, but it nonetheless casts serious doubt on his interpretations.

To begin with, among the versions of the legend there is no absolute agreement on the notion that the two princes were, apart from their martyrdom, nonheroic or remote from virtue. In fact, in one important source Boris, Gleb, their father Vladimir, and one other brother all possess the ideal qualities of exemplary Christian rulers.[6] Next, as Lenhoff shows, there is not even agreement on the claim that Boris and Gleb were ever venerated *at all* immediately after their murders, and to the extent that they were, she shows, it was for any number of possible reasons.[7] In those accounts of the deaths that stress the voluntary nature of the princes' surrender, the motive is not necessarily imitation of Christ. In one source, Boris's motive for giving himself up is his desire to obey God's commandment to love and obey his brother. His martyrdom thus arises not from its resemblance to that of Christ but from the sanctity of his obedience to God's will.[8] In another source, Lenhoff explains, Boris's refusal to fight has two possible meanings: from the perspective of the church, it is a sign of his "willingness to give up his life for the sake of the common good," while from the perspective of his guards, it is "an abdication of his princely responsibilities."[9] Neither of these interpretations is consistent with Fedotov's notion of voluntary suffering as an expression of kenoticism. What's more, a number of sources support their moral point of view on the two princes with scriptural citations drawn largely from the Hebrew Bible, which would certainly weaken Fedotov's assertion that the canonization of Boris and Gleb was an expression of the popular imagination (what did the common Russian people know of the Hebrew Bible?).

To complicate matters even further, when Fedotov comes to compile his *Treasury of Russian Spirituality* (an anthology of primary texts by Russian religious writers) four years after he published the first volume of *The Russian Religious Mind*, he seems to have forgotten that the kenotic ideal has anything to do with voluntary suffering. In the introduction to his selections from the works of Saint Theodosius, he refers to the eleventh-century monk as "the first representative of kenoticism." The entire discussion of the great saint's kenoticism has to do with his humility in imitation of Christ. Suffering is never mentioned.[10]

This notwithstanding, Western critics have fallen in love with the idea that suffering is a kenotic virtue, peculiarly present in Russian Orthodoxy, and that Dostoevsky, because his works focus so heavily on suffering, consistently and almost unthinkingly expressed a sentiment simply indigenous to the culture in which he was raised. We find this idea in Ellis Sandoz's *Political Apocalypse*, which I mentioned in Chapter One. Without bothering to explain himself, Sandoz refers to "the kenotic or humiliated and suffering Christ." He writes, "The doctrine of kenoticism is dominant in Dostoevsky's 'word.' It is that every disciple of Christ must suffer in this world, and that all innocent and voluntary suffering in the world is done in the name and for the sake of Christ."[11] What sense would these statements make without Fedotov (who is cited in a footnote to the second passage)? A recent collection of essays about Dostoevsky and Christianity contains numerous references to kenoticism and includes a casual remark about "a kenotic Christology in which innocent suffering is actually redemptive."[12] Given the absence of any significant tradition, outside the works of Fedotov, associating the adjective *kenotic* with the redemptive value of innocent suffering, the only conceivable source for this remark is, once again, Fedotov.

The Russian kenotic tradition that Fedotov refers to, or to put it more precisely the use of the word *kenotic* to denote broadly a cult of humility and more narrowly a cult of voluntary suffering in Russian Orthodox Christianity, appears to be very much his own idiosyncratic contribution to the West's understanding of the religious tradition that allegedly appears in the works of Dostoevsky. To identify humility as a specifically kenotic virtue is to set humility apart and suggest that it is a trait prized only by certain sects of Christianity, rather than something completely essential to Christianity generally speaking. To identify voluntary suffering as a kenotic virtue might be intellectually defensible, on the grounds that only an "emptied" Christ could physically suffer and that consequently a Christian cult of voluntary suffering is necessarily premised on recognition of the kenosis. But the point in Fedotov is to tell us about the alleged cult of suffering in Russian Christianity, so how does it advance our understanding to call the cult kenotic and thereby to associate it with a virtue (humility) that practically every Christian sect in the world would embrace?

So the scholarly practice of invoking the kenotic tradition in connection with Dostoevsky's works ends up relying on a form of circular logic. First we posit a pair of traits (humility and voluntary suffering) as constituting and defining Russian kenoticism. Then we measure characters in Dostoevsky's novels against these traits for the purpose of determining whether these saints and characters are kenotic. Then we determine that the saints and characters are or are not kenotic, because . . . well, they possess or do not possess the traits we listed at the beginning. But our authority for saying that these are the traits that constitute and define kenoticism is usually, directly or indirectly, George Fedotov, who didn't do a particularly good job of establishing historical credibility for the tradition that in his own eyes is so fundamental to the Russian religious mind.

One thing, however, is clear: whether or not there was a kenotic tradition in Russia like the one Fedotov described, there is no doubt that *Dostoevsky* was interested in the two topics of suffering and humility. It's also clear that he saw the two as associated with religion. To me, this seems to be the truly important point. Take suffering: God will send Raskolnikov new life once he accepts his suffering, Sonia tells the man who murdered her best friend;[13] Stavrogin tells Bishop Tikhon that he seeks "measureless suffering," because he wants to forgive himself.[14] Or take humility: Sonia, a humiliated, fallen creature, reads the Gospel with Raskolnikov;[15] Myshkin finds the whole essence of Christianity in a humble peasant woman as she sees her baby smile for the first time.[16]

But what's not clear is that Dostoevsky necessarily saw voluntary suffering and humility as always and necessarily linked with *each other*, as Fedotov does. Voluntary suffering, whether or not it's associated with religion, is often the expression of vanity and egoism in Dostoevsky's works. The connection between suffering and egoism, in fact, is one of Dostoevsky's favorite themes, appearing throughout his career. For example, in a characteristically unsubtle ploy to alert his reader to this theme in his melodramatic exploration of egoism, *The Insulted and Injured* (1860–61), he italicized the phrase "egoism of suffering" in a key passage, to explain the behavior of Nellie, one of the central characters.[17] The painter in *Crime and Punishment* who falsely confesses to Raskolnikov's crime does so, Porfiry Petrovich the police inspector tells Raskolnikov, because he is a religious sectarian, specifically a *raskol'nik*, and therefore wishes to "accept his suffering."[18] Sectarians like this, Porfiry Petrovich explains, accept suffering for no other reason than that "one must suffer." Admittedly we learn little about the painter's motives beyond what the inspector says, but his utter lack of any actual responsibility for the crime might easily lead us to suspect that, even if the painter is atoning for something (say, the dissipated life he's been living in the city), there's some measure of unreasoned self-gratification in his action.

So in Dostoevsky's universe, voluntary suffering sometimes is and sometimes is not linked with religious fervor. Whether his fascination with the phenomenon stems from the fact of his belonging to the same *Volk* that developed the cult of Boris and Gleb is difficult to say, though it seems unlikely. Tareev, who introduced the term *kenosis* to the Russian lexicon, speaks of suffering in his treatment of the subject but says nothing about any Christian cult of voluntary suffering. It seems quite possible (though certainly difficult to prove) that Dostoevsky partly inspired the voluntary-suffering component of Fedotov's tradition.

Still, the terms *kenosis* and *kenoticism* can be conceptually useful in a discussion of Dostoevsky, because they help describe an approach to Christianity and to the figure of Christ that *is* historically relevant to him. What's necessary, however, is to use the terms with reference to the *process* they denote (the act of emptying). Whether or not the kenosis implies voluntary suffering in addition to humility, it may be viewed in two ways, and it's really a matter of where the emphasis lies. The virtues associated with it may be regarded as the means by which we reach back up and attempt to touch Christ, or they may be regarded as the means by which Christ reached down and touched *us*. If humility is a kenotic virtue, then when we behave humbly either we are doing so in order to approximate the origin of that humility (the prekenosis Christ) or we are doing so because the postkenosis Christ was humble, lived in this world, and thus sanctified our earthly life. One emphasis places us (and Christ, for that matter) near heaven; the other places us (and Christ) firmly in the world.

The second of these emphases is the one many German Protestant theologians adopted in the middle decades of the nineteenth century and the one we often find in postmedieval discussions of kenosis outside Russia. In the 1840s and 1850s, Germany produced a multitude of theological works that emphasized, to varying degrees, the earthly nature of Jesus. No theory of this period denies the divine *origin* of Christ; some insist the divine nature remains with him during his earthly ministry, while others assert that the kenosis resulted in a wholly human Son of God. But the lens is now clearly trained on the earthly ministry, as in the work of such biographers as David Strauss (and later, in France, Ernest Renan). Claude Welch, a scholar of nineteenth-century Protestant theology, describes it this way: "The idea of kenosis seemed a way to conserve the fundamental interests of the classical 'two-natures' Christology and yet to recognize (in a way that the traditional formulas had not) a genuinely human figure in Jesus of Nazareth, a person with actual human limitations of knowledge and power, with a 'gradually dawning infant consciousness' and a real growth—a person for whom sleep and death were real."[19] He gives as the most extreme example Wolfgang Friedrich Gess, a theologian who sees the final result of the kenosis not as a being possessing one person and two natures, according to a doctrine that has been the norm in Christianity since the fifth century C.E., but as a being who is exclusively a man.[20]

Humility and engagement in this world: this appears to be the emphasis that interests Dostoevsky (who did not know the word *kenosis* and who was not directly familiar with the German kenotic theologians) by the time he gets to *The Brothers Karamazov*. This is not to say that this novel or his other late works take a position specifically on the divinity or humanity of Jesus; it's simply to say that, like the German kenotic theologians, he focused on the world as a realm for religious activity and that for him a Christian (or for that matter non-Christian) ministry unashamedly takes place in this world.

## BEING/ABIDING IN THE WORLD

Before he dies, Father Zosima quotes to Alesha the Gospel verse that serves as the epigraph to *The Brothers Karamazov*: "Unless a grain of wheat falls into the earth and dies, it remains just a single grain; but it if dies, it bears much fruit"(John 12:24). He then says, "Remember this. But thee, Alesha, have I many times blessed in my life for thy countenance. Know this. . . . I conceive of thee thus: thou wilt depart from these walls and wilt dwell in the world like a monk."[21]

If Zosima's injunction is meant to follow from the Gospel verse, he's doing something odd because he expresses a sentiment precisely opposite to the one Jesus expressed immediately following this verse: "Those who love their life lose it, and those who hate their life in this world will keep it for eternal life"(John 12:25). But coming from Zosima, the sentiment can hardly surprise anyone. As we read immediately after this scene, in the "Vita" that Alesha has composed, Zosima is all about loving life in *this* world and loving the earth itself—in fact, he's about this far more than he's about any traditional version of Christianity, Russian or non-Russian.

Zosima's earth worship is truly astounding in its departure from the sense of Jesus' message. He passionately embraces the custom of falling to the earth, kissing it, and bathing it with one's tears. "If everyone should abandon thee and even drive thee away by force," he has said, "then, being left alone, fall to the earth and kiss it, wet it with thy tears, and the earth will bear fruit from thy tears, even though none shall have seen or heard thee in thy solitude."[22] Again, having enjoined his disciple to accept his guilt before his fellows and to be humble, he commands him thus: "Love to cast thyself down on the earth and kiss it. Kiss the earth and tirelessly, insatiably love, love all, love everything, seek rapture and this ecstasy. Wet the earth with the tears of thy joy, and love these thy tears."[23]

Dostoevsky's readers have heard these expressions before. Sonia lists kissing the earth as one of the requisite acts in Raskolnikov's repentance for his crime. In *The Devils*, Marie Lebiadkin quotes an old woman at church who spoke of mother earth and watering it with one's tears. Shatov, in his Slavophilic tirade, commands Stavrogin to kiss the earth and drench it with his tears. None of these figures is what you might call a Christian in any traditional sense of the word. Even Sonia, who agrees to read from the Gospel to Raskolnikov, represents a set of practices that either need not or do not conform to Christian belief, Orthodox or other. "Accept your suffering" is not necessarily or exclusively Christian, despite what Fedotov and his followers might say. Forgiving the murderer is certainly consonant with many Christian outlooks, but there is no reason to see it as necessarily tied to Christ in the mind of Sonia. No, Sonia's is a religion of the earth and of suffering, just as is the worldview (if you can call it that) of the lunatic Marie. Shatov, as we've already seen, is anything but a religious man of any kind, unless you consider fanatical nationalism and the absence of belief in God to be a religion.

Be all this as it may, there's no question that Alesha takes to heart the words of his elder. After listening to the Gospel account of Christ's first miracle and immediately before validating Father Zosima's prediction, he throws himself down on the earth:

> He didn't know why he embraced it, he could give no account of why he so irrepressibly wanted to kiss it, kiss it all, but he kissed it, weeping, sobbing, and bathing it with his tears, and he ecstatically swore to love it, to love it forever and ever. "Bathe the earth with the tears of thy joy, and love these thy tears" rang in his soul. . . . Three days later he quit the monastery, which accorded with the words of his late elder, who had commanded him "to dwell in the world."[24]

There are Christian precedents for the commandment "to dwell in the world." For example, the fourth-century Saint Alexis, "Man of God," who came to occupy a prominent position in Russian Orthodox hagiography, is known for having dwelt in the world in place of cloistering himself. Dostoevsky mentioned Alexis several times, and his wife claimed in her memoirs that the late author deeply esteemed the early saint.[25] But Zosima's injunction goes much farther than anything Alexis might have said or done, just as his earth worship extends to far more than kissing the earth and bathing it in tears. It's all-encompassing. "Brothers," he used to tell his fellow monks, "fear not the sin of people; love man even in his sin, for this is the likeness of God's love and is the summit of love on earth. Love all God's creation and the universe and every grain of sand. Every leaf and every ray of light shall ye love."[26] When he knows he is seconds away from death, he falls to the earth and kisses it, praying.

## THE ENDS ALMOST MEET AGAIN

The reader of *The Brothers Karamazov* won't fail to notice that the "opposites" Ivan Karamazov and Father Zosima are very much the same in one important respect: they love the earth. It's astonishing to what lengths Dostoevsky went to establish this parallel (in addition to others I've already mentioned). "I want to live, and I live, though perhaps contrary to all logic,"

Ivan exclaims to Alesha when the brothers "get to know one another."
"Maybe I don't believe in the order of things, but I treasure the sticky little
leaves that blossom in the springtime, I treasure the blue sky, and I treasure
certain people—you know, the ones you love without having any idea why."
He plans to travel to Western Europe, which he describes as "a graveyard."
There he will carry out a rather odd plan: "I shall fall to the earth and kiss
these gravestones and cry over them, all the while convinced with all my
heart that all this has long been a graveyard and nothing more." Once again:
"I love the sticky little springtime leaves, the blue sky, and there you have it!
It's not a matter of mind or logic—it's a matter of loving with your entire
being, from deep down inside."[27] The sticky leaves come up in the conversation twice more before the brothers are finished.

The match-up with Zosima is perfect: loving the earth and its products,
kissing the ground and shedding tears over it, loving people irrationally. For
Zosima, as for Ivan, children enjoy a special status because they are without
sin ("Love little children especially, for they too are without sin, like angels,"
he exhorts his disciples).[28] There are differences, of course. The ground to
which Ivan imagines falling is located in the graveyard that is Europe, he
loves only certain people, and he values all children—*because* they are children—but not all adults. Zosima, by contrast, commands us to love every
grain of sand, every leaf, every ray of light, and, despite the special status of
children, *all* God's creatures—adults, animals, even suicides. They both profess a love for the earth but understand contrasting things by it. One might
be tempted to say that, as in the case of Bishop Tikhon's atheist and man of
most perfect faith, the ends almost meet here. Yet the situation in *The Brothers Karamazov* differs greatly from the one in *The Idiot* and *The Devils*. To
begin with, the earth cannot be said to represent the end of a continuum, as
faith and atheism did for Bishop Tikhon. How could it? The earth is, well,
the earth. It's the point of departure for the twin journeys that Tikhon describes. Because the earth is nothing more than the earth, it's not ideal as
were the ends of the twin journeys Tikhon conceived of. In *The Brothers
Karamazov*, the ends are real-all-too-real and human-all-too-human. Here is
truly where the earthly has come to redress the imbalance of the idealist
model in those earlier works. Zosima may be more inclusive, and his worldview may sound more Christian than Ivan's, in the sense that it promotes
the forgiveness of sins and purposefully overlooks the *apparent* absence of
justice on earth, but, like Ivan's, it ends right where it began: here on earth.
No journey, no true ideal.

So this is how the "extreme blasphemy" of book five gets repudiated in book six! In light of the love for mother earth, it makes even more sense than ever that each book somehow represented the "culminating point of the novel," as Dostoevsky with seeming contradiction explained it to his editor. The closer we get to Ivan's ultimate blasphemy, the closer we get to the earth and its sticky leaves. The closer we get to what is meant to pass for Christianity in Zosima and his disciple Alesha, the closer we get to . . . the earth.

A PATENT ABSURDITY AND A PATENT
HERESY: THE RUSSIAN CHRIST

By the time you've read *The Idiot* and *The Devils*, you'll no longer be surprised to meet up with Slavophilism in Dostoevsky's fictional works, and you're likely to be aware that before he started work on *The Brothers Karamazov* he was turning out his own personal brand of religious nationalism in the *Diary of a Writer*. Prince Myshkin's Slavophilism appeared to come out of the blue quite late in *The Idiot*, so it might even be accurate to say that you shouldn't be surprised *to be surprised* by the appearance of these ideas in the later novel. Still, there can be little doubt that when Father Zosima takes the next step in his earth worship and begins to speak specifically of the *Russian* earth and its sanctity, the author has introduced what appears to be a serious inconsistency. But Zosima does take the next step, so there we have it.

Zosima moves as if seamlessly: he exhorts his disciples to read Luke, the Acts of the Apostles, and the Lives of the Saints; then he sings the praises of the Russian folk (*narod*); and then he declares that "one who doesn't believe in God doesn't believe in God's people."[29] The language grows more explicit in his discourse on the Russian monk. There he speaks of the salvation of the Russian earth and its folk. "The folk will meet the atheist and will conquer him," he goes on to proclaim, "and then the one, Orthodox Rus [he uses the name for the ancient Kievan state] will come to be. Preserve the folk and protect its heart. Bring them up quietly. That is your monastic cause, for this folk is God-bearing,"[30] he says, recalling Shatov's description of the Russian people. In fact, Zosima mentions God and Christ in this connection more than in almost any other; God will save Russia, and we (Russians) are the ones who preserve the image of Christ.[31]

Sergei Hackel, a Russian Orthodox priest, former instructor at the University of Sussex, and widely quoted authority on Russian Orthodoxy, has written that Zosima's creed is quite remote from Orthodox Christianity; it represents a type of "nature mysticism," and it is hardly different from Shatov's Slavophilism. In fact, he claims, Zosima's views closely resemble the nationalism that an Orthodox Church Council in Constantinople in 1872 characterized as *phyletismos*, the heretical belief in the right to establish an autonomous church along purely ethnic lines. The council's decision came in response to the establishment of an autonomous Bulgarian Church. One might say that in the eyes of the council Father Zosima's ideas not only would fly in the face of tradition but would formally qualify as a heresy.

But we hardly need a church council to tell us how odd Zosima's ideas are if they are considered in connection with Christianity. To say that ethnic particularism defies the spirit of the Christian Scriptures is to say something almost too obvious even to pause and think about. It's a patent heresy when it comes from Zosima just as much as it is when it comes from Shatov. "For just as the body is one," wrote Paul to the Corinthians, "and has many members, and all the members of the body, though many, are one body, so it is with Christ. For in the one Spirit we were all baptized into one body—Jews or Greeks, slaves or free—and we were all made to drink of one Spirit. Indeed, the body does not consist of one member but of many."[32] To suggest that God will preserve one nation ahead of or to the exclusion of others is to discard openly one of the fundamental principles by which Jesus distinguished his teachings from those of the Judaism he saw himself as reforming.

But even if one were to argue that various versions of Christianity over the ages have flirted with nationalism and particularism, it still remains true that Zosima's doctrine, like Shatov's, is *unto itself* a patent absurdity. The absurdity of a doctrine like this is far more obvious in a scene with as unappealing and stupid a character as Shatov, who speaks of God as "the synthetic personality of the entire people" and Russians as "the lone God-bearing people on earth" (before going on to confess that he himself does not believe in God). It's perhaps a little less obvious in the earnest and emphatic but fierce and strident man behind the *Diary of a Writer*. The very earnestness of that man can easily divert our attention from the preposterous juxtaposition of the claims that Russia is uniquely Christian among nations and that she represents *vsemirnost'* ("all-world-ness"). Apparently it's least obvious of all in Father Zosima, who is fictional and can therefore be far more compellingly saintly than the man who created him. Yes, absurd is what the doctrine is, no matter how you look at it, and the whole explanation for its absurdity is (1) the conflation of earth, either as Mother Nature or as God's creation, with *this Russian earth*; and (2) the resulting conflation of the truly universal with the *universally Russian*. How can anyone possibly square "love all God's creation" and "you are guilty [in the sense of *answerable*] for everything and everyone" on the one hand and "God will save his [Russian] people, for Russia is great in her humility" on the other?[33]

How can anyone speak of a "Russian Christ" and expect to be taken seriously? Is there a German Christ? A Korean Christ? A Liberian Christ? If the Russians are God's chosen people and Russia has her own God, then what we have is *Judaism* (or, to be more precise, Judaism before the relatively brief, immediately pre-Diaspora period in Jewish history when proselytizing was legitimate). The God of the Hebrew Bible, after all, is the God of a chosen people with whom he has a covenantal relationship: "For you are a people holy to the LORD your God; the LORD your God has chosen you out of all the peoples on earth to be his people, his treasured possession."[34] Yet, like Dostoevsky's "Russian" God, he is to become the God of *all* people: "And the LORD will become king over all the earth; on that day the LORD will be one and his name one."[35] Contrast this with the Christian God: "Or is God the God of Jews only? Is he not the God of Gentiles also? Yes, of Gentiles also."[36] If the Russian God is universal, then he isn't Russian; if he's Russian, then he isn't universal. It's that simple. How else can you possibly play this hand?

Jean Drouilly, author of a book on Dostoevsky's political and religious thought, agrees and says it more forcefully:

> In truth, the system that Dostoevsky presented us was unacceptable. It was teeming with contradictions, and the Christian ideal on which it pretended to be founded not only was incapable of supporting it but flatly contradicted it. . . . The artifice that consisted in affirming that only Russia has preserved Christianity intact and that, as a consequence, Russia is by nature the only one capable of realizing the designs of God on earth was nothing but an artifice and a pseudo-solution.

The reason? "The narrow nationalism that Dostoevsky preached ran counter to the universalist aspiration contained in Christianity."[37] Drouilly, in fact, considers Dostoevsky's thought in general to be incoherent and inconsistent, seeing it as little more than a salad of personal sentiments and disparate, poorly absorbed philosophical systems.[38] I'm not sure I'd go quite this far, but I think Drouilly is right not to take the novelist seriously as the creator of any coherent system of religious thought.

## IS THIS CHRISTIANITY? IS IT EVEN RELIGION?

What does Dostoevsky's "religion" in *The Brothers Karamazov* actually amount to? Think of the funeral speech that concludes the book, unquestionably one of the most sublime things the author (or any author) ever wrote. Only once does the word *God* appear in this speech, and then only as part of an everyday expression ("God forbid") that carries no distinctly religious connotation whatever. There's no reference to Christ. The only reference to religion is the evocation of an afterlife in which we all see each other just as we did on earth. It's a childish picture, totally devoid of any suggestion of judgment, redemption, or salvation. It makes sense that the picture is childish: it's composed by children. Alesha unhesitatingly declares it true, because . . . well, why? Because he himself believes it? Because, though he doesn't believe it, he reckons it's better to keep the children in the fold by letting them enjoy their childishness than to correct them and drive them away? I honestly don't know, but one thing is certain: if this is religion, it's remarkably free of the baggage we might expect in Dostoevsky's world. No "accursed questions" here! No God of Israel sitting in judgment of his chosen people. No suffering Son of God redeeming the sins of *his* people. No human institutions to corrupt the purity of ideal qualities that are inevitably inaccessible to base, fallen human nature. This speech is not about the communion of souls; it's about the communion of people—*children*, for that matter (about whose status Ivan and Zosima are in perfect agreement). It's about eating pancakes: "[This custom] is ancient [read *un-Christian*], eternal, and there's something good in that," Alesha says.[39]

It's not hard to find at least two important reasons why this is so beautiful: it's free of pedantry, and, even better, it's free of all the bawling self-righteousness of Dostoevsky's Slavophilism. Think about it: there's nothing intrinsically wrong with the return to the earth, the sort of pagan pantheism that Zosima professes. As worldviews go, this one has nothing objectionable about it. Its premises are simple and, as far as they go, reasonably consistent internally. What's wrong with loving the earth and everything on it, whether or not you view the earth as the creation of God? What's wrong with loving all one's fellow creatures, even those who have sinned? Acknowledging that some (namely children) are intrinsically free of sin while others (namely adults) are not doesn't disturb the blanket commandment to love them all. If we're going to love them all whether or not they've sinned, then—as far as internal consistency goes—what difference does it make what the source of our conception of sin is?

The problem is not so much that this worldview is different from what we saw in Dostoevsky's earlier works as that now Dostoevsky could not resist converting it into his own personal brand of vulgar, xenophobic, nationalist demagoguery. Suddenly it's Christian, not purely telluric, and suddenly Christianity belongs first to a chosen ethnic group and only later on to all humankind. Suddenly the blanket commandment to love everyone no longer makes sense, since the world is now divided into the favored and the nonfavored. What's more, Dostoevsky's characteristic, idealist habit of mind now appears to be swallowed up in an apocalyptic vision that is as earthly as can be: the vision of a future dominated by a here-and-now, ethnically derived, political entity. I can't help thinking of Southern California's Heaven's Gate cult, whose members donned spanking new running shoes one day in 1997 so that, after their mass suicide, they could eternally travel the universe with extra bounce in their step.

## ASK SOLOV'EV

Toward the beginning of this book, I mentioned Dostoevsky's friendship with the young philosopher Vladimir Solov'ev. When the two made their pilgrimage to the famous Optina Pustyn' monastery in 1877, the twenty-four-year-old Solov'ev had not yet delivered his *Lectures on Godmanhood*, and the fifty-five-year-old Dostoevsky had not yet composed *The Brothers Karamazov*. Much has been written about whether Solov'ev contributed something to the conceptions that Dostoevsky dramatized in his last novel and whether Dostoevsky contributed something to the conceptions that Solov'ev would develop for the remainder of his relatively short life. Of course it's impossible to speak about this matter in its finer details, but there can be no doubt that in 1877 both men were thinking—and would soon be thinking even more—about a universal Christian church and about the place of Russia with respect to Christianity and that church. It's just that Solov'ev came up with a far more plausible way to get to a conception of a universal church than did his much older friend, and this despite the circumstance that the two men had many of the same metaphysical issues on their minds.[40]

If we turn to the *Lectures on Godmanhood*, we quickly see that Solov'ev took as his point of departure an insight almost identical to the one that served as a point of departure for Dostoevsky in the Masha entry and for Ivan in the lead-up to the Legend of the Grand Inquisitor. Solov'ev does not speak of ideal Christian love; instead he speaks directly of the complete inaccessibility of the reality of God. Solov'ev is presenting himself as a philosopher, not as a bereaved husband or as a skeptical Russian former student, so he doesn't indulge in such down-to-earth language as, "Will Masha and I see one another again?" or "In my opinion, it's precisely the people close to you that you can't possibly love and only the ones who are far away that you can."[41] Instead, he puts the problem in Kantian terms:

> It is completely beyond doubt that the reality of the unconditional principle, as something existing in itself and independently of us, the reality of God (like the independent reality in general of any other being besides ourselves) cannot be deduced from pure reason, cannot be proved purely logically. The necessity of the unconditional principle for the higher interests of man, its necessity for the will and for moral activity, for reason and truthful knowledge, for feeling and creation—this necessity makes the actual existence of the divine principle merely *probable* in the highest degree; a full and unconditional conviction in it can be given only by *faith*: and this applies . . . not only to the existence of the unconditional principle but also to the existence of any object and the entire external world.[42]

If Dostoevsky wanted to put his readers to sleep and have Ivan focus from the outset on the existence of God instead of on the realizability of Christian love, he could have his character speak of "the unconditional principle" and then have him move on to speculate about the ideality of the external world. The thought is essentially the same in Solov'ev and in Ivan, including Solov'ev's observation that we can know the divine principle only on faith.

Something else is the same: the impulse to move from the notion of an inaccessible ideal to the notion of a process *toward* the ideal. We've seen how Dostoevsky did this in the Masha entry. By the third lecture, Solov'ev has already begun to speak the language of process, saying that ordinary life itself is a "natural, material-conditional process, subject to the laws of physical necessity."[43] By the tenth lecture, it has become clear that the divine principle, contained within what he terms the "world soul," is both the goal and the "determining principle" of what he calls the "world process": "The eternal idea of the absolute organism must be gradually realized, and the striving toward this realization, the striving toward the incarnation of the divinity in the world, the striving that is general and single in all people and that consequently passes beyond the limits of each person, this striving, which constitutes the inner life and the principle of movement in everything that exists, is the world soul."[44]

But for Solov'ev, the world soul or the divine principle is not the only ideal that can lie at the end of a process such as this. There is also the notion of a universal Christian brotherhood or "church." One of his most dramatic and effective descriptions of this ideal is to be found in his *Three Discourses in Memory of Dostoevsky*, where, oddly enough, he attributes his vision to the late novelist. Dostoevsky's "central idea," Solov'ev says, is "the Christian idea of a free, all-humankind [*vsechelovecheskoe*] unity, an all-world brotherhood in the name of Christ." But as Solov'ev shows, it's not the idea (or ideal) itself; it's how we get to it, and in order to describe the process by which we do he fascinatingly rewrites Dostoevsky so that the novelist can display the rigor of thought we'd expect from a professional Hegelian religious philosopher.

Christianity comes in three stages (recall the brief discussion in Chapter One). The first is called *temple* Christianity, representing a simplistic type of worship in which Christ is a mere dead image of the past and all religious practice is contained within the walls of the temple. The second is called *domestic* Christianity, representing a type of worship that has quit the temple and established itself in the active life, in the very "dwellings of people." If temple Christianity possessed universality (people came together in the temple to worship), it lacked free, individual experience. If domestic Christianity possessed free, individual experience, it lacked universality (people worshiped only in their homes). So the final stage, in a grand Hegelian *Aufhebung*, unites the positive elements and supersedes the negative. It's called *universal* Christianity, in which Christ is neither "a temple image" nor "purely a personal ideal," but "the all-world historical principle, the living foundation and cornerstone of the all-humankind Church." The first two types of Christianity exist as fact, Solov'ev thinks; the third, however, exists only as an "enormous task that apparently exceeds all human forces."[45]

This is fine as a theory. But where did he find it in Dostoevsky? We'll have no trouble finding the notion of process toward an unrealizable ideal, if the ideal is perfect Christian love (or perfect evil). But this is not the way Dostoevsky presented his ideas about a universal Christian brotherhood. As Solov'ev elaborates the theory, it makes more and more sense exactly as it becomes more and more remote from anything Dostoevsky said. Solov'ev even does Dostoevsky the favor of taking some of the novelist's weakest points and representing them as the opposite of what they truly are. Consider this statement, for example:

> The true Church, which Dostoevsky preached, is an all-humankind one, above all in the sense that within it the division of humankind into rivalrous and mutually hostile tribes and peoples must in the end disappear. All of them, without losing their national character but simply freeing themselves of their national egoism, may and must unite in one common effort of all-world rebirth. This is why Dostoevsky, when he spoke of Russia, could not have had in mind any sort of national separatism. On the contrary, he viewed the whole purpose of the Russian people as resting in the service of true Christianity, so that there was in the Russian people neither Hellene nor Jew. To be sure, he considered Russia to be a people chosen by God, but chosen not for rivalry with other peoples and not for dominance and primacy over them, but for the free service of all peoples and for the realization, in fraternal union with them, of true all-humankindness or the universal Church.

He then goes on to say that Dostoevsky "never idealized the people [*narod*] and did not bow to them as if to an idol."[46]

I'm not sure which Dostoevsky Solov'ev was thinking of here. The one I've read advocated Russia's seizure of Constantinople, which he declared to be Orthodox and Russian.[47] The one I've read continually reverted to the idea that the Slavic nations are closer to God than the Catholic. The one I've read idealized the *narod* so often and so vociferously that it's hardly worth citing the evidence. The mere claim that the Russian peasant bears a kind of innate, or at least inbred, Christianity is an idealization too obvious to explain, even when Dostoevsky is at pains to insist that he's not idealizing. As Dostoevsky rhapsodizes in one of the many places where he notes the peasants' Christianity without formal education:

> The chief school of Christianity that he [the Russian peasant] has passed through is the centuries of innumerable and endless sufferings endured by him in his history when, abandoned by everyone, trampled upon by every-

one, working for each and all, he remained only with Christ the Comforter, whom he has accepted into his soul for all eternity and who in exchange has saved his [the peasant's] soul from despair![48]

Passages like this place Dostoevsky squarely and comfortably in the company of all the radical Russian gentry intellectuals in the nineteenth century for whom the Russian peasantry served so conveniently as a mirror for their own theories. Didn't Herzen speak famously of the Russian peasant's "natural" communism in 1851, only three years after the *Communist Manifesto* brought the word "communism" into popular use as roughly synonymous with "socialism?"[49]

In fact, in one of the few places where Dostoevsky uses the word *church*, as Solov'ev does in his speeches, to mean something like "brotherhood of Christians," it is in an historical discussion that pointedly follows a logic exactly opposite to the Hegelian one that Solov'ev describes. It's in the chapters following the text of the Pushkin speech, and Dostoevsky refers to a "new, hitherto unheard-of nationality—all-fraternal, all-humankind, in the form of a common, universal church." But he's speaking of the *early* Christian "church," the one that allegedly existed as a free community of believers before the Catholic Church built a gigantic "anthill" over it, establishing the reign of the man-God on earth. The remnants of that pure, primeval church live today in Russia, and the modern period finds them to be still under attack from the West, though now it is educated, Europeanized Russians that represent the West. There's little about universalism and brotherhood in this picture (though there's no reason why universalism and brotherhood logically must be excluded from it). The focus is on the Russian folk as the "bearer of Christ," and Dostoevsky emphasizes the inextricable connection between "peasant" and "Christian" by simply saying the words for both, implicitly noting the virtual identity of their pronunciation and the semantic association in their roots: *krest'ianin* (containing the word for "cross") and *khristianin* (containing the word "Christ").[50]

None of which is to say that Dostoevsky never preached the gospel of Russia as the great force of reconciliation and brotherhood. This was his message in the famous Pushkin speech, and it seems likely that the speech is what Solov'ev had in mind when he spoke of Dostoevsky's conception of the church. But even though Dostoevsky has abandoned his anti-Westernism here and used a veritable torrent of words beginning with *vse-* ("all-"), and even though he speaks of "the brotherly, definitive concord of all tribes under

Christ's evangelical law," this is not a speech about the church; it's a speech about the supposed universalism of the Russian character.[51]

Nine years after Dostoevsky died, Solov'ev would return to this issue of Russia and Christianity in a book that he wrote in French, titled *La Russie et l'Église Universelle* (Russia and the Universal Church). What's fascinating about the young philosopher's treatment is that he clearly has in mind the same issues that plagued Dostoevsky; he argues with considerably more rigor than did Dostoevsky but now arrives at a conclusion that would have horrified his older friend. After noting early in his book that Orthodoxy and Roman Catholicism materially differ very little from one another and that Russians must proclaim solidarity with their brothers in the West, Solov'ev launches an assault on the Slavophiles. Motivated above all by their hatred of the papacy, the Russian dissidents have promoted a church that merely pretends to universality while in truth being nothing more than a particular, national institution. Eastern Christianity, in Solov'ev's eyes, has existed only in the form of isolated ethnic or national churches. The *phyletismos* for which the Bulgarian Church was officially condemned in 1872 is symptomatic of the entire Greek Orthodox Church.[52]

For Solov'ev, the key principle is the one that Christ enunciates in Matthew 16:18–19, when he addresses Simon Peter:

> And I tell you, you are Peter [*Petros* in Greek], and on this rock [*petra* in Greek] I will build my church, and the gates of Hades will not prevail against it. I will give you the keys of the kingdom of heaven, and whatever you bind on earth will be bound in heaven, and whatever you loose on earth will be loosed in heaven.

The church must be one, not many, and this is the reason the Slavophiles are in the wrong when they advocate (or appear to advocate) a church that is purely national. The significance of naming Peter the prince of the apostles and the rock on which the church is founded is that the church so founded will now transcend "Jewish nationalism."[53]

The church, in fact, represents to Solov'ev the answer to the same conflict between the material and the ideal that troubled Dostoevsky in the Masha entry. Solov'ev agrees with Dostoevsky that a church in all its perfection, as "the *absolute* reign of love and truth," is not conceivable on earth.[54] Solov'ev, however, thinks Christ instituted his church on the assumption that the new edifice would simply "*combat* the Gates of Hades," not on the assumption that it would permanently destroy those gates.[55] But look where Solov'ev's reasoning now irresistibly leads him:

> If one wishes to avoid falling into the opposite extremes of a blind materialism or an impotent idealism, one is forced to admit that the needs of reality and the requirements of the ideal accord with one another and go together in the order established by God. In order to represent in the Church the *ideal principle* of humanity and of concord, Jesus Christ institutes, as the original type of conciliar government, the primordial collegium or council of twelve apostles, equal amongst themselves and united by fraternal love. For such an ideal unity *to be realized* in all places and at all times; for the council of ecclesiastical heads everywhere and always to be able to triumph over discord and cause the diversity of private opinions to end up as the uniformity of public decrees; for debates to be able to come to an end and the unity of the Church to emerge in reality; in order not to expose this unity to the accidents of human conventions—in order not to build His Church on this changing sand, the divine Architect discovers the solid Rock, the unshakable Rock of the ecclesiastical monarchy, and He fixes the ideal of unanimity by attaching it to a power that is real and living.[56]

In other words, Solov'ev finds himself essentially in agreement with the Catholic Church: the rock should be Rome, and unity of faith must rest in "the legal authority of a single head"—the Pope.[57] "*Only* the Roman Catholic Church is *neither* a national Church, *nor* a State Church, *nor* a sect founded by one man," he exclaims.[58]

None of this, of course, should be construed as an unquestioning acceptance or endorsement of all the acts of the historical Catholic Church, which Solov'ev hardly even mentions. For him, the essential feature of Catholicism is its theoretical independence from the authority of the state, something that he says classic Slavophilism, obsessed as it is with freedom of the *individual*, ignores. But that the church should *be* a state or *be like* a state represents no contradiction of Christian principles in Solov'ev's eyes, because for him the church is precisely *not* an ideal institution. It is an institution designed to mediate between the divine and the human, and since the church therefore plays a role in human society, it will apply to that society, through the decisions of *one* leader appointed ultimately by Christ himself, the dictates at which the church arrives. This is why Solov'ev terms the government of the church a monarchy. But above all, we must understand the Catholic Church theoretically, according to its fundamental principles, not historically, according to its acts.

It's easy to imagine what Dostoevsky's reaction to these ideas might have been. Never one for subtleties, he would no doubt have thundered about his friend's willingness to sign a pact with Satan and would have laid all the crimes of the Roman Catholic Church at Solov'ev's feet. But let's face it: even if we keep in mind the difference between the church that Solov'ev describes in the speeches on Dostoevsky and the one he describes in *Russia and the Universal Church*, his solution to the problem of the divide between the real and the ideal makes considerably more sense than the one we find in *The Brothers Karamazov*, or for that matter anywhere else in Dostoevsky. The "church" Solov'ev describes in the three discourses is not a human institution; it is an ideal one, unrealizable on earth. The institution he describes in *Russia and the Universal Church*, on the other hand, is real and human and exists only as an approximation of ideal Christian brotherhood. But real or ideal, the church is *never national*. As we quickly learn in Solov'ev's book, the author could have substituted the name of any country for "Russia" in the title, since the message is that no nationality or state has a unique claim on the Christian church.

By contrast, in his last years Dostoevsky refused to abandon the association of Russia with his vision of a true Christianity (in those moments, that is, when he was in a humor to take seriously the idea of a true Christianity) and increasingly turned toward the earth. The closest thing to a theory of the church in *The Brothers Karamazov* is the conception that Ivan discusses in the early scene set in Father Zosima's cell. Father Paissy frequently steps in to explain Ivan's ideas, and at one point he tells the assembled company why the church of Ivan's vision is something other than "a kingdom not of this world." "Our Lord Jesus Christ came expressly to establish the church on the earth," he says.[59] But the church Ivan speaks of will be quite the opposite of the Roman Catholic Church because in Ivan's view the state will turn into the church, whereas in the case of Roman Catholicism the reverse was true. In Ivan's conception, the church comes about naturally, as the expression of Christian community. Before Roman Catholicism came along, Christianity was *nothing but* the church.[60]

Fine. But then Father Paissy takes up the idea, and suddenly we're back to nationalism. "This star will rise from the East," he incongruously proclaims.[61] If we're meant to understand this comment as following logically from what Ivan has been saying, then we have a big problem, because Ivan has just finished saying that the church under his conception cannot seek out a specific location. But even if we adhere strictly to what Ivan himself has been saying and regard it as a plausible theory of a Christian church, we can't forget that this theory will have to take its place next to the earth worship of Alesha and Father Zosima. Father Zosima, speaking of the *Russian* monks and how *they* (but not other monks) retain the image of Christ, at some moment in his life (as recorded in Alesha's *vita* of him) uttered word for word Father Paissy's sentence about the star in the East.[62]

## BUT LET THERE BE AN UNATTAINABLE IDEAL

In the last months of his life, Dostoevsky returned in his notebooks to a concept that had long obsessed him: infinity. Here is what he wrote:

> If there were an end anywhere in the world, then the whole world would have an end. The parallelism of lines. A triangle, confluence at infinity, one quadrillionth [surely he means "a quadrillion"] is still nothing next to infinity. Yet at infinity, parallel lines are supposed to meet. For all these vertices of triangles still exist in finite space, and the rule must hold that the more infinite they are, the closer they are to parallelism. Parallel lines must meet at infinity, but this infinity will never come. If it came, then infinity would have an end, which is an absurdity. If parallel lines met, that would mean that the world, geometric law, and God would have an end, which is an absurdity, but only for the human mind.

> The real (created) world is finite, while the immaterial world is infinite. If parallel lines met, that would be the end of the law of this world. But they meet at infinity, and infinity, without any doubt, exists. For if there were no such thing as infinity, there would be such thing as finitude either, for it would be unthinkable. But if infinity exists, then God and the other world exist, with different laws from those of the real (created) world.[63]

Never think that Dostoevsky did not keep abreast of developments in intellectual fields far removed from his own. It's likely he wrote this passage in response to an article he had read that included an account of the non-Euclidean geometry of Georg Riemann. In the 1850s, Riemann suggested the possibility of creating a geometry in an elliptical space. In such a curved space, there would be no truly parallel lines; to put it differently, "parallel" lines would actually meet at finite points. For example, on the surface of a sphere (a special case of elliptical space), it's possible to form a triangle with the equator (we'll liken the sphere to the earth) as its base and two north-bound lines that form right angles to the equator. If the two lines form right angles to the base, then in plane geometry they are by definition parallel to each other, and yet on the sphere these two lines will clearly meet at the north pole. This might be what Dostoevsky was thinking about when he wrote his mysterious remark about "triangle" and "confluence at infinity." In elliptical space, then, there is nothing that would serve as a conceptual model for Dostoevsky's idealism, since there is nothing equivalent to infinite approach (as parallel lines are said to "meet" only *at infinity* or a curve is said to approach an asymptote endlessly and finally "touch" it only *at infinity*). In Riemann's non-Euclidean geometry, parallel lines *do* meet *here and now*.

Dostoevsky doesn't like this line of thought. His own thinking on the issue (not the beliefs he embraced, but the way he conceptualized the issue) appears in this entry not to have changed much since the Masha diary entry, so he prefers the tortured notion of lines that meet at infinity and an infinity that never comes. He focuses once again on the theological line of thought he recorded as he sat by the body of his wife.[64] The separation is here once again between the real, created world and the immaterial world, just as the distinction is here between a finite world that we can comprehend and an infinite world that we must merely accept. It's precisely the subject of the Kantian antinomy I used in an earlier chapter for the purpose of illustrating Dostoevsky's own peculiar formulation of paradoxes. Dostoevsky appears to arrive at essentially the same conclusion as Kant did exactly one hundred years earlier, in 1781: that the use of reason to confront problems involving such concepts as endlessness will always lead to insoluble paradoxes. Dostoevsky's assertion that "infinity, without any doubt, exists" signals a leap from the reasoned, "Euclidean" position preceding this claim to a bald and unreasoned declaration of the existence of infinity—from which he infers, again without any reasoned arguments, the existence of God.[65]

So, what to make of it? We can hardly describe the notebook passage as hopeful. The declaration of God's existence offers a solution to the paradox, but the author in no way accompanies it with joyful tidings about taking the unreasoned leap and dedicating ourselves to God and his immaterial world. Instead he offers us a dry exercise in demonstrating the existence of God, an exercise that is founded on the highly suspect claim that the existence of infinity logically implies the existence of God (even Kant devoted two *separate* antinomies to the existence of a world without end and the existence of a "first cause," or God). Small wonder, then, that in his last and greatest novel he took a detour through earthbound pantheism, where the conflict between the terms of his paradoxes appears almost to vanish in the doctrine of love for the earth.

# Conclusion

Let's say we've read every single word Dostoevsky wrote and it's time to say what he's had to tell us about religion. If we're shopping around for a religion, it seems unlikely we'll be in a position to declare ourselves "Dostoevskians" and go forth to do good works of a particular sort. Even in the eyes of the readers who feel most strongly that this author was possessed of a reasonably coherent set of religious convictions, what would a Dostoevskian do? Accept lots of suffering? Embrace poverty? Sin gravely and then seek redemption? Attempt to dissolve into a general synthesis with the all? Fight for the glory of the Russian nation? No, nothing like this seems plausible.

So what *did* he have to tell us about religion?

He had much to say about *us* and religion, or us *in* religion. For Dostoevsky, the human being seems initially to be inescapably an *animal metaphysicum*. Our perpetual position on a continuum between opposing ideal poles indicates that each of us exists in a necessary relation to a metaphysical absolute, just as for Hegel every rational being exists in a necessary relation to Absolute Spirit. We saw how characters who are polar opposites—Myshkin and Stavrogin, for example—are always condemned to live out their existence (before their inevitable destruction, of course) on *this* side of an ideal. The Stavrogins of Dostoevsky's universe, those who pursue an ideal that is oddly nonmetaphysical or antimetaphysical, cannot escape the presence of something that is positively metaphysical. Things grow confused when we get to the earth worship of Ivan Karamazov and Father Zosima, and things grow especially confused when we get to the Slavophilism that so many of Dostoevsky's characters (and Dostoevsky himself on many occasions) professed. Perhaps it wouldn't be too paradoxical to say that the pagan earth worshiper and the Slavophile both *believe* their outlook is founded on something metaphysical, even though that something might not appear to be *Christian* in most traditional senses of the term. At the very least, we can say Dostoevsky has shown as a human characteristic that bears almost no exceptions the tendency to seek—even unwittingly, even against one's will, even in the presence of contradictory intentions—something metaphysical.

What about Christianity in particular? Take, for example, the critique of Christianity we find in Ivan's story about the Grand Inquisitor. For more than a century, readers have persisted in asking the wrong question about this amazing piece of writing. Who cares if we can identify the point of view that is Dostoevsky's? What difference should it really make if Dostoevsky can be proved to stand squarely and permanently on the side of the Inquisitor or on the side of Father Zosima? Dostoevsky had an idea. It's critical of Christianity, and we read it. So he has offered it to us.

Dostoevsky was fond of placing his most interesting ideas at two or more degrees of separation from the reader. Raskolnikov's extraordinary-man theory appears in an article that he, Raskolnikov, wrote. Stavrogin's theories of good and evil appear in the confession that he, Stavrogin, wrote. Ivan's critique of Christianity appears in a work of fiction that he, Ivan, composed, and it is delivered by the Inquisitor, a fictional character, that Ivan, a fictional character, invented. Dostoevsky thus seems to have gone out of his way to distance himself from these ideas. Yet there they are. Like it or not, Ivan's critical observations about Christianity are *true*, at least for any version of it that insists on the personal freedom of the individual worshiper. We can decide as much as we want that the solution to the difficulties Ivan poses is a leap of faith or a decision that the sense of what we do when we believe is unknowable, but this doesn't make the Grand Inquisitor's observations any less true. It's not just that they're true; they're *fundamental*.

I can't help thinking, in this connection, of Dostoevsky's unwitting *alter ego* Nietzsche, himself no mean critic of Christianity. From *Beyond Good and*

*Evil* (1886) till the end of his sane life, but especially in *The Genealogy of Morality* (1887), Nietzsche hammered home the theme of Christianity's inversion of a "natural" morality. The "slave revolt" by which a renegade group of Jews in Roman-occupied Palestine came to redefine morality, so that what was formerly strong and noble now came to be oppressive and wicked, while what was formerly weak and abject now came to be humble and virtuous, led to the lamentable set of features that characterized Christianity and in turn Western morality for almost two thousand years. The Catholic Church established its hold on the Western mind essentially by a type of emotional manipulation: the formerly weak and powerless, through a life devoted to self-denial, gained control over the formerly powerful by inspiring in them a sense of guilt and bad conscience. Hence an institution that has sought, with considerable success, "to become master . . . over life itself."[1]

Nietzsche's condemnation of Christianity is strong stuff. In *Twilight of the Idols* (1889), he referred to the religion as "the hangman's metaphysics," because of the nasty predilection its proponents show for judging, convicting, and punishing.[2] But how much more fundamental is Dostoevsky's critique! In Nietzsche's account, Christianity arose and developed as it did merely owing to an accident of history. The Jewish priestly caste acquired its peculiar character in response to certain conditions, but there was no *necessity* to the emergence of *ressentiment* and the occurrence of the "slave revolt in morality." The priests who established their power on a foundation of bad conscience were, in Nietzsche's eyes, simply opportunists, exploiting human weaknesses in a certain historical moment. The Grand Inquisitor's condemnation, by contrast, is aimed at Christianity's inner core, at the very logic of the ideas on which it is built. If the Catholic Church seized an opportunity, it was one that would have presented itself at any time in history, provided that someone like Jesus came along, claimed divine origin, and asked people to follow him solely on the strength of their own free faith.

This brings me to another observation. Whatever Dostoevsky's attitude toward religion in general and Christianity in particular might really have been, and whatever features he might have endorsed in his moments of faith, he unquestionably made certain assumptions about the religion's basic ideas. For the moment, let's speak only of Christianity as a metaphysical system and leave to one side the more dubious nationalist Christianity Dostoevsky propounded. To him, "Christianity" as a system of thought carried with it certain axiomatic propositions. Here are some of them:

1.   There is a suprasensible world to which we have no direct access.

2.   In that world dwell, among other things, a set of ideals (such as perfect love and perfect faith) and the secrets of God's justice.

3.   The ideal of perfect love is defined as an absolute synthesis of the individual with everyone and everything, with the result that the individual ceases to exist.

4.   We are given a set of commandments that we must obey, but it is beyond our power to obey them perfectly.

These propositions, of course, supply the sense of the Masha entry and of Ivan's rebellion. But they also underlie virtually every religious project Dostoevsky describes in his fiction, except for the nationalist one. Sonia Marmeladova declines to answer the question whether she would let Luzhin die or let her stepmother die, since this is a matter of God's justice and we can't know it. Prince Myshkin is a walking definition of the unattainability of perfect love and faith. Bishop Tikhon in *The Devils* knows that he can't ask God to move a mountain, because this would reveal the imperfection of his own faith. Father Zosima, before he gets to his Slavophilic speech, urges us to celebrate the mystery of God's designs.

This conception of Christianity furnishes especially rich soil for Dostoevsky's ideas about the nature of belief, though those ideas could probably stand on their own. If you're inclined to think that an individual can properly hold mutually contradictory beliefs at different moments, that beliefs often come in antinomic pairs, and that they are never perfect, you'll find a hospitable reception in a system of thought in which it is axiomatic that true belief is unattainable. Dostoevsky's "theory" of belief, if it can be called that, thus has the twin qualities of being remarkable in its own right and of implicitly forming part of the critique of Christianity that surfaces so often in his writings. Christianity, conceived in the way I've just described, irresistibly leads to a type of believing that threatens the wholeness and internal continuity of the individual personality, Dostoevsky appears to say.

This conception of Christianity furnishes equally rich soil for Dostoevsky's ideas about the individual. If the Christianity that Dostoevsky conceives requires an *ideal* brotherhood, then we find ourselves once again facing an impossible commandment: to surrender our individuality to the collectivity. Just as we're condemned to strive for perfect faith without ever attaining it, we're condemned to be individuals while striving not to be. Of course, Dostoevsky muddies everything the minute he introduces religious nationalism, where a kind of tribal brotherhood stands in for the ideal one and where it is never quite clear what the relation is between the two.

It would be irresponsible to omit religious nationalism from an account of Dostoevsky's religion, dubious though its claim is to be treated as religion. The ease with which Dostoevsky's characters make the passage from a truly metaphysical Christianity to the national one suggests that the national one bears some resemblance to the metaphysical one. The chief point on which the two systems resemble one another is undoubtedly their emphasis on collectivity. No doubt a "synthesis with everything" is very different from a feeling of ethnic community with actual, living Russian peasants, but the idea of the collective is present in both. If Dostoevsky regarded humility as a virtue that would necessarily be associated with Christianity and also regarded this virtue as particularly embodied in the figures of Russian religious men who served as models for some of his characters, then it makes sense that he should regard as exemplary the sort of Christianity that (in his eyes) has been practiced in his own country.

## WHAT KIND OF THINKER WAS HE?

I don't mean to make too much of Dostoevsky's modernity and suggest in any serious way that this writer would have chosen to stand resolutely alongside Wittgenstein and other twentieth-century figures in a titanic battle against stability, constancy, and certainty. For one thing, despite all his talk about brotherhood, he was never much of a joiner (hardly surprising, given his incapacity to adopt and retain a single point of view). For another, if his conception of belief stemmed from a critical understanding of the imperfections of Christianity, he would have been inclined to view instability, inconstancy, and uncertainty as the necessary but unfortunate consequences of an idealist worldview. Even when he comments favorably on personal duality in his letter to Ekaterina Fedorovna Iunge, it's not as if he were recommending it as the correct condition for proper people to adopt.

Yet he's identifying it as an inescapable condition in himself and generally in what he calls "not entirely ordinary" people. Scanlan speaks of Dostoevsky's "dialectical method" of philosophizing, by which he means the author's "dynamic counterposing of competing views."[3] Is this really a *method*, in the sense that Dostoevsky on conscious reflection adopted it as an approach? It's hard to say. From the sound of Dostoevsky's letter to Iunge, "division-in-two" is a sort of affliction, not a condition one chooses (or seeks out). Once we suffer from the affliction, however, we get to experience all the exhilaration it brings—together, of course, with the torments. Was Dostoevsky *satisfied* as he sat and madly contradicted the great religious man at Optina Pustyn'? Did he feel he was doing his duty as a thinker, ever mindful of the necessity to apply the dialectical method and look at both sides of an issue? I doubt it. Yet, call it what you like—a dialectical method, a pathological obsession—there it is, a habit of mind that directed the way Dostoevsky thought about all the cursed questions, so we have no choice but to acknowledge that this was, in fact, his "method." Who's to say, for example, that the Antinomies of Pure Reason weren't simply a sign of an obsessive habit of mind in Kant, or the cave analogy in Plato?

Another habit of mind, one that may well have been learned rather than inborn, was the sort of idealism that led Dostoevsky to ponder limits and infinity. Nothing seems to be more characteristic of his style of thinking than the marriage of geometry and metaphysics that we find in the Masha entry, Ivan Karamazov's rebellion, and the enigmatic notebook entry on infinity. In fact, the newfangled geometry he contemplates in the notebook entry is undoubtedly disturbing exactly because it erases the neat, reassuring separation between the possible and the impossible that Euclidean geometry afforded. With parallel lines that meet in finite space, there's no spatial means for representing something that's existent yet infinitely remote. To Dostoevsky's way of thinking, the place where perfect Christian love and perfect Christian faith dwell then becomes just as accessible as the place where parallel lines now meet and where a hyperbola now touches an asymptote. Even when the geometric imagery was not explicitly present, we find limits and infinity lurking just beneath the surface. Many of Dostoevsky's characters appear to be formulated in connection with these concepts. For example, if we don't mind reducing our favorite idiot to a kind of mathematical-metaphysical abstraction, we can say that Prince Myshkin is the idea of earthbound, natural imperfection as it approaches, but never reaches, supernatural perfection, always asserting its finitude the closer it gets to infinity.

But maybe it's not too surprising that Dostoevsky thought this way. So much of intellectual life in nineteenth-century Europe, especially when it came to the metaphysical issues that were important to Dostoevsky, was still under the sway of Kant and Hegel. To put it *very* crudely, Kant was about limits, and Hegel was, with a little tweaking, about infinity. The notion of an impenetrable barrier that separates the world of natural phenomena from the transcendent world of metaphysical ideas was Kant's contribution to German idealism, and the notion of progress toward an absolute (though technically not an *infinite* one, to be sure) was Hegel's. Who actually needed to read the two philosophers in order to be familiar with these simple notions? Nineteenth-century European discussions, from the professional to the popular, were filled with implicit assumptions and explicit ideas from the great Germans.

Nor is it surprising, for that matter, that someone like Dostoevsky should have been perpetually torn between the poles of secularism and religious belief. All those Western European thinkers with whose ideas Dostoevsky carried on a love-hate relationship showed how easily the same philosophical thought patterns could lead to faith or its opposite. Why else would Hegel's successors have fallen into two camps, fighting over whether or not the master was a religious man? It was always just a matter of simple perspective. The "consciousness of the infinite," which persuaded Feuerbach that the religious was simply human, could just as easily have persuaded a religious mind that the human was simply religious. Imagine a continuum on which everything, precisely by existing on the continuum, is connected with everything else, like holiday lights on a single electrical wire. One can choose for one's perspective any point, declare it to be *the* perspective, and see everything else as flowing from *it*. If the infinite is already there, and we're conscious of it, then the infinite dominates and religion is real. If *we're* there first and our consciousness, reflecting on itself, gives us an image of the infinite, then *we* dominate and religion is not real.

Perhaps it would not be too contrived to suggest that Dostoevsky's religious nationalism finds a natural place in this context. German idealism is all about organicism. The spirit that serves as the driving force in the progress toward an absolute is the same one that, in a particular group of people, finds its expression in the nation. The more we adopt the human perspective on our continuum, the more likely we are to settle into the individual and particular. The more we settle into the individual and particular, the more likely we are to divide and classify. The more we do *this*, the more likely we are to focus on the peculiarities of groups and to see those groups as possessed of their own individual spirits. From here to "the Russian Christ" is an easy couple of steps.

So is Dostoevsky just a German intellectual dressed up in Russian clothing? I can imagine *his* response to this question (perhaps one on which he would be inclined to show considerably less doubt than on some others). It's a tricky question, in large part because, in the milieu we're speaking of, "Russian" is not a pure concept and already suggests a healthy admixture of witting and unwitting German culture. No one today would challenge the claim that even the most die-hard Slavophilism in nineteenth-century Russia owed essential features of its ideology to German romanticism. The Russian Christianity that so many writers, among them Dostoevsky, proposed as their own indigenous tradition was to a considerable degree the construct of an intellectual climate imported from Göttingen and other hotbeds of German idealism.

Still, it would be grossly unfair to deny Dostoevsky the national patrimony he so enthusiastically promoted. He *did* read the lives of Russian saints. He *did* focus attention on Russian sectarians. He *did* repeatedly seek to evoke the trappings of Russian religion (icons, for example) that set it apart from Catholicism and Protestantism. It would be equally unfair to ignore features of Dostoevsky's religion that appear to be peculiar to him personally but that don't necessarily betray any sort of debt to a foreign tradition. His love for the book of Job in the Hebrew Bible and the Gospel of St. John in the New Testament seems to stem from a deep engagement with issues of faith and morality that he simply felt very, very strongly.

So Dostoevsky didn't leave us with a Dostoevskian religion. "Dostoevsky's religion" is not that. Instead, it's a hugely powerful commentary on religion—above all, on one religion in particular—and a defined set of issues associated with religion. The *least* interesting part of this, the part that is most topical and that as a consequence is least likely to have a claim on the attention of future generations, is religious nationalism. To my way of thinking, Dostoevsky's most enduring insights are those that concern what he sees as the core structure of Christian thought and those that concern the nature of belief. In the first case, he's left us with some sobering thoughts on a determining tradition in the Western world. In the second, he's left us with some sobering thoughts on religion in general, which is to say on a phenomenon that's not just Western but . . . human.

Reference Matter

# Notes

Biblical passages are quoted from the New Revised Standard edition unless I've indicated otherwise. All remaining translations are mine unless I've indicated otherwise.

*Chapter One*

1. George Gibian, ed., *Crime and Punishment* (New York: Norton, 1975), pp. 647, 648.

2. *Polnoe sobranie sochinenii v tridtsati tomakh* (Leningrad: Nauka, 1972–90), 1:5–6. Hereafter *PSS*.

3. For a book-length treatment of the relationship between Dostoevsky and Solov'ev, see Marina Kostalevsky, *Dostoevsky and Soloviev: The Art of Integral Vision* (New Haven and London: Yale University Press, 1997).

4. Vladimir Solov'ev, *Sobranie sochinenii*, S. M. Solov'ev and E. L. Radlov, eds., 10 vols. (St. Petersburg: Prosveshchenie, 1911–14; rpt. Brussels: Foyer Chrétien Oriental, 1966–70), 3:199.

5. Solov'ev, 3:195.

6. Solov'ev, 3:214.

7. From *Opravdanie dobra* (The justification of the good, 1894–96), Solov'ev, 8:12–14.

8. From "Ideia sverkhcheloveka" (The idea of the Superman, 1899), Solov'ev, 9:272.

9. Vasilii Rozanov, *Legenda o Velikom inkvizitore F. M. Dostoevskogo* (Moscow: "Respublika," 1996), pp. 101, 103.

10. Rozanov, pp. 103–8.

11. Rozanov, pp. 110–11.

12. *PSS*, 25:359.

13. Rozanov, p. 78n.

14. Dmitrii Merezhkovskii, *L. Tolstoi i Dostoevskii; Vechnye sputniki* (Moscow: "Respublika," 1995), p. 317.

15. Merezhkovskii, p. 315.

16. Merezhkovskii, pp. 248–49.

17. Merezhkovskii, p. 249.

18. Sergei Bulgakov, "Ivan Karamazov kak filosofskii tip" (Ivan Karamazov as a philosophical type), in *Ot marksizma k idealizmu* (From Marxism to idealism; Petersburg: "Obshchestvennaia Pol'za," 1903), pp. 83–112.

19. Nikolai Berdiaev, *Mirosozertsanie Dostoevskogo* (Dostoevsky's worldview; Paris: YMCA Press, 1968), p. 20.

20. Berdiaev, pp. 112, 121.

21. Berdiaev, p. 20.

22. Berdiaev, p. 229.

23. Berdiaev, p. 68.

24. Berdiaev, p. 70.

25. There is very little scholarship on Fedotov. A brief account of his intellectual development can be found in V. B. Rybachuk, *Filosofiia kul'tury G. P. Fedotova* (G. P. Fedotov's philosophy of culture; Tver´: Tverskoi gosudarstvennyi universitet, 1996).

26. George Fedotov, *The Russian Religious Mind*, 2 vols. (Cambridge, MA: Harvard University Press, 1946–66). The second volume, which Fedotov never completed, was published posthumously.

27. Fedotov, 1:130.

28. Paul Valliere, "M. M. Tareev: A study in Russian ethics and mysticism" (dissertation, Columbia University, 1974), p. 63.

29. M. M. Tareev, *Iskusheniia Khrista v sviazi s istorieiu dokhristianskikh religii i khristianskoi tserkvi*, in *Osnovy khristianstva: Sistema religioznoi mysli*, vol. 3, *Khristianskoe mirovozzrenie* (Moscow: Sergiev Posad, 1908), pp. 258–63.

30. M. M. Tareev, "F. M. Dostoevskii," in *Osnovy khristianstva*, vol. 4, *Khristianskaia svoboda* (Moscow: Sergiev Posad, 1908), pp. 245–314. The quoted phrases appear on pp. 250, 266, 267, 288, 289.

31. For its place in Bulgakov, see a more recent work by Valliere, *Modern Russian Theology. Bukharev, Soloviev, Bulgakov: Orthodox Theology in a New Key* (Grand Rapids, MI: Eerdmans, 2000), pp. 337–44.

32. E.-M. de Vogüé, *Le Roman russe* (Lausanne: Editions l'Age d'homme, 1971), p. 221.

33. De Vogüé, p. 231.

34. De Vogüé, p. 234.

35. De Vogüé, pp. 242–43.

36. De Vogüé, p. 245.

37. De Vogüé, p. 252.

38. Giorgio Colli and Mazzino Montinari, *Nietzsche Werke: Kritische Gesamtausgabe* (Berlin: Walter de Gruyter, 1969), div. VI, vol. 3, p. 141 (cited hereafter in the format VI, 3:141).

39. *Nietzsche Werke*, V, 6:353.

40. Georg Brandes, *Impressions of Russia*, Samuel C. Eastman, trans. (New York: Crowell, 1966), p. 241–42.

41. *Nietzsche Werke*, III, 5:483.

42. Sigmund Freud, *Gesammelte Werke* (London: Imago Pub. Co/Frankfurt am Main: Fischer, 1940–1968), 14:399–418. The key word in the title of Freud's essay has been translated into English as "parricide," though Freud uses *Vatertötung* or *Vatermord*, both of which contain the word "father" and hence are more accurately translated "patricide."

43. Freud, 14:399.                    44. Freud, 14:406.

45. Freud, 14:408.                    46. Freud, 14:411, 414.

47. Roman Guardini, *Der Mensch und der Glaube: Versuche über die religiöse Existenz in Dostojewskijs großen Romanen* (Leipzig: Jakob Hegner, 1932), p. 181 note 1.

48. Thomas Mann, "Dostoevsky—in Moderation," in *The Short Novels of Dostoevsky* (New York: Dial Press, 1945), pp. vii–xx.

49. Mann, p. vii.

50. Mann, pp. ix, xi, xiii. The passages in Merezhkovsky to which Mann refers include the one I mentioned earlier, in which Merezhkovsky likens Kirillov to Nietzsche. Merezhkovsky's book was translated into German in 1903 by Carl von Gütschow, as *Tolstoi und Dostojewski als Menschen und als Künstler* (Leipzig: Schulze, 1903).

51. Mann, p. viii. Georgii Fridlender has pointed out the mistake in *Dostoevskii i mirovaia literatura* (Leningrad: Sovetskii Pisatel', 1985), p. 268.

52. Mann, p. xiv. Ellipsis is in the original.

53. Mann, p. viii.

54. Mann, p. xii.

55. Mann, p. xv.

56. Proust mentions Dostoevsky for the first time in 1894, when he is twenty-three. For a chronology of Proust's references to Dostoevsky, see Milivoje Pejovic, *Proust et Dostoïevski: Étude d'une thématique commune* (Paris: Nizet, 1987), p. 3.

57. Proust, *À la recherche du temps perdu* (Paris: Gallimard, 1954), 3:377–81.

58. André Gide, *Dostoïevski: Articles et causeries* (Paris: Gallimard, 1923), p. 206.

59. Gide, p. 50. Emphasis is in the original.

60. Gide, p. 130.                     61. Gide, p. 114.

62. Gide, p. 187.                     63. Gide, pp. 212, 106.

64. "The Russian Point of View," in *The Essays of Virginia Woolf*, Andrew McNeillie, ed. (London: Hogarth, 1986–88), 2:181–90.

65. Woolf, 2:186.

66. Woolf, 2:186–87.

67. Woolf, 2:187.

68. D. H. Lawrence, "Introduction," *The Grand Inquisitor*, S. S. Koteliansky, trans. (London: Martin Secker), 1935), p. 10.

69. Lawrence, pp. 6–7.

70. Lawrence, p. 19.

71. Murray Krieger, *The Tragic Vision: Variations on a Theme in Literary Interpretation* (New York: Holt, Rinehart and Winston, 1960), p. 20.

72. "Dostoevsky's 'Idiot': The Curse of Saintliness," in Krieger, pp. 209–27.

73. Krieger, p. 217.

74. Krieger, pp. 214–25n.5.

75. Krieger, p. 212.

76. Jean Drouilly, *La Pensée politique et religieuse de F. M. Dostoievski* (The political and religious thought of F. M. Dostoevsky; Paris: Librairie des Cinq Continents, 1971). See also Konrad Onasch, *Der verschwiegene Christus: Versuch über die*

*Poetisierung des Christentums in der Dichtung F. M. Dostojewskis* (The hidden/silent Christ: Essay on the poeticization of Christianity in the literary work of F. M. Dostoevsky; Berlin: Union Verlag, 1976).

77. Ellis Sandoz, *Political Apocalypse: A Study of Dostoevsky's Grand Inquisitor* (Baton Rouge: Louisiana State University Press, 1971), pp. 212–13.

78. A. Boyce Gibson, *The Religion of Dostoevsky* (London: SCM Press, 1973), p. 41.

79. Nicholas V. Riasanovsky, "Khomiakov on *Sobornost*'," in Ernest J. Simmons, ed., *Continuity and Change in Russian and Soviet Thought* (Cambridge, MA: Harvard University Press, 1955), pp. 183–96.


## Chapter Two

1. *PSS*, 28 book 1:173.

2. *PSS*, 10:94.

3. *PSS*, 10:188–89.

4. *PSS*, 10:196–201. Ellipses are in the original.

5. *PSS*, 10:196–97.          6. *PSS*, 10:34–35.

7. *PSS*, 10:33.          8. *PSS*, 10:199.

9. Kant, *Werke*, Wilhelm Weischedel, ed. (Frankfurt am Main: Suhrkamp, 1956–64), 8:740–41.

10. Kant, *Werke*, 8:782.

11. Kant, *Werke*, 8:825.

12. Friedrich Schleiermacher, *Werke. Auswahl in vier Bänden*, Otto Braun and Johannes Bauer, eds. (Aalen: Scientia-Verlag, 1967), 4:240.

13. Schleiermacher, 4:242.          14. Schleiermacher, 4:285.

15. Schleiermacher, 4:288.          16. Schleiermacher, 4:361.

17. Schleiermacher, 4:382.          18. Schleiermacher, 4:283.

19. Schleiermacher, 4:355.

20. G.W.F. Hegel, *Werke in zwanzig Bänden*, Eva Moldenhauer and Karl Markus Michel, eds. (Frankfurt am Main: Suhrkamp, 1970), 3:495.

21. Hegel, 3:496. Emphasis is in the original.

22. Hegel, 3:568. Emphasis is in the original.

23. Hegel, 12:540.

24. Hegel, 12:53.

25. Hegel, 10:374. Emphasis is in the original.

26. Hegel, 10:394.

27. Hegel, 14:130–31.

28. Hegel, 12:494. Emphasis is in the original.

29. *PSS*, 15:465.

30. David Friedrich Strauss, *Das Leben Jesu kritisch bearbeitet* (Tübingen: C. F. Osiander, 1838), 1:231–32.

31. Strauss, 2:726.          32. Strauss, 2:731.

33. Strauss, 1:86.          34. Strauss, 1:ix–x.

35. *PSS*, 21:132–33.

36. Ludwig Feuerbach, *Sämtliche Werke*, Wilhelm Bolin and Friedrich Jodl, eds. (Stuttgart-Bad Cannstatt: Frommann, 1960), 6:326.

37. Feuerbach, 6:2.                   38. Feuerbach, 6:6, 15.

39. Feuerbach, 6:57.                  40. Feuerbach, 6:325.

41. Feuerbach, 6:148, 168.           42. Feuerbach, 6:278.

43. Feuerbach, 6:222.

44. Feuerbach, 6:59–60. Emphasis is in the original.

45. Feuerbach, 6:297.

46. Feuerbach, 6:335.

47. Max Stirner, *Der Einzige und sein Eigentum und andere Schriften*, Hans G. Helms, ed. (Munich: Carl Hanser, 1968), p. 35.

48. Stirner, p. 36.

49. In *Glauben und Wissen* (Faith and knowledge, 1802), Hegel quoted the verse "Gott selbst ist tot" (God himself is dead), from an early-seventeenth-century Lutheran hymn. See Hegel, *Werke*, 2:432. Toward the end of the *Phenomenology of Spirit*, he mentions "the pain that expresses itself as the difficult saying that *God has died*" (3:547) and "the painful feeling of the unhappy consciousness that *God himself has died*" (3:572). Deland S. Anderson discusses these passages and the entire theme of Hegel and the death of God in *Hegel's Speculative Good Friday: The Death of God in Philosophical Perspective* (Atlanta, GA: Scholars Press, 1996). As Anderson points out, Hegel mentioned the death of God in all his major works except the *Logic* (p. xi).

50. Stirner, p. 105.

51. Stirner, p. 107.

52. Stirner, p. 155.

53. On Dostoevsky and Renan, see the editors' commentary on plans for *The Idiot* in *PSS*, 9:396–99. See also E. I. Kiiko, "Dostoevskii i Renan," in G. M. Fridlender, ed., *Dostoevskii, Materialy i issledovaniia*, vol. 4 (Leningrad: Nauka, 1980), pp. 106–22.

54. Ernest Renan, *Vie de Jésus* (Paris: Calmann-Lévy, 1962), p. 83.

55. Renan, p. 72.                     56. Renan, p. 73.

57. Renan, p. 369.                    58. Renan, p. 349.

59. By far the best account of Dostoevsky's relationship with Belinsky and of Belinsky himself from the perspective of intellectual history, in my opinion, is the one in the first volume of Joseph Frank's critical biography of Dostoevsky. See *Dostoevsky: The Seeds of Revolt, 1821–1849* (Princeton, NJ: Princeton University Press, 1976), pp. 159–98.

60. *PSS*, 21:11.

61. For a good, concise treatment of the subject, see Malcolm V. Jones, "Some echoes of Hegel in Dostoyevsky," *Slavonic and East European Review*, 49 (1971): 500–520.

62. *PSS*, 10:505.

63. *PSS*, 10:506. Ellipses are in the original.

64. *PSS*, 10:486–87.

65. *PSS*, 11:14. Ellipses and emphasis are mine.

66. *PSS*, 12:113.

67. *Nietzsche Werke*, VI, 3:371.

68. *PSS*, 23:130.

69. *PSS*, 25:195.

70. *PSS*, 26:170.

71. *PSS*, 24:309.

72. *PSS*, 25:23.

73. *PSS*, 28 book 2:73.

74. In the crabbed language typical for many German thinkers of this era, Fichte defines *Volk* as "the totality of men living together in society and constantly engendering themselves from themselves naturally and spiritually, this totality of men existing all together under a certain particular law by which the divine develops out of them." *Johann Gottlieb Fichte's Sämmtliche Werke*, J. H. Fichte, ed. (Berlin, 1846; rpt. Berlin: de Gruyter, 1965), 7:381.

75. *PSS*, 5:5.

76. *Sochineniia i pis'ma P. Ia. Chaadaeva*, M. Gershenson, ed. (Moscow, 1913–14; rpt. Oxford: Mouette, 1972), 1:75.

77. Chaadaev, 1:80.

78. Chaadaev, 1:81.

79. Chaadaev, 1:85–86.

80. Chaadaev, 1:88–89.

81. Ivan Vasil'evich Kireevsky, "O kharaktere prosveshcheniia Evropy i o ego otnoshenii k prosveshcheniiu Rossii (Pis'mo k gr. E. E. Komarovskomu)" (On the character of Europe's enlightenment and its relation to Russia's enlightenment [Letter to Count E. E. Komarovsky]), in *Polnoe sobranie sochinenii*, A. I. Koshelev, ed. (Moscow, 1861; rpt. Ann Arbor: Ardis, 1983), 2:276. The word I've translated as "productive," *iskusstvennogo*, is normally translated "artificial," but Kireevsky seems to be drawing a distinction between what we produce and what we feel internally.

82. Kireevsky, 2:238.

83. Kireevsky, 2:243.

84. Kireevsky, 2:256.

85. Aleksei Stepanovich Khomiakov, *Quelques mots par un chrétien orthodoxe sur les communions occidentales* (Paris: Ch. Meyrueis, 1853), p. 34. Khomiakov wrote this and a number of other important essays in French, though most Russians appear to have known them in Russian translation.

86. Khomiakov, "Mnenie inostrantsev o Rossii" (Foreigners' opinion of Russia), in Khomiakov, *Polnoe sobranie sochinenii* (Moscow: Univ. tip., 1900–1911), 1:3–28. The quoted passage appears on p. 9.

87. Khomiakov, "Mnenie russkikh ob inostrantsakh" (Russians' Opinion of Foreigners), in *Polnoe sobranie sochinenii*, 1:31–68. The quoted passage appears on p. 38.

88. Khomiakov, "Russians' Opinion," p. 45.

89. Hegel presents his progression in the *Philosophy of History*, by using the persons of the Trinity. Naturally the highest moment for him is German Protestantism, not Russian Orthodoxy. The "Father" corresponds to the incursions of the German nations into the Roman Empire up to Charlemagne; the" Son" corresponds to the period when the Church was a theocracy and the state a feudal monarchy; the "Spirit" corresponds to the period from Charles V to the present, a

period characterized by the (Protestant) "hegemony of self-conscious thinking." See Hegel, 12:413–18.

90. Khomiakov, *Quelques mots*, p. 46.

91. See Joseph Frank, *Dostoevsky: The Mantle of the Prophet, 1871–1881* (Princeton, NJ: Princeton University Press, 2002), p. 276. The text in question is the article "Tri idei" (Three ideas), in the January 1877 issue of *Diary of a Writer*. See *PSS*, 25:5–9.

92. *PSS*, 27:64.

93. Khomiakov, *Polnoe sobranie sochinenii*, 2:6.

94. Khomiakov, *Quelques mots*, p. 42.

95. *PSS*, 12:234.

96. Nikolai Iakovlevich Danilevsky, *Rossiia i Evropa* (St. Petersburg: Obshchestvennaia Pol'za, 1871), p. 61.

97. Danilevsky, p. 88.

98. Danilevsky, pp. 70–71.

99. Danilevsky, pp. 211–12.

100. Danilevsky, pp. 123–27.

101. *PSS*, 29 book 1:30. Quoted by the editors in *PSS*, 26:401.

102. *PSS*, 29 book 1:146–47. Quoted by the editors in *PSS*, 26:401. Emphasis is in the original.

103. *PSS*, 14:264. Dostoevsky's second wife, Anna Grigor'evna, is the source of the claim that the author learned to read with this book. See *PSS*, 15:565.

104. See the commentary by the editors, *PSS*, 9:511–12.

105. See "St. Tychon: A Westernizing Kenotic," in George P. Fedotov, ed., *A Treasury of Russian Spirituality* (1950; rpt. Belmont, MA: Nordland, 1975), pp. 182–85.

106. On the connection between Parfeny and Zosima, see Victor Terras, *A Karamazov Companion: Commentary on the Genesis, Language, and Style of Dostoevsky's Novel* (Madison: University of Wisconsin Press, 1981), p. 24; and Joseph Frank, *Dostoevsky: The Mantle of the Prophet*, pp. 142–43. See also *PSS*, 15:528, for the editors' comments on this figure.

107. See *PSS*, 11:305–7.

108. *PSS*, 6:347–48.

109. *PSS*, 6:348. In *Notes from the House of the Dead*, the similar story appears in *PSS*, 4:29.

110. *PSS*, 29 book 2:43. Quoted in Frank, *Dostoevsky: The Mantle of the Prophet*, p. 146 (though this is my translation).


*Chapter Three*

1. *PSS*, 30 book 1:210–11.

2. Quoted in Frank, *Dostoevsky: The Mantle of the Prophet*, p. 222. The passage from *The Adolescent* appears in *PSS*, 13:379. The passage from the *Diary of a Writer* appears in *PSS*, 23:37.

3. *PSS*, 21:95.

4. *PSS*, 23:42.

5. *PSS*, 24:212.

6. *PSS*, 27:52.

7. *PSS*, 30 book 1:104–5.

8. Dostoevsky, *Pis'ma*, A. S. Dolinin, ed. (Moscow and Leningrad: Academia, 1934), 3:380.

9. Dostoevsky, *Pis'ma*, 3:381.

10. *PSS*, 29 book 2:281.

11. *PSS*, 29 book 2:138–41. Emphasis is in the original.

12. David I. Goldstein, *Dostoyevsky and the Jews* (Austin: University of Texas Press, 1981), p. 114.

13. *PSS*, 25:75.

14. *PSS*, 25:77–81.

15. *PSS*, 25:86, 88.

16. *PSS*, 25:87.

17. Goldstein, p. 132.

18. *PSS*, 25:92.

19. *PSS*, 29 book 2:147.

20. Goldstein, p. 138.

21. Geoffrey Kabat, *Ideology and Imagination* (New York: Columbia University Press, 1978), pp. 51, xi.

22. Kabat, pp. 171–76.

23. Kabat, pp. 93–110.

24. Gary Saul Morson, "Dostoevskij's Anti-Semitism and the Critics: A Review Article," *SEEJ*, 27, no. 3 (1983): 302–17. For a more recent summary of scholarship on this topic, see Maxim D. Shrayer, "Dostoevskii, the Jewish Question, and *The Brothers Karamazov*," *Slavic Review*, 61, no. 2 (Summer 2002): 273–91.

25. For two recent and differing approaches to the complexities of Dostoevsky's attitude toward the Jews, see James P. Scanlan, *Dostoevsky the Thinker: A Philosophical Study* (Utica, NY: Cornell University Press, 2002), pp. 209–11; and Frank, pp. 310–19.

26. *PSS*, 28 book 1:114.

27. *PSS*, 18:54–55.

28. Frank, *Dostoevsky: The Stir of Liberation, 1860–1865* (Princeton, NJ: Princeton University Press, 1986), p. 53.

29. *PSS*, 19:57–66.

30. *PSS*, 20:9–11.

31. *PSS*, 28 book 2:154.

32. *PSS*, 29 book 1:207.

33. *PSS*, 24:106–7.

34. *PSS*, 25:195–96.

35. *PSS*, 25:240.

36. *PSS*, 27:120.

37. *PSS*, 26:148.

38. *PSS*, 26:133.

39. Marshall S. Shatz says that Nechaev, not Bakunin, was probably the primary author of this document. See Marshall S. Shatz, ed. and trans., *Statism and Anarchy* (Cambridge: Cambridge University Press, 1990), p. xxiv.

40. *PSS*, 21:129.

41. *PSS*, 21:129. Ellipses are in the original.

42. *PSS*, 21:131.

43. *PSS*, 27:54.

44. *PSS*, 27:57. Quoted in Frank, *Dostoevsky: The Mantle of the Prophet*, p. 374.

45. Frank, pp. 256–57.

46. Frank, p. 186.

47. *PSS*, 11:303. Quoted in Frank, p. 303.

48. *PSS*, 27:56. Quoted in Frank, p. 711.

*Chapter Four*

1. Frank, *Dostoevsky: The Mantle of the Prophet*, p. 385. The story comes from an eyewitness account that was discovered only recently and first published in 1995.

2. *PSS*, 20:75.

3. *PSS*, 20:75.

4. *PSS*, 30 book 1:149.

5. *PSS*, 15:77.

6. *PSS*, 27:85–86.

7. *PSS*, 22:123.

8. *PSS*, 25:102.

9. *PSS*, 25:103.

10. For a discussion of the second article, see James Scanlan, *Dostoevsky the Thinker*, pp. 223–26. For a different view of the relation between the two articles, see Frank, *Dostoevsky: The Mantle of the Prophet*, pp. 273–74.

11. *PSS*, 23:84–99.

12. Ia. E. Golosovker, *Dostoevskii i Kant: Razmyshlenie chitatelia nad romanom "Brat'ia Karamazovy" i traktatom Kanta "Kritika chistogo razuma"* (Dostoevsky and Kant: A reader's meditation on the novel *The Brothers Karamazov* and Kant's treatise the *Critique of Pure Reason*; Moscow: Akademiia Nauk, 1963), p. 39.

13. *PSS*, 10:197.

14. *PSS*, 30 book 1:63.

15. *PSS*, 30 book 1:102.

16. *PSS*, 14:265.

17. *PSS*, 14:289.

18. *PSS*, 14:292.

19. *PSS*, 14:275–76.

20. *PSS*, 14:65.

21. *PSS*, 14:123.

22. *PSS*, 14:223.

23. *PSS*, 6:248.

24. *PSS*, 6:313.

25. *PSS*, 6:322.

26. Kant, *Werke*, 3:33.

27. *Nietzsche Werke*, IV, 2:367.

28. *Nietzsche Werke*, IV, 2:368.

29. *Nietzsche Werke*, IV, 3:60–61.

30. Ludwig Wittgenstein, *Werkausgabe* (Frankfurt am Main: Suhrkamp, 1989), 1:386, Joachim Schulte, vol. ed. (*Philosophische Untersuchungen*, §337). Emphasis is mine.

31. *PSS*, 6:54–55.

32. *PSS*, 6:199–200. The ellipses are in the original.

33. *PSS*, 6:246–49.

34. M. M. Bakhtin, *Problemy tvorchestva Dostoevskogo/Problemy poetiki Dostoevskogo* (Problems of Dostoevsky's creative art/Problems of Dostoevsky's poetics; Kiev: NEXT, 1994), pp. 284–308.

35. Speech—or literally "the word"—as a social phenomenon is the underlying thought in his long essay "The Word in the Novel." See *Voprosy literatury i estetiki* (Questions of literature and aesthetics; Moscow: Khudozhestvennaia literatura, 1975), p. 72.

36. Bakhtin, *Problemy*, p. 265.

37. Scanlan, pp. 4, 231.

*Chapter Five*

1. Matthew 22:30. The entire verse reads, "For in the resurrection they neither marry nor are given in marriage, but are like angels in heaven." In the text, I've modified the New Revised Standard translation to render literally Dostoevsky's "angels of God." The original Greek has "angels in heaven," but many translations have either added "of God" ("angels of God in heaven") or replaced "in heaven" with "of God."

2. Matthew 10:34: "Do not think that I have come to bring peace to the earth; I have not come to bring peace, but a sword."

3. Revelation 10:6. I've translated literally from Dostoevsky's text.

4. Pierre-Joseph Proudhon (1809–65) was known as one of the founders of modern anarchism. In his *Système des contradictions économiques, ou, Philosophie de la misère* (System of economic contradictions, or Philosophy of poverty; Paris: Guillaumin, 1846), he characterizes the notion that humanity is an emanation of God as "humanity's first affirmation."

5. John 14:2. This is Jesus' farewell speech, in which he describes to his disciples death, resurrection, and a final place of brotherhood.

6. *PSS*, 20:172–75. Emphasis is in the original.

7. Kant, *Werke*, 4:512–13.

8. Hegel, *Werke*, 20:359.

9. Joseph Frank points out that this was an issue on which Dostoevsky and his younger friend Solov'ev differed: "For [Dostoevsky] this notion [of the Kingdom of God] presumably remained speculative and transcendent. . . . Solovyev, however, genuinely believed in the possibility of a free Christian theocracy, one in which the Christian law of love would entirely penetrate and spiritualize the workings of earthly life." See *Dostoevsky: The Mantle of the Prophet*, p. 387. For the passage in *The Devils*, see *PSS*, 10:188.

10. Matthew 19:5–6. The material that Jesus quotes is from Genesis 1:27 and 2:24.

11. Hegel, 10:374. Emphasis is in the original.

12. See Chapter One.

13. *PSS*, 8:187–89. Dostoevsky may have read the legendary stories about Mohammed's epileptic fits in a Russian translation (1857) of Washington Irving's *Mahomet and his Successors* (1849). The translator was Petr Vasil'evich Kireevsky, brother of the Slavophile Ivan. See the editors' commentary, *PSS*, 9:442.

14. *PSS*, 8:195.          15. *PSS*, 8:195.

16. *PSS*, 8:451.          17. *PSS*, 8:459.

18. *PSS*, 12:113.

19. Some years ago René Girard made a similar claim about the heroes of these two novels. See *Dostoïevski, du double à l'unité* (Dostoevsky: from the double to unity) (Paris: Plon, 1963), pp. 81–90. Girard's understanding of the characters and the issues they raise is different from mine. To begin with, his ultimate interest is what sort of man Dostoevsky was on a personal level. His conclusion from the discussion of Prince Myshkin and Stavrogin is that they are "two opposite images of the novelist" (p. 90)—quite true, possibly, and quite interesting. My focus is less on

what kind of man Dostoevsky was than on the conceptions forming the outlook he expresses in various genres of writing. Girard speaks of Myshkin's perfection and of Stavrogin's detachment and indifference. My view is that what balances the relation between the two characters is precisely the distance of both from a perfection that neither can attain. For Stavrogin, detachment is almost the same as absolute evil, or better, it is the prerequisite of absolute evil. But perfect detachment for him is no more attainable than is perfect synthesis for the prince.

20. *PSS*, 11:10.                     21. *PSS*, 8:182.

22. *PSS*, 8:184.                     23. *PSS*, 8:182–84.

24. *PSS*, 8:458–59. The words in single quotation marks are a paraphrase of Luke 9:42.

25. *PSS*, 20:172.                    26. *PSS*, 6:419–20.

27. Matthew 24:30.                    28. *PSS*, 14:275–76.

29. *PSS*, 6:421–22.                  30. *PSS*, 14:328.

31. *PSS*, 30 book 1:149.

32. Irina Paperno, *Suicide as Cultural Institution in Dostoevsky's Russia* (Ithaca and London: Cornell University Press, 1997), pp. 8–9.

33. *PSS*, 8:189.                     34. *PSS*, 10:470.

35. *PSS*, 14:26.                     36. *PSS*, 13:76.

37. *PSS*, 13:385.                    38. *PSS*, 13:446.

39. *PSS*, 30 book 1:149. See Chapter Four.


## Chapter Six

1. Fedotov, *The Russian Religious Mind*, 1:104.

2. Fedotov, 1:95.                     3. Fedotov, 1:121.

4. Fedotov, 1:127–30.                 5. Fedotov, 1:123.

6. Gail Lenhoff, *The Martyred Princes Boris and Gleb: A Socio-Cultural Study of the Cult and the Texts* (Columbus, OH: Slavica, 1989), p. 99.

7. Lenhoff, p. 13.

8. Lenhoff, p. 85.

9. Lenhoff, p. 110.

10. George Fedotov, *A Treasury of Russian Spirituality* (New York: Sheed and Ward, 1948), pp. 11–14. Thanks to my student Anders Engberg-Pedersen for calling this to my attention.

11. Sandoz, *Political Apocalypse*, pp. 87, 213.

12. George Pattison and Diane Oenning Thompson, eds., *Dostoevsky and the Christian Tradition* (Cambridge: Cambridge University Press, 2001), p. 149.

13. *PSS*, 6:323.                     14. *PSS*, 11:27.

15. *PSS*, 6:250–52.                  16. *PSS*, 8:183–84.

17. *PSS*, 3:385–86.                  18. *PSS*, 6:348.

19. Claude Welch, *Protestant Thought in the Nineteenth Century*, 2 vols. (New Haven and London: Yale University Press, 1972), 1:233.

20. Welch, p. 234.

21. *PSS*, 14:259.

22. *PSS*, 14:291.

23. *PSS*, 14:292.

24. *PSS*, 14:328.

25. See the editors' comments in *PSS*, 15:475–76; and Valentina A. Vetlovskaya, "Alyosha Karamazov and the Hagiographic Hero," in Robert Louis Jackson, ed., *Dostoevsky: New Perspectives* (Englewood Cliffs, NJ: Prentice-Hall, 1984), pp. 206–26.

26. *PSS*, 14:289.

27. *PSS*, 14:209–10.

28. *PSS*, 14:289.

29. *PSS*, 14:267.

30. *PSS*, 14:285.

31. *PSS*, 14:286–87.

32. 1 Corinthians 12:12–14.

33. *PSS*, 14:286.

34. Deuteronomy 7:6.

35. Zechariah 14:9. Thanks to Richard Elliott Friedman for directing me to this passage.

36. Romans 3:29.

37. Jean Drouilly, *La Pensée politique et religieuse de F. M. Dostoievski* (The political and religious thought of F. M. Dostoevsky; Paris: Cinq Continents, 1971), p. 422. Drouilly comments on the resemblance of Dostoevsky's religion ("this vision of a God bestowing his graces on a new chosen people, the Russian people") to Judaism; see p. 409.

38. Drouilly, p. 175.

39. *PSS*, 15:197.

40. In what follows, I've taken many ideas and references from my article "The Shape of Russian Idealism: From Kant and Hegel to Dostoevsky to the Russian Religious Renaissance," in Gennady Barabtarlo, ed., *Cold Fusion: Aspects of the German Cultural Presence in Russia* (New York and Oxford: Berghahn, 2000), pp. 137–52.

41. *PSS*, 20:172, 14:215.

42. Solov'ev, *Sobranie sochinenii*, 3:32–33.

43. Solov'ev, 3:27.

44. Solov'ev, 3:144–45.

45. Solov'ev, 3:200.

46. Solov'ev, 3:201–2.

47. *PSS*, 24:173, 225; 25:74; 26:82–87.

48. *PSS*, 26:151.

49. Alexander Herzen, in his essay "The Russian People [*narod*] and Socialism" (1851), in *Izbrannye filosofskie proizvedeniia* (Moscow: OGIZ, 1946), 2:142.

50. *PSS*, 26:169.

51. *PSS*, 26:147–48.

52. Vladimir Solov'ev, *La Russie et l'Église Universelle* (Paris: Stock, 1922), p. 64.

53. Solov'ev, *La Russie*, p. 97.

54. Solov'ev, *La Russie*, p. 101.

55. Solov'ev, *La Russie*, p. 102.

56. Solov'ev, *La Russie*, p. 102–3.

57. Solov'ev, *La Russie*, p. 120.

58. Solov'ev, *La Russie*, p. 157.

59. *PSS*, 14:57.

60. *PSS*, 14:57.

61. *PSS*, 14:62.

62. *PSS*, 14:284.

63. *PSS*, 27:43.

64. On Dostoevsky's acquaintance with the non-Euclidean geometry of Georg Riemann, see *PSS*, 27:324.

65. James P. Scanlan discusses this notebook passage in *Dostoevsky the Thinker*, pp. 42–43.

## Conclusion

1. *Nietzsche Werke*, VI. 2:381.
2. *Nietzsche Werke*, VI, 3:90.
3. Scanlan, *Dostoevsky the Thinker*, p. 231.

# Index